Recruitment and Selection

Gareth Rober ... ...agement and has assisted many organisations in the development of HR strategies including improved selection and employment brand strategies, and the development and application of competencies in selection, pay and performance. Prior to his consulting role, he held senior HR positions in financial services, pharmaceutical and confectionery manufacturing, and the health service. Gareth is a member of the Employment Tribunals and a CIPD consultant and trainer. gareth@m3c-uk.com

The Chartered Institute of Personnel and Development is the leading publisher of books and reports for personnel and training professionals, students, and all those concerned with the effective management and development of people at work. For details of all our titles, please contact the publishing department:

tel: 020 8612 6204

e-mail: cipd@cipd.co.uk

The catalogue of all CIPD titles can be viewed on the CIPD website:

www.cipd.co.uk/bookstore

Recruitment and Selection

2nd edition

Gareth Roberts

Chartered Institute of Personnel and Development

Published by the Chartered Institute of Personnel and Development,
151 The Broadway, London, SW19 1JQ

This edition published 2005

Reprinted 2006, 2007

First published in 1997

Reprinted 1999, 2000 (twice), 2002, 2003, 2004

Typeset by Ferdinand Page Design, Surrey
Printed in Great Britain by The Cromwell Press, Trowbridge, Wiltshire

British Library Cataloguing in Publication Data
A catalogue of this publication is available from the British Library

ISBN 1 84398 117 3
ISBN 13 978 1 84398 117 6

Chartered Institute of Personnel and Development
151 The Broadway, London SW19 1JQ
Tel: 020 8612 6200
E-mail: cipd@cipd.co.uk   Website: www.cipd.co.uk
Incorporated by Royal Charter.   Registered Charity No. 1079797

For Denise – the best selection decision I ever made

Preface

This book is intended as a practical guide to the process of recruitment and selection. It aims to provide an explanation and insight into the key aspects of all elements of the selection process, which will be of interest to students of the subject, but its main purpose is to provide practical advice and guidance to those involved, at whatever level, in the recruitment and selection of people.

ACKNOWLEDGEMENTS

In the first edition of this book I acknowledged the great value I placed on its predecessor, written by Philip Plumbley, from which I had gained both enjoyment and invaluable advice. I hope that in the first edition I continued to provide a useful source of reference and practical guidance for those involved in recruitment, with sufficient coverage of the issues for those interested in its study. In this edition I have sought to reflect the changes that have taken place in recent years, in academic research, the changing role of work, opportunities from technology, best practice, and the ever-changing law (stated as at May 2005).

I am grateful to many people for their help and advice in the preparation of this book but particular mention must go to some. Russell Drakeley of CGR has been a great source of advice on biodata as well as being a patient martyr to the lost cause of trying to make me understand statistical correlation, selection ratio, and all the other heavy stuff. Adrian Furnham, Professor of Psychology at University College, London has helped me greatly on psychological testing, as well as making me understand the importance of an open mind. Lawrence Warner of the International Graphology Association has provided very helpful insights into graphology as well as general support. David Rayner has been the legal eagle, to whom I am indebted for keeping me up to speed on legislative changes and case law. Denise Roberts has worked wonders on turning around the manuscript.

Thanks must go to Andy Roberts of Knight Chapman Psychological Ltd and Gareth Edwards of aia, and to Virgin Atlantic Airways, Ladbrokes Telebetting, and BECTA for the opportunity to share their material. Thanks also to Stephen Partridge and his team at CIPD for their support and encouragement.

Contents

Part 1

Overview

1

The importance of selection

The purpose of selection is to match people to work. It is the most important element in any organisation's management of people, simply because it is not possible to optimise the effectiveness of human resources by whatever method, if the quantity or quality of people is less than the organisation needs.

Well-designed organisations cannot excel by the quality of design alone, and neither can praise or pay motivate people to perform beyond their capabilities. The best training programme cannot make a silk purse from a sow's ear. Without the basic match of people and work, it is not possible to gain a proper return on all the other investments in human resources programmes.

'Work' is more than the range of tasks and activities undertaken; it includes the physical, economic and social environment in which the activities take place.

In the twentieth century selection was primarily concerned with matching people to specific jobs. However, in the twenty-first century the importance of flexibility and the rapid pace of change make it more important to look at matching work in the wider context. It has now become necessary to look beyond the skills for the specific job in hand in assessing people, and to look at the potential range of matches for the person. Matches such as future work, mobility in and out of the organisation, interaction with a wide range of potential colleagues, fit with the current and 'social' environment of customers, suppliers, culture, and the 'physical' environment, particularly technology.

Mintzberg has said that strategy is the stream in which a range of disparate activities takes place. Continuing that train of thought, selection is often strategic and can be linked to a range of activities undertaken in the general 'stream' of finding people to 'fill a role'. Effective selection is more akin to a total quality approach, in which measurement is a vital tool. The specification must be clear and all activities carefully orchestrated to play a specific part in a grand design in which the whole is greater than the sum of the parts.

2

Using the book

The aim of this book is to help recruiters to make decisions on the way they will go about the recruitment process. The principles involved in selection are the same whether the organisation is in the public or private sector, a large multinational with dedicated recruiters, a small enterprise with limited resources, or whether employing staff directly or recruiting on behalf of others. How these principles can be applied is the key issue. The book therefore covers the principles involved in the various stages of recruitment, provides advice on 'how to' and gives some case studies by way of example. It is not the intention to set down a 'one size fits all' approach to recruitment and selection, but to break down and consider the various components so that recruiters can determine the approach that best suits them.

The key attributes of effective selection are:

- a clear and precise specification

- effective use of multiple techniques

- elimination of redundant processes

- measurement

- evaluation and continuous improvement.

The book is designed to cover these elements.

Part 1 provides an overview so that recruiters can stand back and look at the process 'in the round'. Recruiters should then be able to map their processes against this background and determine whether there are any specific areas that need particular attention.

Part 2 takes a look at the way the process is managed, including the way that the recruitment strategy fits into the wider HR strategy, the extent to which it can be managed directly or by others, the use of specialists, and the role of systems. The tools and techniques that make up the selection process are also considered.

Part 3 looks at how people can be attracted to the organisation. Starting with the need for a clear picture of what is looked for, including the use of competencies, how to define the requirements, and how to market the job on offer so that the right people will want to apply for it.

Part 4 looks at how to gauge whether the person applying is the right person for the job. The range of tools and techniques available is discussed, with the advantages and disadvantages of each tool or technique considered.

Part 5 looks at how to ensure that the process is right starting with effective decision-making, the need for checks and safeguards, consideration of equal opportunities, the importance of settling the new person into the role, and the process of measuring the effectiveness of the recruitment itself.

3

The selection process

The flow chart for a typical selection process is illustrated in Figure 1.1.

PERSON SPECIFICATION

The process begins with a very clear specification of the person being sought. Selection is like searching for the proverbial needle in the haystack. Good selection techniques may effectively remove the hay, but it is critical to be able to recognise the needle.

The specification embraces a profile of the role and the ideal person to fill that role. Since selection is about matching people to roles, it is important that both sides of the equation be clearly specified. Poor selectors overlook the necessity of clear role information, whereas good selectors understand that one of the best judges of a candidate's suitability is the candidate; and helping candidates to gain a clearer understanding of the role will help them make a more effective judgement. Careful scrutiny of the role provides other hidden benefits beyond pure selection. It enables decisions to be made on whether the role is necessary; whether it should be redesigned or reviewed; whether its 'pecking order' and reward status in the organisation are correct; whether it should be a training role for higher positions; and a host of other HR management issues not purely connected to selection. Since most employment tends to be for a significant duration, it is important to look to the future and consider planned and potential changes to the role.

COMPETENCIES

Competencies play an important part in the selection process: their use and development are discussed in Chapter 8. The term 'competencies' is used to describe all the personal attributes, knowledge, experience, skills and values that a person draws on to perform their work well. In many HR applications, such as training or performance management, the competencies are described in terms of behaviours and patterns of work and the focus is on those competencies that differentiate between effective and superior performance. For selection purposes a slightly broader approach needs to be taken, for the following reasons.

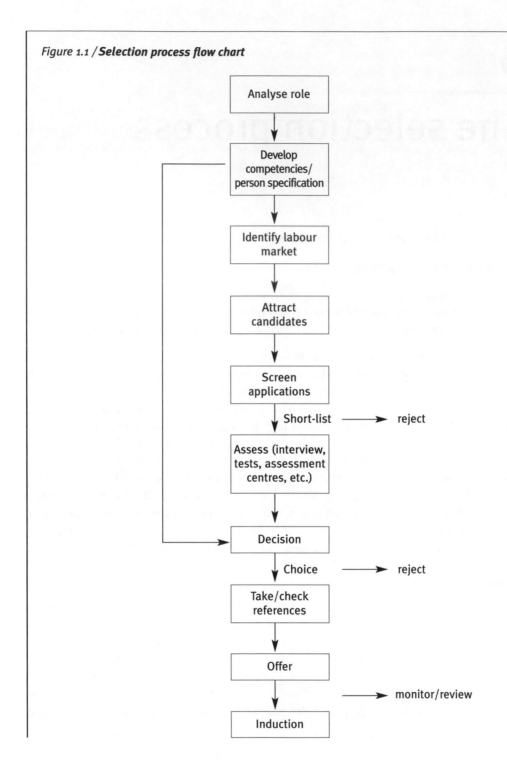

*Figure 1.1 / **Selection process flow chart***

First, it is not appropriate to focus on only the competencies that differentiate superior from effective performance. In selection there needs to be a great concern with all the competencies that underpin effective performance, as the selection process will be the threshold that separates the suitable from the unsuitable. None of the 'basic' competencies can therefore be ignored.

Secondly, providing descriptions of the competencies in terms of everyday work behaviours is of limited value. It is likely that candidates will not be familiar with the organisation or will be from a different area of work. They may therefore not be able to fully understand the descriptions if they are tied too specifically to the organisation.

Thirdly, there are major practical constraints that may make it difficult to obtain examples of the candidate displaying the required competencies in everyday work behaviour. This may be because the candidate has no directly comparable work experience or because it is not possible to seek the opinions of those currently able to observe the candidate, particularly if they are in another organisation.

Finally, and perhaps most importantly, observing the behaviours in the current setting does not necessarily mean they will be repeated in the new role. It may be a reflection of the environment, the organisation style or the way the person is managed, and which may not transfer easily to a different environment, culture, or role. It is important therefore to consider the competencies that will provide clear evidence of potential performers in addition to those that give evidence of a track record.

The use of competencies extends beyond simply 'measuring' the candidate. It is important to match the candidate and the role. The candidate can play an important role in self-assessment of suitability. Competency-based role descriptions help candidates to get a feel for the role in a way that 'logical' job information and traditional job descriptions do not. The inclusion of values and standards helps to ensure that the hearts as well as the minds of potential candidates are attracted to the role.

ATTRACTING

The initial part of the selection process is concerned with 'selling' the role. Considerable thought needs to be given to this part of the process, particularly where external advertising is being used. Very few organisations would allow their products to be marketed in 'one-off' disparate, uncoordinated advertisements. The expenditure on selection advertising rarely achieves the same levels as product advertising, but neither is it loose change. A single newspaper advertisement can represent a significant proportion of starting salary. The advertising spend therefore need to be carefully targeted within an overall marketing strategy for employment. This means a coordinated on-going campaign in which key messages are communicated cost-effectively through the appropriate media. A similar process that is used for developing a product brand strategy needs to be followed for the development of an employment marketing strategy. Essential elements of this process would comprise setting the values, the selling proposition, the target audience, and the communication channels. This aspect is considered further in Part 3.

The process of attracting people to apply for the role requires achievement of a balance. There need to be sufficient candidates to afford an opportunity for choice, but the quality of candidates needs to be good enough to make such decisions meaningful. Line managers get a much greater sense of satisfaction in making a difficult choice from a high quality pool of similar candidates, than they would in selecting a candidate who stands head and shoulders above the others. There is also a very important cost consideration in the processing of unsuitable applications. Some organisations, notably some 'professional' selection consultants, choose to reduce costs by deciding not to acknowledge the application or keep the candidates informed of progress. This is a false economy and carries the disadvantage of creating a poor image of the organisation. The correct approach is to manage the response rate proactively through the provision of useful information, and other related techniques, to assist in self-selection.

The information on the organisation and role will be useful, but more is not necessarily better: there is an optimum amount of information. Research, for example, on candidates' use of glossy company brochures has shown that little of the information is used to influence the candidates' actual decision to apply. Such material is most frequently used to help the candidate prepare for the interview. The most useful way of providing information is to give candidates a preview of the work or to provide a job information questionnaire. Job previews are very useful but logistically difficult to organise in large volume recruitment, although open evening, temporary postings, and work experience have been run effectively in a range of organisations. The job information questionnaire is a method by which information is 'drip fed' in response to a range of questions about the role that the candidate completes and self-scores. Information linked to the level of score can discourage potentially unsuitable applicants from proceeding further. This has dual benefits in avoiding administration costs and avoiding the hostility of rejected candidates. For many organisations there is always a risk that rejected candidates become lost customers.

RESPONSE

The response process is usually based on application forms or curricula vitae, whether paper or electronic. Use of application forms means a standardised response against which volumes of candidates can be assessed. Care needs to be taken in designing a form so that the necessary information can be gleaned from it. This may seem an obvious point, but the form serves a dual purpose: it is a mechanism for screening but it is also a reference source for such information as addresses or references. There is sometimes a tendency for the 'reference source' requirements to overwhelm the 'screening information' requirements. The form should concentrate on a small number of key competencies capable of being assessed from it. There is a temptation to attempt to extract too much information from the form. Motives, values and personality characteristics cannot be gleaned from an application form; they are better identified through testing and interviewing. The form, and its screening process, needs to focus on the acquired knowledge, skills, and experience pertinent to the role.

It is usually most effective to incorporate monitoring forms with the initial response. These forms ought to be separate from the application form so that they are seen to be unrelated to selection decisions. They will be used to monitor compliance to legal requirement on race, sex, disability and other discrimination.

SCREENING

The application screening process has attracted little research attention, but a research project undertaken by Herriot and Wingrove (1984) revealed that the process is generally subjective, inconsistent and lacking in focus. The quality and consistency of the selection process will be significantly improved if selectors are provided with a clear idea of the competencies to focus on when screening the application form, together with examples of good or poor evidence. A similar principle can be applied to the screening of curricula vitae, although the very nature of each candidate's CV makes the task more difficult and time consuming.

Variations on the screening process occur in a number of ways. In telesales and other telephone-based services it is customary to undertake the initial screening over the telephone. The advertisement will provide a telephone number, with set call times. The candidate's call is answered by a screening person, who uses a defined script (for consistency) and scoring methods for rating the answers. Candidates are not rejected (because of the adverse reaction to telephone screening), but 'streamed' with a fast stream proceeding quickly to the next stage.

A variation on the application form is the use of biodata (biographical data). This is a technique that dates from the 1920s but, despite high levels of predictive validity, still does not enjoy common usage. This technique can be best described as a set of questions framed around 'coincidences' in the lives of people who are good performers. The concept is widely used in the financial services industry for approval of loans or insurance. People are generally accustomed to the concept in car insurance, where the model of car and postcode of address dictates the level of insurance premium payable. It is, however, much less common in selection processes, and carries with it some degree of sensitivity. For selection purposes the approach would be to ask a group of employees to provide information about themselves through their responses to a wide-ranging questionnaire, and then to look for correlations in the answers that seem to differentiate between high-performers and low-performers. The reasons for the differences may not be known or understood, but their occurrence will provide the basis on which to screen applications.

Following the initial screening process, the use of selection methods varies more widely between organisations and between different kinds of recruitment. Some organisations will use interviews, some will use psychometric tests, some will use work simulation or role-plays and some will use an assessment centre comprising a range of techniques.

INTERVIEWING

Interviewing is the most frequently used selection technique and it is very unusual for people to be hired without an interview. Interviews may be either structured or unstructured. The unstructured interview generally takes the form of a free-ranging discussion, sometimes with the interviewer using a set of 'favourite' questions, but giving the interviewee free rein to answer in a general way. In an unstructured interview, the interviewer uses his or her judgement about the overall performance of the candidate in deciding whether or not they match the role.

The unstructured interview is the most commonly used interview. It is frequently used by professional selectors from search and selection agencies who are confident in their ability to assess candidates without the constraints of a structured interview.

Research suggests that the unstructured interview is half as effective as a structured interview. The structured interview is focused on a set number of clearly defined criteria, usually competencies. The questions are carefully structured to obtain specific information about the criteria and the answers are scored against a consistent scoring range. The structured interview may be a situational or behavioural interview. In situational interviewing candidates are presented with a future hypothetical situation and asked to explain how they would deal with it. The answers are assessed for evidence of relevant ability. In the behavioural/experience interview, the questions are aimed at drawing out past examples of behaviours, linked to specific competencies. The interviewer compares the answers to positive and negative descriptions of the behaviours, scores each of the competencies and makes a judgement based on the scores. Recent research shows that behavioural/experience interviews are a more effective form of structured interview.

Although interviewing is one of the best established selection techniques, it suffers from a number of problems. It is difficult for the interviewer to sustain attention throughout the interview, with interviewers sometimes able to remember only the opening and closing stages of the interview. Judgement of interviews can sometimes be clouded by prejudices or influenced unduly by stereotyping the candidate with, for example, others in his or her organisation, or by 'mirroring' in which the interviewer looks more favourably on candidates matching the interviewer's own profile. Perhaps the most common failing of interviews is the lack of preparation on the part of the interviewer.

Regardless of its problems the interview remains one of the most popular selection techniques. Whatever its 'technical' value in the selection process, it is of great perceived value to selectors and a very important aspect for candidates.

TESTING

Psychometric tests have gained significantly in popularity in recent years, but are by no means commonplace. Tests can be either ability or personality. Ability tests measure specific aptitudes such as vocabulary, numeracy, spatial awareness, typing speed and accuracy. They are used most commonly in selection for clerical positions. Ability tests are generally more accurate in predicting potential than are personality tests. The most frequent cause of legal claims arising from test use is with ability tests, often because selectors use the test without taking into account whether the ability it measures is essential for the job. For example, testing train drivers for vocabulary may discriminate against those whose native tongue is not English, and may bear no relation to potential ability to drive trains.

Personality tests are used to measure the range of personal characteristics, values and attitudes that shape an individual's beliefs and behaviours. There are various theories of personality, but most psychologists agree on a basic five-factor model, known as the 'big five', the permutations of which will form the many varieties of 'personality'. Most proprietary personality tests measure one or all of the five factors, however, some tests may subdivide these factors into a larger number of dimensions. There is dispute over whether or not personality tests can predict job performance, with plentiful evidence to back both views. In the UK there are constraints imposed by The British Psychological Society on the use of tests, so that only someone trained to BPS Level B or a psychologist may use personality tests. The constraints are imposed because the interpretation and feedback of test results requires expertise.

Ability tests are tests in the true sense of the word, since they measure in an absolute sense the degree of aptitude required for a job. The higher the score on the ability test, the better that person will be in that ability. Ability tests usually have the feeling of a test, have exam-type questions and strict time limits for completion. On the other hand, personality tests are not tests as such and do not have pass or fail elements. Each aspect of personality is a continuum with good and bad features at both extremes. The measures on a personality test are benchmarks (known as norms) with others in the group, so it is important to know which aspects are causally related to a job performance. It is also important to have benchmark information (normative data) on actual job holders in order to judge the results. Personality tests do not usually look like tests but are often a series of questions or adjectives with which the candidate simply agrees or disagrees. In addition to 'omnibus' tests measuring the full range of personality, there are specific tests measuring single dimensions or specific values or particular attitudes. There are about 100,000 types of psychometric tests available worldwide.

EXERCISES

There are no foolproof selection techniques and there is nothing that comes close to total accuracy in predicting future job performance. The only way to be certain that someone can do the job is to offer them the job. This is technically sound, perhaps, but it is fraught with practical difficulties and cost implications. The next best thing may therefore be to give candidates a preview of the role and provide some work simulations on which to base a judgement of their performance. Such role plays and simulations are frequently to be found in assessment centres, although there are occasions when they are used alone.

Exercises used in establishing work simulations should have the following key elements: they must be realistic, capable of being observed and evaluated, encourage true rather than artificial behaviours from candidates, and be cost effective. Developing realistic exercises means measuring those aspects that are causally related to job performance. One of the criticisms of work simulations is that they tend to seek idealised responses, which are based on assumed good behaviours, rather than being anchored in any empirically-based researched examples. It is sometimes said that candidates in a work simulation are assessed against the designer's idea of how the work should be done rather than the way jobholders work in real life.

The nature of exercises varies. Sometimes they take the form of individual work. For example, a candidate may be given an in-tray of sample mail and asked to prioritise and respond in order to assess prioritisation, work organisation and understanding. The exercises can also be abstract assignments designed around teamwork so that the interpersonal skills of candidates can be observed. In observed exercises the judgement of observers is highly important and requires clear instruction and training.

The limited use of exercises and work simulations is mainly a reflection of the high cost involved. There are some off-the-shelf exercises but they may require customising; most exercises however need to be designed from scratch. There are also significant resource costs involved in providing and training sufficient observers. There is also a discomfort factor in candidates 'playing games', which tends to target such exercises on school leavers and graduate recruitment. There are, nonetheless, some novel adaptations. The use of 'trial by sausage roll' is popular in the selection of salespeople or public profile roles, and usually takes the form of an informal buffet reception for candidates but during which a number of 'hosts' are required to assess the candidates on the way they 'work the floor' and identify, and build relationships with, key influencers at the reception. In high-cost or high-risk occupations the use of simulations, e.g. flight simulators for pilots, can be a very cost-effective and safe means of assessing potential candidates.

ASSESSMENT CENTRES

Assessment centres involve the application of a number of techniques over a prolonged period in order to build a comprehensive picture of the candidate. A typical assessment centre will last at least one day, and often a number of days. It will usually comprise some visits and presentations of information on the organisation, one or more structured interviews, testing, work simulations and exercises, and perhaps some element of 'trial by sausage role'. Assessors are brought together for debriefing and provide their evaluation of candidates based on overall performance through all the assessment elements. Assessment centres are most often used in graduate recruitment, partly because the investment in graduate trainees is usually high, and partly because candidates already in employment find it difficult to commit themselves to a long assessment process.

Assessment centres have the highest predictive validity of all the selection techniques, but they are an amalgam of techniques rather than a technique in their own right. In developing cost-effective assessment centres, it is important to ensure that the candidate specification is clear, that the different techniques are matched most effectively to particular criteria, and that there is an effective evaluation process for bringing the results of the various techniques into an overall assessment.

CHECKS AND OFFERS

The information on candidates needs to be checked for authenticity. This may include documentary checks on qualifications or licences; statutory checks on work eligibility; specialist checks on health, credit or criminal records; and taking up references. The use of references is one of the most universal aspects of selection even though there is unease when giving them, and cynicism when receiving them. There are legal obligations, in providing references, to the recipient and the subject. References are generally more useful when the request is framed around specific questions. Offers of employment may be conditional or unconditional. Conditional offers are sometimes based on pre-conditions such as receipt of satisfactory references or achievement of an academic qualification. Some offers are post-conditional, for example they may be subject to satisfactory completion of a probationary period. Offers need to be clear and explicit, and although there are no legal requirements for a written contract of employment, there is a legal requirement for a statement of main terms and conditions to be provided within two months of taking up employment. It is unlawful discrimination to make a different offer to people based on gender, race, or disability even if the person turns down the offer.

STARTING-UP

Recruitment and selection is often viewed as the process up to the decision point on the candidate. The information gained on the candidate is often placed with the recruitment file and retained in case of any discrimination claims or other complaints. The information gathered is, however, of great potential value in managing the person. It is often the case that the final selection is a compromise, that no candidate perfectly matches the specification, and that an offer is made to the person who most closely matches the specification. It is important, therefore, to plan the induction process to meet the needs of that person, to review the role design to see whether it requires changing (the new person may need more or less supervision than envisaged, for example), and to provide the candidate's manager with information on the way in which they can be managed for best results. The more structured the selection process, the easier it will be to identify these key elements. In competency-based selection there is the added advantage of being able to track development, manage on-going performance, and link pay to competencies so that selection becomes the start of a process rather than the end.

As well as concentrating on ensuring the candidate adjusts to the new role, it is important to review the process itself. Using utility analysis techniques, described in Chapter 16, it is possible to calculate the cost-effectiveness of the selection process but some key data needs to be collected to support this. Organisations find it useful to track costs and measures along each stage of the process. At the advertising stage, the response rate to each form of publicity needs to be monitored, not only in absolute terms but also showing proportions of respondents going on to the different stages and to final selection. The correlation of interview, test and exercise success to application form and CV information needs to be analysed, to identify future targets. The cost of each stage and technique needs to be clearly identified (including internal labour costs) both in gross terms and as a ratio to successful candidates. The effectiveness of the different stages and techniques needs to be assessed. This is best done by reference to the subsequent evaluation of the candidate's work performance to see whether the techniques accurately predicted the outcome. Where different techniques provide the same clues, the question has to be asked whether both are needed or whether it is effective to just rely on one.

In addition to information on the cost and effectiveness of the process, standards need to be monitored. These include both quality and legal aspects. Quality will be reflected in the speed of response: whether all applications were acknowledged and may include service questionnaires for clients (including internal) and candidates (both successful and unsuccessful). The legal aspects will need to include monitoring or response rates and success rates for ethnic minorities, male and female, or candidates with disabilities, and other protected groups. Care should be taken to monitor the effect of mechanistic processes such as tests and biodata in creating indirect discrimination.

Part 2

Managing the process

4

Strategy

There is an old saying that 'you can't make a silk purse of a sow's ear'. This holds equally true in the context of an organisation's human resources strategy. Without the right people in place a human resources strategy will be expending effort on making good the shortfall rather than capitalising on the assets and leveraging for optimum organisation performance. One of the frequent appeals of business leaders today is the need to change the organisation's culture, which on closer examination often means trying to get people to do the things they should be doing in the first place, and in the way in which they should be doing them. It may not be over-simplistic to say that it would be more effective:

- to employ people who are capable of doing the work to be done

- to employ people who are inclined to work the way the organisation would wish them to work

- to have mutual obligations and expectations which are clearly defined from the beginning of the employment relationship.

Significant amounts of money and effort are expended in many organisations on organisation design strategies. These strategies could involve, for example, improving the problems of misplaced people, or redundancy programmes to rid the organisation of people who should never have been selected or of jobs that should never have been filled. Similarly in some organisations, precious training resource is 'squandered' in trying to train round pegs to fit square holes. It is also the case that pay policies are sometimes made to sweat too hard in order to condition patterns of behaviour that the organisation should really be able to take for granted. These are of course bold statements and they have no universal truth, but neither are they universally irrelevant. The point is that many organisations can carry out improvements to business performance by simply improving recruitment and selection practices.

In recent years selection in the UK has seen an improvement as successful organisations recognise the pivotal role it plays in the overall human resources strategy. Selection is pivotal however in more than the fact that the quality of the people determines the quality of the organisation. There is also the role recruitment can play in shaping people's expectations and in conditioning their attitudes and contribution on entry. Recruitment also helps in gathering a rich source of information on people's skills, values, and motives, which can play an essential part in providing the intelligence upon which other human resource policies can be shaped. The links between the selection practices and other human resource policies need to be made explicit.

SPECIFICATIONS

One of the most important parts of the selection process is the development of a clear specification upon which the selection activity is based. Good selectors have always followed this discipline rather than 'shooting in the dark'. It has however been a fairly transient phase; once the successful candidate has been appointed, the specification has been disregarded. Over the last decade or so many organisations have adopted a competency-based approach to selection and, in defining such competencies, have made use of them in the wider context of human resource management generally. Similarly, some organisations have adopted a competency framework for other purposes and then made it available for the selection activity. Regardless of the origin, the important benefit is that there is a consistency in identifying and measuring 'people quality' at all stages in the employment cycle. The use of competencies is further discussed in Chapter 8 and for the present it is sufficient to say that this can be defined as the identification of skills, motives, personality characteristics, and other attributes which give rise to performance, and which differentiate between poor, average and superior performance; expressed in plain terms as descriptions of such people qualities which are in action in everyday work. The use of these competencies means that it is possible to select against them, but also possible to use them to predict the workplace behaviours of the candidate and monitor their performance against them, aligning performance management and training programmes to support and enhance optimum performance. Thus the creation of a competency-based specification provides clear, quantifiable measurement of people and allows the principles of total quality management to be applied to the management of human resources. Since a properly prepared person specification will have been generated from thorough role analysis, it also means that there is very clear information about their roles in the organisation, and their purpose and contribution to the overall business aims.

HUMAN RESOURCES PLANNING

Effective human resource planning must begin with an analysis of the needs of the business in order to identify the requirements of people within it, both in terms of numbers and the role required. Good planning needs to be soundly anchored in reality since it is not an end in itself – the art of prediction – but an integral part of human

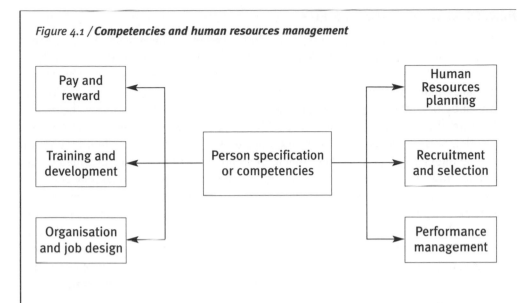

Figure 4.1 / *Competencies and human resources management*

resource management, setting the demand for the strategies which will be put in place. There is therefore a very close iteration between HR planning and selection. The planning output will create the target for selection quantity and quality in the sense of specifying the number and skills required and the type of people needed. In the course of planning, labour markets and movements will have been analysed together with other trends, and flows within the organisation will have been analysed in terms of promotions, labour turnover, and retirement. Sophisticated HR planning will also gather information on causes behind past trends, for example research into reasons for leaving, in order to make meaningful predictions on future trends. Such information is of great importance to the selection activity since it will define the attractions and reservations influencing potential employees and applicants. In the course of selection activity, information will come to hand about trends in the labour market that will be valuable to HR planners, along with information on the difficulties or ease of recruiting appropriate numbers and types. Thus information on selection ratios at each stage of the process can help HR planners to determine the viability of achieving increases or reductions in staff numbers through increased recruitment or natural wastage. In order to make decisions on candidates, information needs to be obtained on their alignment with the person specification; this information needs to be captured within an integrated human resource information system. Planners will thus be able to determine whether such skills are available from the existing workforce, when they make plans which require certain levels or availability of skills.

PERFORMANCE MANAGEMENT

During the course of selection, a great deal of information will have been obtained about candidates and there should be clear measures of their competencies. This will be invaluable for both day-to-day general management of performance and the formal performance management process. The day-to-day management of performance will be enhanced by providing managers with a clear understanding of the nature of the people working for them, their potential and their limitations, their preferences and dislikes, information on what 'makes them tick' and ways to motivate them. Such information will allow managers to determine how much freedom of action can be provided to an individual, how much support they are likely to need, and to predict how they will cope and react in certain circumstances. If a manager knows, for example, that an employee is likely to be a risk-taker, this will aid the manager to see that this individual needs a tighter rein or perhaps clear guidelines or limits on their degree of risk. Additionally that individual's role could be redesigned so that high-risk elements are reallocated to more prudent people. In so doing, the manager may be informed, from the employee's selection profile, that they will perhaps dislike completing forms or perhaps react adversely to close supervision. Using all the information available, the manager is able to select the most appropriate course of action to avoid undue risk without adverse impact upon the motivation and performance of the employee. It has long been held that situational leadership, the ability to apply different styles of leadership to different types of followers in different circumstances, is the most effective form of leadership, but it has been difficult for leaders to secure information on their staff to give the cues they need to adapt their leadership style. The selection profile should provide this kind of data.

Formal processes of performance management, such as performance appraisal, often suffer from some common faults. One of these faults is that the process favours senior people over junior people in the allocation of good performance ratings, as the schemes themselves often provide less opportunity for junior staff to be recognised given the bias towards projects or one-off objectives. Managers, and other senior people, whose role is characterised by the setting of such goals and targets or milestones (but where day-to-day standards and routine are less important), find it clearer to be appraised against them. For junior staff, where there is less discretion over the nature of the work (and less opportunity usually to become involved in projects or other goals), they often find that the performance appraisal process overlooks the on-going, day-to-day routines and standards which are important in maintaining the organisation's performance. Performance appraisals still seem in many cases to be derivatives of management by objectives. Competency- based appraisal processes provide a balance of targets (*what* is to be achieved) and behaviours (*how* it is to be achieved). This provides a more balanced system and can accommodate the differing nature of junior and senior work, since senior people will have more emphasis on the 'what' than the 'how', whilst junior people will have more emphasis on the 'how' rather than the 'what'. A competency-based appraisal system takes a balanced view of overall performance and will embrace outputs (in terms of specific projects or objectives, or other measurable dimensions of performance such as productivity or sales) and inputs (behavioural descriptions of the standards expected in fulfilling the role, i.e. the competencies).

The selection process should be able to do two things, particularly when using competencies. First, it should provide predictions on how the new employee is likely to perform and provide an assessment of how the individual will behave in comparison to the desired behaviours. Secondly, it should pinpoint where areas of attention are required such as potential weakness.

PAY AND REWARD

The pay bill is often the most significant area of an organisation's expenditure. There is always the danger that it can be viewed as an overhead rather than an investment, with little attention being paid to how the organisation can maximise its return on such a large annual investment. It is true that legal obligations or other restraints mean in practice that there is little choice but to continue paying people on an on-going basis; the workforce is not a truly disposable component. Yet, although not 'avoidable', there is no reason why pay should not be expected to 'sweat'. It can be used as the foot on the accelerator or the brake. It can be used to push the motivational button and reinforce people's desire to achieve certain goals, or it can be used to press the shock button, to make people think twice about pursuing goals the organisation does not regard as important, or displaying behaviours that it does not regard as desirable. It is not unusual in the design of pay systems to press the wrong button accidentally. This occurs when there is insufficient information about the psychological make-up of the people working for the organisation, and therefore little opportunity to predict accurately the likely outcome of changes to the pay system. Beauty is in the eye of the beholder, and the motivational aspect of pay is in the mind of the recipient. The psychological make-up of the workforce will, for example, determine whether performance-pay systems will work or not. It is of course always possible, and desirable, for pay designers to undertake research as part of the design process, but difficult to embark on the same degree of research around the individual that is afforded in selection activity. It should prove invaluable to capture the information on employees gained as part of the selection process, and feed the data into decisions on pay design. Figure 4.2 illustrates the importance of psychology on pay design.

In addition to the 'soft' data, there is also the 'hard' data that is available to recruiters, on the sufficiency of the employment package to attract new candidates. Some care needs to be taken with this, given that poor recruiters will often blame lack of a competitive salary, rather than their own failings, as excuses for failure to recruit. Simple amendments to the application form asking for details, for example, of current salary can nevertheless provide some very good raw data for development of local pay intelligence.

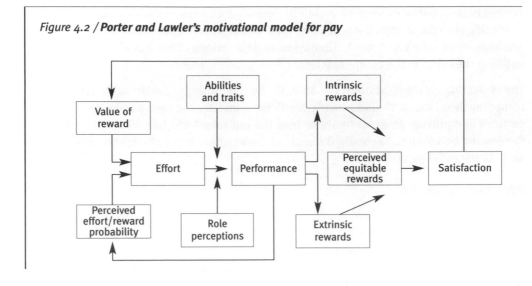

Figure 4.2 / **Porter and Lawler's motivational model for pay**

TRAINING AND DEVELOPMENT

The use of a competency-based approach to human resource management means that measures of individual ability can be more precisely and objectively defined. It is possible to build up a very robust analysis of individual training needs from the performance management process, and of course the individual training plan for induction and early development can be tailored precisely to the needs of the new employee. Equally, collective training needs can be gathered from the output of the role analysis, contrasted with the aggregation of data from individual competency-based assessment. Since the role analysis and the person specification are expressed in exactly the same definition of competencies, it is possible to be very clear and specific in targeting the shortfall. Using the competencies, it is also possible to see where the training and development investment is likely to yield the greatest return. Innate behaviours or competencies (such as the deep-seated underlying personal characteristics) are less receptive to training and development interventions, and money spent in such areas can be regarded as extravagant. Similarly, in looking at whether the 'deficiencies' are in acquired skills or adapted behaviours, it is possible to see whether they would be better served through education (for acquired) or training/development (for adapting).

There is an element of a two-way street here. It should not be assumed, in making selection decisions, that deficiencies in skills that can be acquired or behaviours that can be adapted are less important than innate qualities simply because training can be provided. To take an obvious example, it would be unwise to select a company legal adviser without legal qualifications, or a typist without typing skills, on the basis that the candidates' judgement, resilience, and interpersonal skills are excellent and that the 'shortfalls' are capable of being trained. These may be farcical examples but they should serve to make the point that recruiters and trainers need to be in close liaison to ensure that they are aware of, and supportive of, each other's demands.

INTEGRATION

Some organisations choose to adopt a competency framework as the architecture for their human resource policies and practices. In so doing, they define the competencies required in the organisation that can be used for selection purposes as the specification, and the recruitment activity can be subsequently 'bolted in' to the framework. Some organisations choose to begin with the recruitment function, developing competency-based people specifications as the basis for selection, and then use the specifications as the framework to drive other HR practices. The starting point is not important. It is important that integration takes place and that the following conditions are met:

- Selection of people into the organisation is tied into the needs of the role.

- The induction and development of people is built around such demands for the role and their compatibility with it.

- Reward creates the connectivity between the needs of the business and the values/expectations of the workforce.

- The requirements of the role are clearly explained to those undertaking it.

- Insights into those people are clearly conveyed to those responsible for managing them.

Furthermore, decisions on the design of the organisation will need to take account of the character of the current workforce, and so too will plans for any future change.

5

Management

IN-HOUSE OR EXTERNAL?

Organisations large enough to support a dedicated recruitment function face a choice on whether to resource the function internally or externally. Where outsourcing occurs, it generally takes one of two forms:

- using an external agency to undertake all the functions expected of an internal recruitment and selection department or

- contracting out individual assignments as required.

There are no hard and fast rules as to why a recruitment function should or should not be resourced in-house. It is simply a matter of judgement which takes account, as in any other decision, of cost, convenience and suitability. It is true that in theory internal recruiters will be more familiar with the business and the personalities, but in practice they can sometimes be more remote and less supportive than an outsourced agency, who would be acutely aware that its very existence depends upon the quality of service provided. Equally, although specialists should be able to provide a higher quality or lower-cost service than an in-house team, it is often the case that in-house teams can provide higher levels of proficiency, innovation and technical expertise at lower cost than some external specialists. The key considerations will therefore be:

- Is there likely to be sufficient frequency/volume of recruitment/selection to justify an in-house function?

- Can the organisation afford the salaries of a skilled team or the training costs to bring generalist staff up to speed?

- Are there any sensitivities or information about the organisation which need to be closely guarded?

There has been a trend in recent years for larger organisations to streamline and re-position HR Managers as 'Business Partners' or 'Strategy Advisers' so that the role of

HR in supporting the business is more clearly evident. In tandem with this approach has been the centralisation of other HR activities, most notably Personnel Administration, into HR Service Centres. This is usually undertaken as part of a process re-engineering exercise or greater use of technology to facilitate 'remote delivery' of services. Inevitably, as with any new idea, it has been adopted in many different ways to mean different things, from simply relocating HR people in 'business' offices to a radical reconfiguration of HR services and displacement of routine functions. For some organisations there has been a move to centralise some functions such as recruitment into specialised HR centres to achieve economies of scale alongside enhancement of expertise. In moving to the HR centre approach the organisation has the following broad choices:

- to centralise the administration of recruitment activities such as advertising, response handling and employment contracts, taking the opportunity to streamline and make better use of technology

- to centralise recruitment specialists with expertise and skilled support for aspects such as interviewing, testing and assessment centres, taking the opportunity to streamline and raise standards

- to decentralise recruitment expertise so that it is at the point of delivery, within the business unit, making use of the HR Centre for administration and support

- to use external providers or specialists to provide the administration service centre and support in-house recruiters, or use external recruitment specialists supported by an in-house service centre, or to have both either in-house or outsourced.

A number of large agencies in the UK have successfully established outsourced HR service centres in both the public and private sector, although these tend to be dedicated services for an organisation rather than 'call off' arrangements available to groups of small or medium sized enterprises.

RECRUITMENT CONSULTANTS

It is possible to outsource ad hoc assignments to a recruitment consultant. At one time, recruitment consultants were mainly used for specialist or senior appointments where a particular expertise was not available in-house. Nowadays their use is more widespread as Human Resource departments have faced cutbacks and changed their role from being 'providers' of service to 'procurers' of services. Similarly, many organisations have devolved human resource management to line managers who will not have the time or expertise to cope with recruitment 'blips'. There are three main ways in which consultants are used: registers, selection and search.

Registers: Registers were traditionally restricted to temporary agencies (and similar), who maintained a database of candidates sourced primarily from their own advertising. The major advantage of this approach is that candidates were pre-screened and available fairly immediately. In more recent years their use has widened. The incidence of executive redundancy has created interim databases of experienced managers and professional staff capable of undertaking short-term assignments. Many large-scale redundancy programmes have been assisted by out-placement consultants who have developed a database of redundant staff, and are pro-active and professional in marketing their services to prospective organisations. Many specialist recruitment agencies maintain a database of candidates seeking new employment, since they are aware that many organisations express a sense of urgency when assignments arise.

Selection: Consultants may be assigned to a specific project, such as specialist managers or professional staff, and will work with the client to take (or help develop) a clear brief of the candidate, make all the necessary arrangements for advertising, receive applications, screen them on behalf of the client, and provide the client with a shortlist of recommended candidates, usually accompanied by a report on each. The benefits of using a selection consultant are the ability to devote time to the urgent task, the knowledge of the market and how/where to begin advertising, their professionalism, and, where required, the opportunity for the client to remain anonymous.

Search: Consultants operate differently from selection consultants (although many provide both kinds of service) in that selection consultants aim to hold out the job as an attraction for suitably qualified people to apply, while search consultants actively seek out those people with a view to persuading them to work for their client. Using the search approach can be particularly appropriate where there is a small pool of people with potential suitability for the role. It has thus tended to be restricted to executive and very specialist positions. The advantage of using the search method is that it is more targeted, and more pro-active than simply relying on appropriate people to apply. The downside is that it can be expensive, carries high discrimination risks, and is very dependent upon the skills and network of the 'head hunter'.

The costs of the three approaches vary widely. The register method can cost from 10 per cent to 30 per cent of the employee's first year salary, depending on the availability and demand for particular skills. Selection consultants normally operate on a fee equivalent to about 20 per cent of the first year's earnings of the selected employee. Search consultants generally charge a fee of around 40 per cent of the first year's earnings. Some consultants charge fees on the basis of time spent rather than related to the earnings of the person recruited, and will apply the charge regardless of the assignment's success. Consultants charging a fee linked to the employee's salary will often only charge (apart from expenses) where the assignment is successful. There is of course the opportunity, though not always taken, to negotiate the scale of fees.

How to choose consultants

In choosing consultants, care should be taken to check out their suitability. It may be appropriate to look at their track record and seek out references on their behalf but, even with satisfactory commendations, their method of operation should be carefully checked since professionalism is not always present. The following points should be checked:

- Will the consultant undertake to prepare a detailed specification to form the basis of the selection assignment and which will be agreed with the client?

- Are guarantees provided on time-scales, with penalties if appropriate?

- Will all elements of decision-making, including screening applications and interviewing be undertaken by the consultant rather than 'delegated' to junior untrained staff?

- Will all candidates be treated courteously, particularly paying regard to the acknowledgement of applications, advice on progress, and promptly notified of decisions?

- Will all ethical and legal requirements be fulfilled and the client indemnified for any liability incurred?

- Will proper methods be used to make the selection, including the use of structured interviews, tests, and other techniques?

- Will they undertake not to 'poach' appointed people at a later stage, or in any other way breach the confidence or trust of the client?

- Will they undertake all appropriate checks such as references and verifying certificates/qualifications claimed?

It is not out of order to question consultants and agencies on these points since they will be the outward face of the organisation and, however confidential the assignment, will at some time cause candidates to connect the reputation of the client organisation with the standards of the consultant/agency.

ADVERTISING AGENCIES

It is possible 'to go it alone' with the employment marketing strategy or any other element related to the process of attracting candidates. It is particularly tempting, where a low level of local recruitment is being undertaken, to draft and place advertisements directly. The use of an advertising agency may seem an extravagance, but it is an area in which any time and money will be well invested. In the simple placing of advertisements, many agencies will work free of charge, using discounts negotiated from the media to 'subsidise' the work undertaken for the client. Sometimes agencies will pass on part of the discount to the client. The benefits of using an agency extend beyond the basic creativity and technical expertise that they can provide. Although this in itself is valuable in reinforcing a proper image of the organisation, some of the greatest benefits come from the process of explaining requirements to the agency. The need to crystallise and present thoughts on the candidate requirements, the opportunities the role affords, and the current state of the organisation, provide an invaluable step in preparing to lay such information before applicants in a clear and attractive fashion. Furthermore it is extremely rare to find an agency being profligate with the client's advertising budget; it is almost universally true that agencies will take great time and care in advising the client on the best possible use of cost-effective media. The use of a well-drafted and attractive advertisement (or any other form of announcement) will pay dividends in improving the response ratio, such as raising the proportion of candidates who are more suited to the role and reducing the proportion and number of unsuitable applications. It is also of course far more efficient for selectors to be devoting their time to selection activities rather than trying to master copywriting or layout skills.

In choosing an advertising agency, it would be appropriate to seek evidence of previous assignments undertaken, and the way in which they were handled. In showing examples of any previous work, the agency should be able to demonstrate how it took the brief and developed a strategy aimed at the target audience, how the advertising was received by that audience, and be able to provide specific measures of response rate, selection ratios and other statistics to illustrate the success of their work. A very clever or visually appealing advertisement may be evidence of a very creative mind but creativity, although important, is much less important than suitability.

LINE MANAGERS OR HR SPECIALISTS?

Where it is decided to bring the recruitment function 'in house' wholly or partly, the degree of line manager involvement needs to be carefully considered. Generally speaking it is safer, given the risks involved in checks, offers and discrimination legislation (see Chapter 18), to ensure that the management of recruitment and selection is in the hands of a consistent group of knowledgeable and experienced recruiters. It is overly ambitious to expect general line managers to keep up-to-date on developments in selection, the markets and the law. Small organisations will not have the luxury of such dedicated resources and it is essential therefore to take time to map out the processes and develop a policy and framework that can be applied consistently. This would reduce the demands in 'getting back up to speed' on the occasions that recruitment is undertaken.

Whatever the size of the organisation and whatever the availability of skilled expertise, it is essential to involve in the process the line manager with whom the new person will work. Such involvement will be valuable in ensuring that the specification is up-to-date but, more importantly, will ensure that the 'chemistry' between the new candidate and their boss is workable, and will also ensure that the manager is committed to the appointment and therefore putting effort into making it work.

A survey conducted by CIPD showed that, for most organisations, the responsibility for advertising, making job offers, and recruitment administration was vested in the HR function, but that the screening and selection of candidates most often involved line managers, either solely or jointly with HR. See Figure 5.1.

Figure 5.1 / *Primary responsibility for recruitment activities*

	Line managers	HR/ personnel	Joint (HR and line manager	Outsourced (e.g. (employment agency)
	%	%	%	%
Placing adverts	8	77	21	8
Screening candidates	33	37	50	9
Selecting candidates	42	13	68	2
Making job offers	19	67	28	2
Recruitment-associated administration	6	91	8	3

6

Systems and support processes

Since recruitment is the shop window of the organisation for new employees it is vital to create a good impression. It is equally important that the image portrayed is the correct one, as unsuccessful and insincere candidates can still become loyal customers or shareholders. All too often it is the 'back up' service that can make the difference between a perception of a slick sophisticated organisation or a bunch of amateurs. A letter containing the wrong name or an offer that never actually gets posted can quickly undo the image created by a professional interview in a prestigious office. It is important therefore to consider the amount of support work involved and resource it effectively.

Whether the resource should be in-house or external, dedicated or ad hoc, will depend on the cost and administrative resource available. In making that decision, consideration should be given to the frequency and scale of recruitment, taking into account the volume of applications rather than the number of positions to be filled. Efforts to improve marketing should help to raise standards so that there are fewer applications but a higher quality. It may still be the case, however, that extra resources need to be allocated to the work involved in supporting the recruitment activity. This work could involve activities such as sending out applications or literature; acknowledging applications and CVs; arranging interviews and assessment; ordering test materials and stationery; obtaining references; and preparing offers and contracts.

MANUAL VERSUS AUTOMATED

There are plenty of opportunities to automate significant parts of recruitment and selection activity. To be cost-effective however there needs to be a high level of homogeneous recruitment. The example of a medium-sized retail organisation with a wide distribution of small stores and where recruitment is undertaken on a store-by-store basis would be illustrative: it would probably not be cost-effective to invest in automated systems at each store. A low-key manual system would probably be more suitable and the administrative burden on each store may not be manageable. Conversely it may be appropriate to develop a central automated system that is shared through a network, or to set up an HR Centre to handle recruitment support remotely.

Given that all word-processing software nowadays provides the opportunity for standard letter templates and mail merge facilities, it is unlikely that a small organisation, with limited recruitment activity, would find it cost-effective to further invest in automated systems, but a large organisation with significant recruitment activity should actively seek opportunities for automation. The benefits of automation go beyond simply the timesaving aspects. There are significant advantages in the following areas:

- storing data effectively

- displaying every candidate's data in a consistent format and organised to match appropriate data in the right place for the right occasion

- sharing the data between different people involved in selection decisions

- accessing all the data for all candidates to correlate with other data in order

- testing the effectiveness and legitimacy of selection decisions and techniques.

RESPONSE HANDLING

Consideration needs to be given to responding to applications and CVs. Where the practice is to accept unsolicited applications it may be appropriate to have information packs available at the 'point of sale' (e.g. reception desk). The pack should contain information about the organisation, the employment proposition and, preferably, self-score questionnaires, together with information on the selection process. Where jobs are specifically advertised the arrangements for response handling will depend on the anticipated volume of response. For large campaigns such as graduate recruitment exercises it may be appropriate to set up a dedicated department or commission a specialist response-handling service.

The options for automation include *telescreening, testing, biodata* and *résumé* scanning. In *telescreening* the candidate makes a telephone call to an automated response line that poses a series of questions and the answers are then decoded against a scoring criteria using voice recognition systems. A partially automated system would involve a live response with questions posed by the operator from a script and keyed into the scoring system. In *testing*, the candidate will complete an ability or personality test that will be machine scored. This can be done through an optical scanner or 'light reader', or can be completed 'on line' over the Internet, at a workstation or booth on the recruiter's premises. *Biodata* will entail a response to a set of biographical questions either on paper to be scanned, or 'on line'. *Résumé* scanning uses text or character recognition systems to detect key words or phrases and score against key criteria, either on the basis of 'on line' completion of a form or scanning typed or handwritten applications or CV. These processes can be fully automated to the extent that no human intervention need take place between the candidates applying for the job. The biodata system is able to acknowledge their application, assess it for fit against the specification, and send a letter of rejection or invitation to interview, or (depending on the degree of faith in the system!) a job offer.

DECISION-MAKING

In making final selection decisions it is important to ensure that all the relevant data assembled during the selection process is collected into an accessible format. Where a competency-based selection is undertaken this would include a score for each competency with the scores derived from a series of tools or an aggregate for each candidate. This, for example, the application screen may have provided a score of 15 and 20 for competencies A and B, the interview produced a score of 18 and 28 for competencies C and D, with a score of 15 and 25 for competencies D and E derived from psychometric tests. The final score of 121 may be used to place candidates in rank order, but the data would be presented as a profile for the candidate against the competencies. See Figure 6.1.

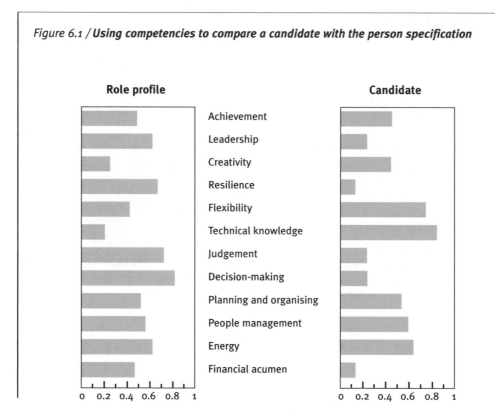

Figure 6.1 / **Using competencies to compare a candidate with the person specification**

An important point, but often overlooked, is that in using the data from different techniques a common and consistent approach should be used so that, for example, the interview and tests use the same scoring systems and the same descriptors of competencies.

There are plenty of opportunities to automate the process of data gathering and most proprietary HR software will include a selection suite that will collect the data, re-present it effectively, and link it to standard letters for rejection, interviews, assessment, or job offers. Collecting the data can also be automated through the use of bar codes and 'light readers' or optical scanners that can ensure that, for example, tests can be scored and the results/report inserted in the candidate's file alongside other data. There are options to automate the process fully so that decisions are automatically taken. In practice, however, there are problems with this because recruitment is not an exact science and the acceptability of a 'machine picked' candidate is a strong challenge to full-time recruiters and line managers alike.

INTERNET

The explosive growth of the Internet in the twenty-first century has made it a widely accepted part of business communication. In the 2004 CIPD Survey of Recruitment more than 70 per cent of employers received applications and CVs by e-mail while 24 per cent provided online completion of applications. The reasons cited for using the Internet are often cost savings (either in advertising or administrative support) or speed of response and hire. Inevitably, as the growth of Internet recruitment continues, the decision will simply be made on the basis that it is the accepted norm.

There are various options for using the Internet in recruitment from a very simple experimental approach to a fully-fledged 'e-recruitment', on-line process. It is possible for organisations to use their own sites, to use agencies to undertake the process on their behalf or to make use of commercial sites. Research has shown that over 40 per cent of job seekers begin their search from a search engine. There are, however, dedicated job sites where candidates can search for a wide range of opportunities. There has been significant volatility in the job site business and today's market leaders quickly become tomorrow's casualties. To identify key sites enter 'jobs' and country into a search engine or in the UK use the National On-line Recruitment Audience Survey website (www. noras.co.uk) to gather information. Whatever decision is taken on the use of the Internet for recruitment, it is essential for recruiters to check their own company's website to ensure that there is information on the nature of employment in the company (preferably setting out the employment brand) and how to set about securing it (even if that isn't through the Internet). Recruiters have the following options available to them:

- Use the organisation's own website, setting up dedicated pages with hyperlinks to current vacancies and methods for submitting applications and CVs electronically, and completing online applications.

- Appoint a third party to provide the organisation's job site, often 'attached' seamlessly to the organisation's main website.

- Use an agency or job board (web sites dedicated to recruitment advertising) to post vacancies or career opportunities.

Successful recruiters often use a mixed approach. This is because candidates interested in a particular organisation will look at that organisation's web site and will be missed if there is sole reliance on a job board. This situation is particularly relevant to passive job seekers who may, for example, be buyers searching for a supplier or scientists researching data and who 'stumble across' very suitable opportunities. Conversely someone looking for a job change may be seeking an opportunity but had not thought about a specific organisation. This type of person will be more likely to be captured by a job board. Since a number of job boards are linked directly or indirectly to newspaper publishers, it is often the case that recruiters are persuaded to use both media; this however must be of questionable value. There are some concerns over access to the Internet and the potential for unfair discrimination against certain groups. The practical evidence however seems to be that age, gender, or ethnicity are not barriers to Internet access or usage. Particular care however needs to be paid to people with disabilities; the Employers' Forum on Disability provides a guide to barrier-free e-recruitment on their website (www. barrierfree-recruiment.com).

It is probably true to say that recruiters have not yet grasped the full potential of the Internet. All too often Internet recruitment involves the grafting-on of traditional adverts and brochures with little real conception of user interaction and image projection. Given that the Internet is half a century old and has been widely available for the last quarter, it will be interesting to see when recruiters stop talking about the 'new technology' and instead think fundamentally about the processes for attracting and selecting people, list the barriers to speed and effectiveness, and then examine how the Internet can be fully exploited to overcome them.

7

Using the right tools and techniques

There are numerous tools and techniques to assist in the screening and selection of candidates, and choices will need to be made on which of them to use. Descriptions of the techniques follow, but the choice of any technique will need to be based on one of the following:

- suitability
- resource and cost constraints
- effectiveness
- acceptability.

Suitability is concerned with whether the technique is appropriate for the specific aspect it is attempting to assess. Looking at qualifications, for example, will not provide an indication of personality characteristics nor will measures of personality give an indication of expertise in a particular subject area. This is not to say that application forms or personality tests are not effective selection techniques, simply that they are only effective when applied to a suitable purpose. Consideration of resource and cost constraints may be an affront to purists looking at the effectiveness of techniques, but such is the reality of life in modern organisations that the proverbial coat needs to be cut to fit the cloth. This is not an entirely negative viewpoint and it is sometimes the case that organisations adopt too great a sophistication in selection practices, whereas a clear focus and some more 'basic' techniques would provide a very effective selection system. It is important to look at the effectiveness or validity of any particular technique if reliance is to be placed upon it. Great emphasis is often placed by researchers on this particular aspect, often to the exclusion of any other consideration. In practice, although important, it needs to be considered alongside the other three factors. The acceptability of a technique is of great importance. 'Acceptability' includes acceptability to the client (whether a formal external relationship or an internal 'colleague' relationship), acceptability to candidates, as well as compliance with ethical and legal standards.

SUITABILITY

It is important in choosing the technique to focus on the aspect that it is intended to measure. This becomes much easier when a competency-based approach is used. Using the competencies framework outlined in Part 3, it is possible to look at the most suitable techniques for innate or natural qualities, acquired skills, and adapting behaviours. Natural competencies (i.e. the underlying personality traits and characteristics) can be identified through the use of personality tests, graphology or structured behavioural interviews. The acquired competencies lend themselves to identification through techniques such as the application form or curriculum vitae, ability tests and structured interview. Similarly, work simulation or telephone screening can also be used to identify the acquired competencies. Techniques suitable for the adapting competencies include personality testing, structured behavioural interviewing, structured situational interviewing and graphology. Assessment centres that comprise a range of techniques such as testing, interviewing and exercises can have individual components of the assessment centre targeted on natural, acquired or adapting competencies. Biodata is suitable for identifying natural, acquired and adapting competencies, but the nature of the technique means that it is not possible to identify which particular competency (and therefore which particular type) is being identified since it works on matching rather than analysis. Generally speaking, clearly defined requirements such as experience or qualifications that come under the acquired competencies are suitable for identification through explicit measurements such as application forms or straightforward interviews or tests of ability. The less visible aspects such as personality characteristics that are to be found in the natural competencies are better identified through indirect or 'subtle' techniques such as testing or graphology. The adapting competencies are more suited to identification through dynamic techniques such as interviewing which enable elements to be explored on an interactive basis, but personality testing can identify the propensity to be adaptable and assessment centre exercises and work simulations can attempt to replicate the real workplace dynamics.

RESOURCES AND COSTS

Selection techniques differ widely in their resource requirements and cost to support. It is however important to look at costs in the complete sense of development costs, production costs and usage costs. Consideration also needs to be given to whether the technique is to be used for screening or selection decisions, since the number of applicants screened will usually be greater than the number of candidates being assessed in the final selection. In some cases the screening process will need to deal with very high volumes indeed.

Of the main screening techniques, CVs have no development or production costs because such costs are borne by the applicant, but the usage cost is generally higher than application forms or biodata. This is because CVs are not standardised and therefore screeners will be 'inefficient' because of the need to familiarise themselves with different layouts and perhaps missing information. Application forms are generally cheaper to design and produce, even if undertaken professionally, and although the final unit cost will be dependent upon the shelf life of the form and the volume of applications processed, unit costs are usually measured in pence rather than pounds. Usage costs with application forms are usually lower than with CVs, because screeners can become proficient in finding and assessing the information, particularly where proper training is provided and a scoring system used. Biodata and telephone screening are higher cost options. It is possible to develop a biodata form 'in-house' but it is more usual to employ consultants to develop the form, and consultant fees of around ten to fifteen days would seem an appropriate guide for total development costs. Printing will be on a par with application forms if scored manually, but where a decision is taken to use light-reading machines, specialist printing equipment will be necessary. This may push the unit costs into pounds rather than pence. Using light-reading machines for scoring biodata necessitates a capital investment, usually a few thousand pounds, but since such a machine can score a biodata form in less than a second it can, with large volume campaigns, reduce usage costs to such an extent that even with all the development expenditure it becomes the lowest-cost screening option. There is also the opportunity to link the biodata scoring to applicant databases and word processing or mail merge software to automate the administration of selection still further. Telephone screening has a high development cost particularly where online scoring and appointment logging systems are used, since programmes need to be written, scripts prepared and telephone interviewers trained. Production costs are also high since call centres need to be staffed to respond to applicants, leading to equipment and staffing expenditure. The usage costs will be high because of the need to staff the call centres and the overall costs of telephone screening can therefore be significantly higher than paper screening, running into unit costs of several pounds. There is however the opportunity to offset costs of later selection techniques such as the interview or to conduct the interview within the telephone operation.

The cost of assessment techniques can vary significantly, not simply because of the comparative costs of the techniques themselves, but because for each technique there may be a variation in costs between different providers. Interviewing can be seen as a low cost activity since most people are capable of establishing a dialogue with a candidate, but an effective interview will incur some development cost in the development of an interview system and the training of interviewers whilst the usage costs of the interview (effective or ineffective) will be significant because of interviewer time. These costs may be 'hidden', where internal resources are used, or explicit, where external consultants are used. Unit costs of a one-on-one interview are expensive when measured in labour cost terms and the unit costs of panel interviews are of course significantly greater. Some organisations choose to develop their interviewing system in-house and provide training accordingly, whereas others choose to use proprietary interview training costing a few hundred pounds or go for proprietary interviewing systems. These systems may vary in cost between providers from a few hundred to several thousand pounds.

The cost of psychometric testing varies widely. There are some published tests that are available freely and therefore cost nothing to develop or acquire. The most expensive option is probably the development of a bespoke test that would take anything upward from twenty days of consultant time. For larger organisations with in-house psychologist expertise and significant recruitment demands, this may however be a very cost effective route. The cost of proprietary tests differs between providers but, generally speaking, ability tests cost less than personality tests – the former being in pounds and the latter being in tens of pounds. Some organisations sell their tests as single usage tests and charge a unit price, others provide re-usable tests and charge a one-off purchase fee, whereas others provide multiple usage tests but charge an annual licence. Costs are sometimes attached to the test itself; sometimes they are attached to the scoring system. In addition to the cost of the tests there is the cost of training. Organisations employing occupational psychologists will not incur additional training costs, but for all others it is usually the case that British Psychological Society rules will be applied and users of ability tests will need to undergo level A training of six days, and users of personality tests will be required to additionally undertake level B training at a further six days. In addition to the explicit test costs there are also the 'hidden' costs of time spent in administration and scoring, even taking into account the fact that most scoring nowadays is computer based. It should be noted that training in test administration is provided to individuals, not organisations, and the loss of selectors can therefore necessitate further costs in the training of their successors.

Graphology has no development or production cost since it is based on the handwriting of candidates in a free format. There are, however, significant usage costs in that the handwriting analysis will need to be performed by a trained graphologist at an average cost of a day's consultancy per analysis.

Assessment centres are probably the most costly of any of the selection techniques because they usually comprise a combination of techniques. The design of the assessment centre can often represent significant development cost and, if undertaken by an external consultant, will take around five to fifteen days consultancy time depending on the balance of original or 'off the shelf' material used. In addition to the development costs, there is a significant degree of training required for assessors and usage costs are high because of the numbers of assessors used and the range of materials employed.

It is difficult to make a straightforward cost comparison between the various assessment techniques, but in simple terms it is fair to say that testing, graphology and third-party interviewing are high on 'hard' (visible) costs but light on resource requirements, whereas in-house interviewing is low on hard cost but high on resource requirement, and assessment centres are high on resource requirements and medium to high on hard costs.

EFFECTIVENESS

The effectiveness of any selection technique is of great importance since the amount of resource or cost devoted to it, or the degree of reliance placed upon it, must be influenced by its accuracy. It may therefore seem surprising that hard evidence on the comparative effectiveness of different selection techniques is not available, although some studies have been undertaken to compare results of the studies of each technique carried out separately. Closer consideration of the problem of measuring effectiveness helps, however, to reveal the difficulty of establishing valid results. In shortlisting or selecting a candidate it may, for example, be possible to review the extent to which the particular technique helped to predict successful performance of that candidate. It is highly unlikely that there will be a chance to evaluate whether the rejected candidates would have been less, equally or more able to perform than the selected candidate, because they were rejected and no opportunity was therefore afforded to evaluate their subsequent performance. There are very few true 'control' experiments in which suitable and unsuitable candidates are selected as a means of assessing the effectiveness of the selection technique. Consider further the difficulty of assessing the performance of the successful candidate. Failure to perform may be attributable to the candidate, but equally it may be attributable to the way in which they were managed, the support provided, relationships with colleagues, the quality of the product which they were working on, or a host of other variables. It is rarely the case that success or failure can be wholly attributed to the individual. Consider also the measures of success. Is the measure the achievement of targets regardless of other aspects such as team relationships, or is it the quality of performance possibly measured in team relationships or customer service, irrespective of volume of output or targets achieved? Is success wholly a matter of performance, or does the length of time the new person stays or the amount of absence they incur, or their level of work satisfaction play any part in evaluating 'success'? In looking at the effectiveness of the selection technique, can it be assumed that the results of that technique contributed wholly, partly or not at all to the decision to select? Is the rating of a supervisor a reliable indicator of successful performance?

The imponderables and variables outlined above are all reasons why care must be taken in accepting or rejecting the research into the effectiveness of any selection technique. Furthermore when looking at the failure of techniques, consideration needs to be given as to whether the technique itself was inadequate or whether the way it was used rendered it ineffective.

Allowing for the above considerations, it is still possible to gain a general view of the effectiveness of the various techniques. Taking a common scale from 0 to 1 it is possible to undertake some guarded comparison. The value 0 reflects random choice, the equivalent of the toss of a coin. Choosing every sixth person to walk through the door would of course score 0 because as a random method it is no more effective than any other random choice. It needs to be remembered that occasionally the sixth person through the door will be an effective performer purely by chance. Thus selectors who believe in always choosing candidates with blue eyes, and rejecting ones with white socks – or some other arbitrary factor – will inevitably be able to point to examples of where 'their technique' brought measurable results. Perfect selection is measured as 1, that is to say, that the technique identifies the suitable candidate for the position every time. It is interesting to note that no technique has been proposed as, or found to be, a perfect selection system. Good selection is therefore about improving the odds of success rather than guaranteeing it.

The **application form** has been reported as having a predictive validity (that is to say effective at predicting job performance or some other success factor) of 0.2. On the face of it, this is a fairly low predictive validity. However, care needs to be taken because much of the research on application forms has been on how they are used and what they measure rather than the effectiveness of the things they measure. The low rating is therefore more a reflection on the poor use of application forms than on the technique itself. Given the wide diversity of application forms it is also very difficult to bring a standard assessment of them. Notable research by Herriot and Wingrove (1984) highlighted the idiosyncratic nature of assessors' evaluation of application forms. This research showed that the likelihood of success by the candidate in securing an interview was attributed more to the amount of space taken up on the form than on the quality of the information contained within it, or any other significant factor. Notwithstanding the results of the studies, it must be true to say that, even allowing for occasional dishonesty, an application form must be an effective technique (far greater than 0.2) of assessing whether an individual possesses certain academic qualifications, or professional certificates, or relevant experience. As long as it is used to screen for appropriate matters (i.e. acquired competencies), then it will be an effective technique, particularly if it is used properly with a clear rating system.

Various studies on **interview** effectiveness have demonstrated a significant difference between structured and unstructured interviews. Unstructured interviews generally have predictive validity of 0.2 with structured interviews averaging about 0.4, but with structured situational interviews scoring less, and structured behavioural interviews scoring more. Given that users of structured interviewing will have usually received training in such interviewing, there is the possibility that the heightened skill of the interviewer raises the results of the technique. Recent research has identified that behavioural interviews (experienced based) are more effective predictors of success than the situational (future scenario) interview. Both types of interviews might benefit from the following enhancements that could improve their effectiveness:

- proper job analysis to identify the key factors or competencies

- consistent and structured interview questions

- a panel of interviewers

- examples of effective questions

- a consistent rating system

- note-taking during the interview.

It has been concluded that, using this approach, the effectiveness of the interview is raised from 0.14 for traditional interviews to 0.56 for structured interviews, which makes it one of the most effective selection techniques.

One of the least researched aspects of selection is around the way in which the individual fits with the organisation culture or team. The limited research that has been undertaken indicates that the structured interview is one of the most effective ways of assessing the person-organisation fit.

The effectiveness of **psychometric tests** for predicting performance has been subject to a significant degree of research. It is however not without contention, and results need to be carefully considered. The received wisdom is that ability/cognitive tests have a higher predictive validity than personality tests. Ability tests score at around 0.53, whereas personality tests score from 0.2 to 0.5 dependent upon the research used.

Ability tests are fairly robust because the aspect they seek to assess – an observable or measurable skill – is easily measured and the test itself can therefore be validated. Designing a typing test or a spelling test or some other form of ability test is therefore, to a great extent, foolproof. Why do ability tests then not score more highly? The answer is that the abilities which they measure are not always wholly or directly related to job performance. This is particularly the case where cognitive tests have been used to identify 'intelligence' for managerial posts, but where no causal relationship has been shown between intelligence and management performance. There are also some problems with test construction because many of the tests have been developed using school children or university students in the development stages but later applied to mature adults, and it is an accepted phenomenon that mental ability deteriorates with age. The additional benefits that the mature worker enjoys however, such as experience and decision-making, may allow 'wisdom' to more than compensate for any 'deficiencies' in mental ability and therefore enable a higher performance than their youthful counterparts. Consequently, there may be doubts cast over the test, whereas it may be the hypothesis that is unsound. Generally speaking, where an ability test is designed to measure an ability, and that particular ability is directly related to job performance, then the test will be an effective predictor.

Personality tests have been the subject of greater contention. One of the difficulties in establishing the effectiveness of personality tests is that research has been undertaken for many decades but, until the last two or three decades, there was no consensus on the components of personality. It was therefore difficult to conclude that they would predict anything if it was not known what they were trying to predict. For the last three decades there has been consensus on the big five factors of personality and it has therefore become easier to research the effectiveness of personality tests in gauging personality and predicting work performance. Personality tests have a predictive validity of around 0.4. Behind the statement, however, lies a considerable degree of academic controversy. The prevailing view is that personality remains fairly constant over time. It is entirely feasible therefore that accurately gauging personality at any point in time will enable us to predict the broad patterns of behaviour which will be displayed by that person in subsequent life. Translating that prediction directly to work performance is however a quantum leap. It is not necessarily certain that a particular personality characteristic will contribute positively or negatively to work performance, and there are difficulties in excluding consideration of the knowledge of the individual, or the fit with the environment, or the way in which they are managed. One of the difficulties of assessing the effectiveness of psychometric tests is the degree of contention that they provoke. Those who oppose them, often do so from a viewpoint of ignorance or because they have been let down by placing too much reliance on a particular test. Those who promote their use can often do so with a conviction and enthusiasm that outstrips their validity. For certain positions, personality may be less important than other aspects such as acquired knowledge. It is therefore stretching a point to argue that a psychometric test, which properly predicts personality, can be predictive of job performance since job performance may only be attributable in part to personality. In choosing a legal adviser, for example, greater importance would be attached to legal knowledge and qualifications than to personality characteristics. Conversely, selection of a sales representative in certain industries may not demand any prior knowledge or qualifications, and the personality characteristics that drive selling skills may be more important, perhaps critical, selection criteria. Periodically, in the UK, there is a barrage of criticism vented against personality tests; such assaults are usually promulgated by one or two prominent individuals and generally coincide with publication of their new ability tests. Care needs to be taken therefore to assess the motive for such criticisms. Whilst the research evidence on the predictive strengths of personality tests is interesting it is not always consistent. Invariably the results will also include the outcome of poorly applied or unsuitable tests which will bring down the overall validity. It is more pertinent that very few organisations that use personality tests take the trouble to make the information generally available on their use and success. Many organisations that are satisfied with the use of the test and find it valuable in predicting job suitability of candidates are not prepared to collect information on their success. There are many unpublished examples of the use of personality tests to identify predictors of job performance that are being used to improve significantly the effectiveness of selection.

Assessment Centres generally have a very high predictive validity. This has to be a generalisation because assessment centres take many forms and there is difficulty in applying a common standard to them all. It is nevertheless the case that assessment centres, which comprise a range of selection techniques such as structured interviewing, testing, and exercises, will provide a higher validity than other techniques operated in isolation. There is however a need for a word of caution: psychologists are very favourably inclined towards assessment centres and there is the danger that studies of their effectiveness may have been tainted with optimism. More concerning, perhaps, are the criteria used to assess effectiveness. Two of the most commonly quoted are supervisor ratings of performance, and promotion success. It is of course the case that assessment centres are most frequently used for graduate selection or selection on to management development schemes. There is therefore a very strong influence of self-fulfilling prophecies since most organisations that have a graduate intake or management development scheme tend to give preference for promotion to those on such schemes. It is also the case that people on these schemes are rated by the person in charge of the graduate training scheme or management development programme rather than solely by the trainee's line manager. Even where assessment is undertaken by the line manager, it is often the case that such managers take a lenient approach to rating because of the effects of the rating on the career prospects of the trainee. It is also not unusual for eligibility to be restricted by certain criteria to pre-qualify for entry to the assessment centres; for internal centres this may be a supervisor's pre-assessment and for external centres it may be a degree qualification. Where there is pre-selection, the possibility cannot be ruled out that all candidates would have been suitable. Notwithstanding these caveats, the assessment centre is almost certainly the most effective selection technique.

Graphology is not widely used in the UK and, where it is used, it does not have a high visibility. There is therefore a paucity of information on its effectiveness in the UK. The technique is widely used in France, Germany, Switzerland and Israel but there seems to be a similar paucity of effectiveness studies. This may not be entirely surprising given that the most popular selection techniques in the UK, the application form and interview, have similarly attracted scant research attention. The studies that have been undertaken are mostly in the United States.

Although there have been few studies undertaken, those which have been properly undertaken demonstrate that graphology can be an effective predictor of performance and other aspects. In the UK there has been a concerted body of opposition to graphology, most notably from the British Psychological Society. In mounting opposition, the opponents cite 'hostile' research studies to disprove graphology but omit mention of those that support their effectiveness and, more lamentably, state that such studies do not exist. A review of the 'hostile' studies shows an alarming lack of objectivity and thoroughness. In one oft-quoted study, researchers asked the subjects to copy a piece of text. This, in terms of graphology, is like asking a third party to complete a personality test on one's behalf. In two other studies conducted in 1984 and 1986, graphologists competed with psychologists and laymen to predict job success in candidates. The results showed that graphologists had a higher success rate than both the psychologists and the laymen but the researchers dismissed the success by claiming that the psychologists could have based their predictions on the content of the text as much as the writing itself.

A study undertaken in 1995 provided a number of graphologists with forty pairs of handwriting. Each pair consisted of one random sample and one successful entrepreneur (chosen from Chief Executives of INC Magazine 500 companies). The graphologists were asked to identify the 40 entrepreneurs and the study was carefully constructed to remove any content in the writing to serve as a clue. The three graphologists were successful respectively in 31, 34, and 34 out of the 40 samples.

Studies of 'researcher effectiveness' has revealed that researchers often fail to assess evidence correctly before them if such evidence does not fit in with their preconceptions and beliefs. There seems to be a strong case of such 'data blindness' creeping in to evaluations of effectiveness in graphology. It also needs to be remembered that ten years ago psychologists were dismissing the interview as an ineffective selection technique with similar scores to those attributed to graphology but, as with graphology, provided little hard evidence to support their views. More recent research has revealed the effectiveness of interviews, particularly of a structured nature.

Although **biodata** is not extensively used in selection in the UK, it has an extensive body of research to provide an insight into its effectiveness. Most of the research has been undertaken in the United States, but research undertaken in the UK has mirrored the findings of US research and served to demonstrate that cultural differences do not distort the research findings.

Biodata has been impressively validated in predicting a number of work-related factors including performance, absenteeism, job tenure and income. The most-quoted review has not been an academic study but a practical study of biodata in use in Standard Oil of Indiana in the 1960s. Biodata was administered to a group of petroleum research scientists, validated and cross validated against three different criteria of overall performance ratings, creativity ratings, and number of patents. The validations for the criteria were 0.61, 0.52 and 0.52 respectively, which provides a very significant degree of correlation. In the 1980s a flurry of large-scale research projects and meta-analysis of other studies consistently demonstrated the effectiveness of biodata as a predictor of performance and other work-related aspects. The studies varied in their rating of biodata from 0.34 to 0.46. Many of the researchers have placed a high value on the predictive validity of biodata; in some cases running second only to assessment centres and in some cases slightly less than ability tests. In addition to predicting performance, however, biodata has been seen to be very effective as an indicator of potential absenteeism and retention. See Figure 7.1.

Figure 7.1 / Comparisons of candidate profile

The reports below relate to the same person and are real results. They are three extracts taken from interview, graphology analysis, and psychometric testing. The three were undertaken independently of each other or any other technique.

Report from a structured interview	Analysis of two pages of abstract handwriting	Feedback from psychometric test
Confidently infer a strong ability at both the implementation and strategic level ...	Exhibits a sense of purpose which contributes to continuing determination when faced with a task ... an added streak of persistence which makes him welcome challenges and difficulties ...	... thinks ahead, organises, plans, and makes a systematic effort to reach objectives on schedule.
Leaves me in no doubt he can take people with him ...	He has an instinctive feel for a situation. This sensitivity helps him to maneouvre others to do what he wants even without their realising it.	Responds to opportunities for taking the lead and being given responsibility but may be resistant to too much direction from others.
An individual able to see what a given problem is and then select one or two of the major options for resolving and to drive through to good effect.	... he thinks quickly, addressing his attention to what he considers to be major issues. His incisive intellect enables him to pick up quickly on ideas although he is unlikely to analyse them in depth. This carries with it the danger of jumping to conclusions.	... stimulated by problems where he can find and implement new solutions ... run the risk of deciding too quickly before firstly examining the situation.
... works as a team player ...	... he adopts a friendly approach to others on the basis that this will bring best results ...	... will enjoy demonstrating being part of a group.

ACCEPTABILITY

In addition to consideration of the suitability of the technique for the aspects being measured, the effectiveness of the technique in measuring such aspects, and the resource/cost to apply it, consideration also needs to be given to the acceptability of the technique. Acceptability may be looked at in the following ways:

- client acceptability
- candidate acceptability and
- ethical/legal acceptability.

Acceptability to clients is an important point because, for example, a line manager who does not endorse the use of psychometric testing will dismiss it as a 'black box' and disregard any information, however valuable, which comes from it. It is of course, not only the client but sometimes the selector who may be fazed by a particular technique. It is often true that biodata scores are at odds with interviewers' perceptions and can cause some difficulty if used as a shortlisting technique. Given that biodata can be a more effective predictor than certain kinds of interviews an interesting conflict arises as to which technique should be given the greater credence. In practice, acceptability will usually win over effectiveness and underlines the importance of this aspect in choosing techniques. There is no comprehensive research into the reasons behind discomfort with certain techniques, but the following general conclusions may be relevant:

- Interviewers can feel uncomfortable with interviews, as they may be more conscious of their own performance in the interview than that of the interviewee and an awkwardness of knowing what questions to ask and how to gauge the suitability of answers given. Structured interviews overcome these problems, but then create other problems, such as the interviewer feeling awkward in coming to terms with the structures of a controlled process or avoiding structured questions which lead to a staccato rather than a fluid dialogue of investigation.

- Biodata creates discomfort because it cannot provide substantiated reasons for its conclusions and is therefore difficult to grasp. It is seen as a black box and often differs with interview ratings.

- Ability tests create discomfort in treating candidates as school children rather than adults, which may have to do with the way in which they are administered. Personality tests, however, are sometimes seen as rather vague and meaningless questions that cannot be relied upon to support conclusions drawn. Sometimes the reports from personality tests are as impenetrable as the tests themselves and peppered with psycho-babble that leaves line managers 'cold'. Tests that use bar chart profiles and other diagrammatic devices to present the data are more popular with clients.

- Assessment centres can be seen as tedious, time consuming, and often overly academic and impractical with many line managers attributing a low validity at great odds to the published data.

- Graphology has received so much assault from certain psychologists that many selectors dismiss its effectiveness without any consideration and some clients feel that handwriting is too 'juvenile' an element for consideration in selecting adults (although it is more frequently used in senior selection than others).

These are of course generalisations and they are not universal beliefs. There are many interviewers who praise biodata, many line managers with an evangelistic zeal for psychometric testing, and some senior executives place great reliance upon the outcome of handwriting analysis. Acceptability of selection methods to clients is like acceptability of anything else – one person's meat is another person's poison. Some investigations into client preferences for selection techniques have been undertaken. In the United States in 1996, executives were asked to rate various selection methods in their perceived effectiveness for identifying high performing employees. It should be noted that this was not a wholly subjective process and that many of the organisations relied upon internal studies of the validation of the various techniques. The results were rated on a scale of 1 for 'no good' through 3 for 'average' to 5 for 'extremely good'. The results were:

work samples	3.68
references/recommendation	3.49
unstructured interviews	3.49
structured interviews	3.42
assessment centres	3.42
specific aptitude tests	3.08
personality tests	2.93
cognitive ability tests	2.89
biodata	2.84

A study in the UK of small businesses – a third of the UK workforce is employed by the 88 per cent of businesses who employ less than 25 people – showed that 92 per cent used formal interviews (of whom 66 per cent used unstructured interviews and 34 per cent used structured interviews), 44 per cent used work trials or realistic work previews for a week or so, 18 per cent used job simulations, 18 per cent used literacy and numeracy tests, 15 per cent used ability tests and 3.6 per cent used personality tests. Less than 20 per cent used a formal application form in order to gather information on candidates,

27 per cent used a CV and 20 per cent relied on general letters, but 58 per cent used face-to-face interviews to gather the data and 20 per cent obtained it on the telephone. In terms of usefulness the interview was deemed to be the most useful method with references, CVs and application forms some way behind, and work trials, ability and personality tests as the least useful.

In a survey of over 800 UK organisations undertaken by CIPD in 2004, the most frequently used selection methods were interviews (66 per cent based around the application form and 62 per cent using a competency-based interview), tests for specific skills (60 per cent), ability tests (53 per cent), personality questionnaires (46 per cent), literacy and numeracy tests (48 per cent), and assessment centres (43 per cent). The screening was mainly undertaken by application forms, used by 81 per cent and CVs by 75 per cent. On-line application forms accounted for 24 per cent, although 56 per cent accepted applications by e-mail. Telephone screening was not covered in the survey but previous research has shown this to be a growth area with around a third of employers using it.

The respondents were not asked to nominate the best selection methods but another survey of over 200 employers, conducted by IRS Employment Review in 2004, asked employers for the single most effective technique:

interviews	53.6 %
assessment centres	23.1 %
application form/CV	8.8 %
ability/aptitude tests	5.1 %
personality questionnaire	1.0 %
references	0.5 %

Smaller organisations were more likely to rate the interview highly, while the larger organisations rated assessment centres highly. Nearly all employers used references, but it was an area of concern since many were more inclined to ask for references than to provide them, and many were wary of the reliance that could be placed upon references given. Just over half of the respondents requested references before offering a job, but the survey did not indicate how many took up references before making their selection decision.

One of the interesting facets of the IRS survey is that it highlights the contrasting views of academics and practitioners. Until the last decade, academics wrote off interviews as little better than chance selection and, even now, only afford limited recognition to the effectiveness of structured interviews. Yet practitioners cited the interview as not only a very common technique, but also a very useful one. Academics give a high regard to ability tests. However, their opinion is not shared by practitioners and furthermore the IRS survey would suggest that where literacy and numeracy tests and some other ability tests are used, their use is more of an 'excuse' to reduce unwanted volumes of applications. It is also noteworthy that the great body of academic research amongst psychologists confirms the five factor theory of personality and that efforts to replicate the findings of Cattell's 16 factors of personality have not been successful. Efforts to justify greater numbers of factors such as the 32 used in the Occupational Personality Questionnaire have been similarly unsuccessful. Similarly, instruments such as Belbin's team roles or the Myers-Briggs Indicator have not been corroborated by independent research and, though useful for development purposes, are not regarded as having any reliance for selection purposes. The Personal Profile Analysis (hitherto known as the Thomas International or Disc) is not without significant concern over its validity. In the IRS survey, the most popular proprietary selection tests were the OPQ, 16PF, the Personal Profile Analysis, Belbin, FIRO-B, the Myers Briggs Type Indicator and the Perception and Preference Inventory, none of which adhere to the established principle of the big five factors of personality, or enjoy widespread academic support. On a similar note, biodata, which has very high predictive validity and is popular with academics, is not so popular with practitioners.

It may be the case that rationality is not a prime determinant in favouring selection techniques whereas ease of use, understanding and the presentation of data are more important considerations than effectiveness or cost. It is also the case, of course, that the most popular tests in use are those which are marketed most effectively and it may be that selectors respond to the sales overtures of test publishers rather than deciding on the need for a test and then undertaking a survey of available choices. Finally the influence of fashion should not be ruled out and in choosing techniques, recruiters may be more influenced by those in use in other organisations and their 'track record' than deciding to embark on protracted investigation into the efficiency of the techniques or products. Certainly practical considerations alone would not explain differences in the popularity of techniques differing between countries. One study of selection techniques in French and British firms gave the following comparisons of usage:

Technique	Use in French firms	Use in British firms
Assessment centres	18.8%	58.9%
Biodata	3.8%	19.1%
Personality tests	17.0%	9.6%
Graphology	77.0%	0%

There is little reason to suspect that practitioners in either country are less concerned than the other with issues of effectiveness, usability and cost.

Acceptability to candidates, of selection techniques, has not been greatly researched. There has been some academic research including research into the impact on morale and performance, but it has generally been contradictory. Research by practitioners is similarly uncommon although some organisations take time to canvas the views of both successful and unsuccessful applicants/candidates to gauge their perceptions of the process, their feelings about the company, and concerns about fairness (particularly equality of opportunity).

The degree of familiarity will of course influence perceptions of the process; whilst candidates may be irritated by the need to complete an application form, particularly if poorly designed, they are unlikely to condemn it as inappropriate or intrusive since they will expect it to be part of the standard selection process. Allowing for differences in the results of the various forms of research, perceptions of candidates seem to be as follows:

- Application forms are generally an expected and uneventful part of the selection process and taken in their stride by most candidates. They are most resented at senior levels where candidates prefer to prepare their own CV (and can be particularly irritated if asked to complete after a CV has already been provided), and they are intimidating for manual workers unaccustomed to completion of 'official forms'.

- Interviews are similarly regarded as an expected part of the process and the lack of interview is viewed more unfavourably than 'failure' at interview. It is the case however that candidates' perceptions are more strongly influenced by the conduct of the interview than the interview itself, and a badly handled interview is more damaging than no interview at all. There seems to be no evidence that panel interviews are regarded as any more intimidating to candidates than one-to-one interviews, and structured interviews are not seen as any more demanding by candidates than unstructured interviews. The structured situational interview is however regarded as a hurdle by some candidates, particularly for manual workers where the ambiguity of non-specific future situations and the need to describe hypothetical responses in an abstract language contrast sharply with the specificity of current circumstances and the limited 'earthy' language in everyday use. The behavioural or experience-based structured interview does not suffer such a drawback and although it may appear to be an interrogation from the interviewer's viewpoint, feedback from candidates indicates that they are more at ease with the process and consider it to be wholly relevant to the selection procedure.

- Biodata has a mixed review with some studies showing that candidates perceived it to be less invasive than ability tests and other techniques whilst some showed that there was candidate hostility to the process. In some cases biodata has ceased to be used because of hostility from candidates and although its use is most frequently with graduates there is some evidence that even graduates find it unwelcome. It tends to be most acceptable when included as a supplementary part of an orthodox application form.

- Ability tests have a mixed blessing. Graduates and school leavers accustomed to examinations and tests are rarely fazed by them but some groups find them deeply offensive. Ability tests are proven to be more difficult for older workers and, since test norms are usually developed using graduates and school children, may be viewed as unduly hard and resented by older workers. Candidates for managerial and professional roles can be puzzled by 'school tests' which bear little relation to the realities of their roles. Ethnic groups, to whom they may be discriminatory, can be offended by their use particularly where the tests are for abilities that bear no relation to the qualities needed for the position being filled. More legal actions have been taken against employers over the use of ability tests than any other technique.

- Assessment centres are generally well received and, if properly handled, can even be enjoyed by candidates. There is clear evidence that where feedback is provided to candidates (a frequent feature of assessment centres) the candidate's perception of the selection process is very favourable regardless of success or failure.

Given the lack of hard evidence of perceptions of candidates to the selection process, it is important that organisations undertake periodic surveys of candidates' reactions to the selection process. This should particularly be the case where the selection is undertaken by a third party, such as a recruitment agency, on behalf of the organisation since it is not uncommon for administrative convenience and economic consideration to outweigh consideration of courtesy to candidates. It is regrettably not uncommon for some agencies to fail to acknowledge applications or advise on the outcome. It is not uncommon for agencies to write to candidates *'should you not hear from us in the next x weeks you should presume that...'* Disaffected candidates can all too easily become disenchanted customers. In the United States, for example, it has been estimated that one in four of the population has either worked for, or applied for, employment with McDonalds; the potential impact upon the business, of the way such candidates are treated, is very clear and provides sound commercial reasons for handling them with care.

Ethical and legal acceptability are important because there are many opportunities for unfair discrimination to creep into the selection process, from the development of a person specification based on stereotypes of race, gender or physical ability, through to prejudices in decision-making. There is, however, also the opportunity for direct and indirect discrimination to creep into the selection process through the choice of technique.

Application forms and biodata are not in themselves discriminatory except in the case of people with sight difficulties and where there is insistence upon the application being completed in 'your own handwriting'. (How do you complete in someone else's handwriting?). Discrimination can however creep into the components of the application form or the questions within the biodata. Questions on the application form about marital status could be held to be an intention to discriminate. Similarly, asking questions around gender and race; which is why many recruiters now use a separate section to gather this information for equal opportunities monitoring where they are clearly seen to play no part in the decision making process. Great care needs to be taken in the design of biodata to avoid it becoming a discriminatory instrument particularly since it uses the principal of coincidences and may therefore perpetuate a workforce which is not truly balanced in terms of gender and race. Generally speaking, both biodata and application forms can be carefully designed to ensure they become an objective part of the assessment process which promotes the equality of opportunity.

The interview is the most frequently used selection technique in the UK. There is evidence – both from research and legal cases – that discriminatory decisions can be made from the interview and, of course, the prejudices of the interviewer can directly impact on whether the process is discriminatory or not. These are however aspects of how the interview is used rather than the interview itself. Is the technique itself discriminatory? The answer seems to be 'perhaps'. An investigation by the Commission for Racial Equality in 1984 looked at a Leicester engineering company and concluded that Afro Caribbean and Asian candidates had been unsuccessful either because of an inability to communicate or an inability to answer interview questions to the panel's satisfaction. Other ethnic candidates were unsuccessful for other reasons, but such reasons were consistent with reasons given for the failure of white candidates. None of the white candidates, however, suffered because of the communication difficulty. The investigation also looked at the interview structure that used a situational interview, which asks people to think ahead to a hypothetical future situation and answer how they would respond to it. It was concluded that ethnic minority applicants, with less likelihood to have English as their first language, would suffer unfairly by being hampered in inferring the panel's intentions from the language used to phrase the questions, and being able to frame a response in a similar way. It was also found that the vocabulary and tone of answers from Asian candidates made it more difficult for the interviewers to evaluate the response. There is a further concern, which is that in many cases the interview is used to measure the person-organisation fit. The likelihood of an ethnic minority candidate 'fitting' a predominantly white workforce or of a female candidate 'fitting' a predominantly male workforce or a physically disabled candidate 'fitting' a sports oriented workforce is the rationalisation of prejudice. The unstructured interview has the potential to be more discriminatory, particularly where the questions are loosely and thoughtlessly phrased. Even where the answers are not taken into consideration for decision-making, such questions as '*when do you intend to start a family?'* or *'can you wear a hard hat on your turban?'* may, not surprisingly, lead the candidate to believe that they are likely to be discriminated against. Note-taking in unstructured interviews can reveal unconscious discrimination as in the Commission for Racial Equality investigation into the recruitment of chartered accountant trainees in 1987.

Psychometric testing has not been without its challenges for discrimination. Generally speaking, most proprietary personality tests have been carefully designed to ensure that the questions they ask are not discriminatory and that the scoring mechanism does not disadvantage racial or gender types. Ability tests have however probably been the greatest source of discrimination cases than any other selection technique. Well-publicised cases in the UK against British Rail and London Underground, though being settled before being heard, have focused much attention on such parts of the selection process. In broad terms an ability test that discriminates against a protected group but which properly tests an appropriate indicator of performance will not be held to be unfairly discriminatory. There are some potential problems with age discrimination because most ability tests measure skills that deteriorate with age. In itself that may not be alarming but the standards for the tests are usually set by university students or school children rather than real performers in the work place. The primary reason however for actions against ability tests involves careless selection of the tests. Tests of verbal prowess will obviously discriminate against those whose first language is not English and to use them for the selection of manual roles where language is unimportant is, at best, a waste of money. The widespread use of IQ, literacy or numeracy tests without full consideration of their relevance and purpose is perhaps the most worrying aspect of the use of ability tests.

Graphology fails to predict the gender, race, or age of the writer and since graphologists are concerned with the form and shape of the writing rather than its content, it seems that graphology is a technique that is remarkably free of discrimination. It is however in low use in the UK and therefore perhaps not wholly 'tested' for discrimination in practice.

The key elements in ensuring ethical and legal acceptability of any selection technique are as follows:

- to ensure that the criteria which have been set for selection are free of bias and wholly relevant to the performance of the role

- to ensure that all candidates are treated in a consistent way

- to ensure that redundant items are excluded from the application form, interview, or structure

- to ensure that questions on application forms and in interviews are carefully framed around the key requirements and competencies and phrased in a non-discriminatory way (and interpreted and scored accordingly)

- to ensure that tests are only used where they measure aspects pertinent to the role and the performance of the techniques, and are monitored for equal opportunities

- to ensure that they do not discriminate unfairly on gender, race, disability, sexual orientation or religion.

How to decide on selection techniques

It can be seen that the decision on which technique to use to support selection decisions is one requiring a balanced judgement. It may be feasible to develop a scorecard to assist in the selection by adding weight to each of the criteria discussed above:

- suitability

- resource and cost constraints

- effectiveness

- acceptability.

There is however a danger in becoming overly rigid and mechanistic in such an approach and it may be better simply to keep the four criteria in mind when making a final choice. There are however three key preliminaries that need to be addressed in order to make an effective choice. These are:

- The selection ratio for the positions to be filled. This is the likelihood of people being able to do the job. A selection ratio of 0.5 means there is a fifty/fifty chance of people being able to perform the job if picked at random, 1 means that anybody picked would be able to do the job and 0.1 means that only one in ten people selected at random for the job would be able to it. This is merely applying a statistical device to the common-sense notion that some simple jobs can be done by most people whereas more complex jobs will mean that fewer people would be available to perform them. This may seem an obvious point but all too often decisions are made to apply expensive selection techniques to fairly straightforward selection.

- The interplay of techniques is important and it has been shown that where all parts of the selection process contribute to the final decision, often building up as independent pieces of the jigsaw, the success rate is much greater than where each of the techniques is used as a hurdle to screen out for the next part of the selection process and then ignored once that latter part is

---

underway. This is a significant point because it is all too often the practice that application forms and the information on them are ignored once later stages, such as the interview or testing, are under way and do not feature in the final decision making. The selection will be more efficient if all parts of the process are combined and reviewed at the final selection decision point.

- The most important pre-requisite is that there is a clear idea of the criteria for selection, a specification of the person needed, preferably in the form of defined competencies. The development of a clear specification is discussed in Part 3; without such clarity it is difficult to identify which techniques are the most useful for assessing the various criteria and though the techniques are all to varying degrees efficient at removing the hay from the haystack, they cannot in themselves provide a clear picture of the needle.

With these three pre-requisites in mind, it is then possible to proceed further. First, having set down the criteria for selection by developing a clear person specification, determine the priorities for selection (i.e. the skills people really must have before they can be considered for the job, and those it would be good to have but could be developed later if necessary). Secondly, consider the suitability of the technique for assessing each of the criteria (keeping in mind the relative importance of natural, acquired, and adapting competencies, as discussed above). Thirdly, consider the resources available and the cost constraints, keeping in mind the selection ratio, the importance of the job and a broad cost-benefit analysis. Think about the acceptability to clients/candidates and the ethical/legal considerations, remembering that the selection process will be the shop window of your business. Finally, consider the effectiveness of each technique, bearing in mind of course that the more difficult the selection ratio the more weight will be attached to the effectiveness of the technique.

Part 3

Finding people

8

Defining the requirements

SPECIFICATIONS

Selection has been described as the process of finding a needle in a haystack. Maximising the effectiveness of selection is therefore not only about improving the methods for removing the hay but also about improving the recognition of the needle. One of the difficulties of selection has always been the subjectivity of decision-making. It is an area in which many selectors feel uncomfortable and it is also the source of greatest disagreement between those undertaking the selection and those on whose behalf they undertake the assignment. Such disagreements can take place between a selection consultant and the client, or between the personnel adviser and the line manager.

Many years ago the IT industry recognised the problems inherent in vague and loose approaches to defining requirements for new systems, which often lead to a breakdown in the relation between the IT providers and their customers, resulting in overly expensive or under-performing solutions to IT needs. The IT people responded by placing great emphasis on detailed specifications of customer requirements so that there was a clear understanding of the requirements, the solution, and the deliverables, before any work commenced. Such a slow and measured approach can seem alien to recruitment in which the nature of the exercise is a more rapid event, usually requiring a quick recruitment of the new person to the organisation and, on the face of it, a lower cost issue with far fewer players involved. After all, in most IT projects other people will be involved in maintaining or using the system, its impact can spread widely, and it may need further amendment from time to time. It is, however, not unrealistic to consider selection in similar terms.

Just as the IT designer is unlikely to be the person operating the new system, so too the selector is unlikely to be the person managing the new recruit. In the same way as the IT system may potentially have a wide range of end-users or recipients of the information, in today's organisations the new recruit will be networking widely and impacting a great number of customers both internally and externally and will be relied upon for information and service in the same way as many IT systems. Nor are there many IT systems which compare with the cost associated with the employment of people, both in terms of salary and related employment costs spread over the average length and service with the organisation. Coupled with the knock-on cost of the decisions they make, or the services they use, the high-spend on IT projects can pale into insignificance, particularly for more senior appointments. It is unlikely that many IT projects, pound for pound on a par with selection costs, measured in such terms, would go through on the nod and wink and the informality which accompanies many selection assignments.

PERSON SPECIFICATION

One of the problems of selection is that of 'mirroring' in which selectors often choose candidates who mirror their own values, beliefs or abilities, rather than stepping back and searching for the candidate best suited to their client. Good selectors adopt the practice of drawing up a clear specification of the ideal candidate and agreeing the specification with those on whose behalf they are undertaking the assignment. Such a specification needs to be very comprehensive and embrace not only the skills, background and experiences of the ideal candidate, but also the individual qualities and working style of such people. The chances of success are much improved by drawing up an agreed specification not only because of the inherent improvement to the process of selection, but also because the likelihood of subsequent disagreement between selector and client is minimised.

A useful approach is the **PERSON** specification covering:

- **P**ersonal qualities and attributes which are inherent in the person's character, not easily changed, and pertinent to good work performance. Does the person need to be creative, or resilient, or able to follow detail and routine, or be 'good with people'?

- **E**xperience, whether of a particular industry or type of work, or dealing with certain types of customers.

- **R**ecord of achievement or evidence that the potential has been applied and realised, such as projects completed or sales achieved.

- **S**kills or qualifications needed to perform the role. Some roles may necessitate certain qualifications, such as law or accountancy, perhaps as a statutory requirement, others may have a specific requirement, e.g. Driving Licence, or qualifications may be used as a guide, e.g. degree-level.

- **O**rganisation-match, which may cover the fit with the style and culture of the organisation if it is significant (perhaps very 'laid back' and informal or perhaps very formal and 'bureaucratic') but more usually aspects such as shift-work or travelling requirements.

- Needs and expectation of the candidate; what does the organisation require? Should the potential candidate be someone looking for a long-term career, someone looking for a short-term fill-in, someone wanting routine or someone seeking new challenges?

Care must be taken to prioritise between essential and desirable requirements and to avoid any form of discrimination. 'Physically fit' may be a requirement for a professional sports player; however, incorporating it into the specification for a sales representative may create an offence under the Disability Discrimination Act 1996. Similarly, specifying the requirement for 'O' levels has been found to be race discriminatory. So too, the use of stereotyped personal qualities such as 'assertive' or 'aggressive' may be deemed to be sex discrimination. Great care needs to be taken therefore to incorporate aspects which truly relate to job performance and are objective and defensible. Although the use of informal approaches such as PERSON specification can help in odd cases as a better option than '*I' ll know it when I see it*', it is a poor substitute for proper role analysis. Undertaking role analysis and adopting a competency-based approach to selection will significantly improve effectiveness, objectivity and fairness.

COMPETENCIES

In recent years the development of a specification has become much easier due to the use of a 'competencies' approach.

The competencies approach was developed in the 1980s and 1990s as a way of providing the measurement of people which is so elusive in day-to-day human resource and general management. Two approaches took different paths at similar times. In the UK, greater integration within the European Community and moves for greater mobility of labour across the EC necessitated the definition of national qualifications and skill levels for meaningful measures and comparisons across countries. This was accompanied by a concern bordering on embarrassment about the levels of skills In the UK, particularly in managerial roles where it was felt that the acquisition of management skills was much more haphazard than in other European nations. In particular it was perceived that in Germany many managers were highly qualified and skilled, whereas in the UK the pattern had been for people to drift into management through the 'university of life', gathering experience and hopefully expertise 'along the way' without any underpinning of a formal body of knowledge or qualification in management.

To address the mobility of labour and portability of qualifications, the development was begun of National Vocational Qualifications (NVQs/SPQs). Furthermore, to put the art of management into a science with a professional standing, the development of the chartered manager was initiated, which eventually became the Management Charter Initiative (MCI). These approaches received considerable government funding and support from large companies and academic institutions as well as government agencies.

Since their primary concern was to ensure that standards were achieved and developed, these qualifications became focused on training and development approaches. They specified minimum standards for achievement of set tasks and activities, expressed in ways which were capable of observation and assessment with a view to certification and thereby qualification. Since an integral part of the approach was to provide the opportunity for people to receive training and development to achieve the required skill, it became necessary to break jobs down into significant detail and put in place a robust assessment process. This approach became rather bureaucratic, unwieldy and the cause of much criticism in recent years, which has since been addressed.

In a parallel time frame, a move was growing in the United States to improve the competitiveness of US industry. A highly successful management book called *In Search of Excellence* became influential and sought to examine successful US corporations and identify the recipe for their success, a recipe which could be adopted and copied by others. A natural extension of such an approach was to look at successful managers and see whether it would be possible to replicate their approaches and their qualities in others. The American Management Association commissioned McBer Associates to undertake research into successful managers and attempt to identify the qualities and features of them. The consultant, Richard Boyatzis, concluded in his research that there was no single factor but rather a range of factors which differentiated between the successful and the less successful managers. He concluded that these were a variety of factors including personal qualities, experience, motives, and various other attributes.

Boyatzis coined the term competency (plural competencies) originally used by Harvard Professor David McClelland in his work on motivation. The term was defined as 'an underlying characteristic of an individual which is causally related to effective or superior performance in a job'. In the UK the term 'competence' was adopted (with the plural competences) to indicate the range of standards. The Training Standards Agency drew up a definition of competences which was 'an action, behaviour or outcome which the person should be able to demonstrate'.

The difference between the UK and US approaches is more than simply words and phrases. It is a fundamental difference between the following choices:

- Looking at a small number of key aspects which differentiate between performance regardless of whether they are visible or hidden.

- Looking at the full range of skills needed to perform a role, regardless of whether they differentiate between levels of performance, but confined to those aspects which can be observed or assessed (and therefore able to be trained and developed) in people performing the work.

*Figure 8.1 / **Defining competences and competencies***

Competences

Things that a person who works in a given occupational area should be able to do. Each one is an action, behaviour or outcome that the person should be able to demonstrate.

The Training Agency, *Definition of competence and performance criteria*, 1988

Competencies

Those characteristics that differentiate superior from average and poor performance ... motives, traits, skill, aspects of one's self--image or social role, or body or knowledge.

Richard Boyatzis, *The Competent Manager*, 1982

It is a difference between drivers of performance and standards of work. The US approach does not confine itself to only the observable aspects, but includes also the underlying values or characteristics which contribute to performance. This approach does not look at all the requirements of the role, merely those which differentiate between levels of performance.

In the UK the approaches have tended to merge in companies and sometimes the loose use of the language masks or confuses the real nature of the approach. This has often occurred because many of the UK companies adopting the approach were themselves parents of US corporations and their adoption of the competencies route came through their parent organisation rather than from the external business world. Often it is a mix of the external influence and the internal customisation which has led to a hybrid approach. In practice neither approach should be regarded as inappropriate since they both have something to value. A pragmatic route is to adopt both approaches – but being very clear on their use. Using the competence approach has limitations for selection since it bases an emphasis on looking at people doing the work, and the assumption that with sufficient effort they can be trained and developed to do the work. In such an approach it is therefore implicit that there is little point in differentiating at selection and that the effort should be placed on training and developing people for whatever role they can be equipped. This has some serious limitations in practice. The US route can be particularly helpful in making selection decisions because it is looking at the underlying characteristics which may not yet have had the opportunity to surface in an entirely similar environment, and therefore it is concerned with potential rather than accomplishment. The limitation here however is that selection is about bringing people in to do a job of work and it is important to know about the way in which they will perform. It is useful, for selection purposes, therefore to have a framework which accepts principles from both the US and UK route.

Emotional Intelligence

In recent years there has been significant growth of interest in the concept of emotional intelligence. Arising from a book by Daniel Goleman that stressed the importance of managing one's own emotions and being aware of others' emotions in forming effective relationships, there has been a 'cottage industry' in positioning emotional intelligence as the key ingredient for successful management. Much attention has been paid to helping people become more aware of their own emotions and the effect on their dealings with others, and to become more sensitive to the emotional needs of others. A simple – and doubtless oversimplified – explanation is that emotional intelligence is the ability to sit on your own shoulder and take an objective view of how you are interacting with others, and providing yourself with 'live' commentary and coaching to handle the interaction effectively. Whilst emotional intelligence may be an effective coping strategy and a learned behaviour that may help improve effectiveness, it is of limited value in the selection context, because we need to consider all aspects of personality in selection and to prioritise on the areas that are less receptive to training (see *Competency-based person specifications* below).

COMPETENCY FRAMEWORK

The true potential of the competency approach can best be exploited through combining rather than choosing between the disparate approaches and using them as an integrated balanced framework. This involves looking at:

- innate qualities

- acquired skill

- adapting behaviours.

The labels are not important but it is important to make a clear distinction between each element, since this facilitates a practical balanced system for managing competencies.

The 'innate qualities' comprise all the 'underlying traits' (to use Boyatzis' terms), and thus the 'big five' dimensions of personality (see the chapter on Psychological Testing in Part 4). These are:

- extroversion/introversion

- emotional stability

- agreeableness

- conscientiousness and
- openness to experience.

The 'acquired' would include knowledge and skills, whether achieved through work or elsewhere, with which people are not naturally gifted. Thus professional knowledge or business awareness would be covered here.

The 'adapting' form the set which enables the individual to succeed in his/her work environment. All too often people in a new position fail to continue their previous track record of success. This can be true of highly rated people failing to make a transition to a new department or organisation, or of people being promoted. Success will flow from the ability of the individual to adapt their natural talents and acquired knowledge to current circumstances, whether this involves coming to terms with a different culture, a different operating environment, or a different set of priorities/demands.

In using the competency framework for performance management it will be more user-friendly simply to have a set of example behaviours for those competencies that are causally related to superior job performance and over which the individual has control. The candidate profile for selection may therefore contain some innate qualities or threshold skills that may not feature in on-going performance management or training programmes. Additionally care should be taken with the following aspects:

- **Cloning**: The criticism aimed at the Competency approach about defining a single, prescribed way of operating needs to be kept in check by paying attention to adapting behaviours and flexibility. Behavioural descriptions should be examples not checklists.

- **Know-how:** There is an argument that in some roles or occupations, *what* the person does is more observable but less important than *how* they do it or what they *know*. In such situations greater weight can be applied to acquired skills and adapting behaviours.

- **Personality:** Over-emphasis on observable behaviour ignores the personal characteristics necessary for success. Behaviour can be transient and is sometimes more a reflection of the environment than the person; although important for gauging current success it is not a reliable predictor of future success in a different arena. Recognising the importance of the 'innate' qualities provides the appropriate balance.

The key message is that the management of competencies requires a broad view. In practice there is a tendency to flexibility. Even those who insist on restricting the definition to observable behaviour include competencies such as 'judgement' or 'resilience' which are easier to recognise as personality traits than as behaviours.

COMPETENCY-BASED PERSON SPECIFICATIONS

Preparing the specification in the form of competencies ensures that both the selector and the client have a clear understanding of the person being sought, and a clear agreement on what is meant by those terms. It can often be the case that selector and client have failed to agree that the candidate possesses a certain quality when there is no common understanding of the quality itself. The term 'flexibility' is an example of this confusion: the client's view of flexibility may mean *the willingness of the person to perform tasks outside the normal range of duties, and not to be too rigid in their outlook,* whereas the selector's view on flexibility may be *the ability of the person to undertake a number of tasks in different areas, or to switch between routine and complex tasks easily.* Neither interpretation is incorrect in their view of flexibility nor is either perhaps incorrect in their assessment of the candidate's 'flexibility'. The difficulty is that 'flexibility' for one is different from 'flexibility' for another. Thus the benefit of taking a competencies approach is that people can identify and isolate the key characteristics which would be used as the basis for selection, and that those characteristics will be described in terms which both can understand and agree. Furthermore, using the description of behaviours of the competencies in everyday work, it is possible to identify good and bad answers to interview questions or good and bad responses to assessment exercises.

The competencies therefore become a fundamental part of the selection process. They become the technical terms for the specification in precisely the same way that the IT professional would use technical terms to describe the software being developed on behalf of their client. A further benefit of a competencies approach is that it breaks down the specification of the candidate into meaningful parts. Thus the elements of the selection process can be best aligned to identify it and the whole process can be used to build a complete picture component by component. This avoids the difficulties of 'whole picture' assessments in which selectors are trying to make an overall judgement of a candidate, but not able to specify clearly the elements where they believe the candidate may or may not fit the requirements of the role. This often shows itself in concerns about subjective judgements of candidates and inevitable 'school report' type of assessments.

Using a competency framework it is possible to target the particular elements of the selection process so that, for example, the innate competencies which are deep-seated can become the focus of psychological testing to reveal the underlying characteristics. In addition, the application form can be used to gauge the appropriate experience or knowledge of the candidates, and assessment centre exercises can be used to gauge the performance behaviours. This therefore uses each technique to its best advantage without techniques competing or conflicting, and creates a better overall picture of the candidates. Occasionally in selection a selector may prefer one approach to another. They may for example think that psychometric tests are the best means of assessing candidates and they will therefore place a heavy reliance on the psychometric techniques,

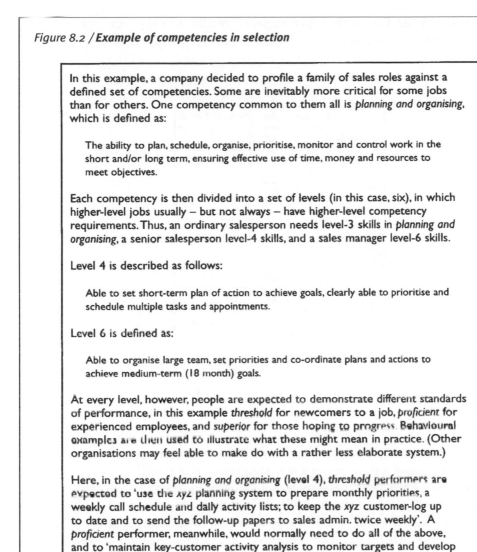

Figure 8.2 / *Example of competencies in selection*

In this example, a company decided to profile a family of sales roles against a defined set of competencies. Some are inevitably more critical for some jobs than for others. One competency common to them all is *planning and organising*, which is defined as:

> The ability to plan, schedule, organise, prioritise, monitor and control work in the short and/or long term, ensuring effective use of time, money and resources to meet objectives.

Each competency is then divided into a set of levels (in this case, six), in which higher-level jobs usually – but not always – have higher-level competency requirements. Thus, an ordinary salesperson needs level-3 skills in *planning and organising*, a senior salesperson level-4 skills, and a sales manager level-6 skills.

Level 4 is described as follows:

> Able to set short-term plan of action to achieve goals, clearly able to prioritise and schedule multiple tasks and appointments.

Level 6 is defined as:

> Able to organise large team, set priorities and co-ordinate plans and actions to achieve medium-term (18 month) goals.

At every level, however, people are expected to demonstrate different standards of performance, in this example *threshold* for newcomers to a job, *proficient* for experienced employees, and *superior* for those hoping to progress. Behavioural examples are then used to illustrate what these might mean in practice. (Other organisations may feel able to make do with a rather less elaborate system.)

Here, in the case of *planning and organising* (level 4), *threshold* performers are expected to 'use the xyz planning system to prepare monthly priorities, a weekly call schedule and daily activity lists; to keep the xyz customer-log up to date and to send the follow-up papers to sales admin. twice weekly'. A *proficient* performer, meanwhile, would normally need to do all of the above, and to 'maintain key-customer activity analysis to monitor targets and develop six-month plan'.

even for those elements that may be better gauged by other means. So too there may be those who distrust techniques such as psychometrics and prefer to stick to interviews or perhaps references, and may then place undue emphasis on those elements and fail to recognise information that could come from sources such as the psychometrics. The pity is that all of these techniques are useful for gauging certain things and ought to be considered as good evidence of certain elements and rejected as insubstantial evidence for others. Breaking the specification into competencies means that the appropriate technique can be used to gauge that competency, and the overall picture is built up on a piece-by-piece basis and becomes more reliable. See Figure 8.3.

Figure 8.3 / *Deciding the techniques to use for assessing the competencies*

	Screen	Test	Interview	Exercise
Achievement		✔		
Leadership				✔
Creativity		✔		
Resilience		✔		
Flexibility			✔	
Technical knowlege	✔			
Judgement		✔		
Decision-making		✔	✔	
Planning and organisation				✔
People management	✔			
Energy			✔	
Financial acumen				✔

Use of the competencies enables the correct answer to be applied, in addition to providing the built-up picture. While it is not suggested that selection should be seen as a test in which candidates pass or fail, it is nevertheless the case that selectors, particularly those who undertake the task only occasionally, need to have some benchmark against which to measure. They need to know whether answers are good or bad in the sense that they provide evidence that the candidate either possesses the competency in depth or not at all. Similarly in using structured techniques such as psychometrics there is a need for some form of benchmark.

A further benefit of the competencies approach is that it becomes the thread extending beyond simply the selection process. The recruitment of the candidate should only be the first stage in the on-going relationship, and it is not an end in itself. All too often selection processes are seen as a discreet activity, the appointment of the individual being the culmination of the process. Thereafter the information is filed away with the rest of the assignment information and does not somehow form part of the further development of the appointed person. In using the competencies approach it is possible to give the new manager information about their recruit which specifies how they are likely to perform against each of the competencies. In describing the output of the assessment in terms of the performance behaviours it becomes easier for the manager to see how their 'new recruit' will perform. It will therefore provide the basis upon which their performance in the early days can be monitored to judge whether they actually live up to the predictions flowing from the selection process. It is also the case that the ideal candidate rarely does step forward fully meeting all of the requirements of the role. There are often compromises to be reached or choices to be made. By using competencies it is possible to show how the candidate broadly fits the specification, but that there are some areas in which they are exceeding the particular requirement for that competency and in other areas where they may fall short. In this way their induction can be planned so that attention can be paid to providing additional help, whether in the form of training or development or additional guidance to address shortfalls, or, if such shortfalls cannot be made good, ways in which the role can be re-designed, perhaps with additional supervision or a change of duties, to compensate and adjust for the deficiency in that particular competency.

The greatest benefit of a balanced framework is the practical application it affords for a system of integrated human resources management. The following points summarise the benefits of a balanced framework:

- 'Innate' characteristics will have their focus in the selection process. The possession of natural-born qualities, as every selector knows, will not guarantee that the person will successfully apply his/her talents. However, selecting people with the raw ingredient is an essential pre-requisite. Attempting to train or artificially create such natural talent is unrealistic.

- 'Acquired' skills may be a centre of attention for some selection decisions but there are also important as the focus for on-going education. There is likely to be increasing emphasis on education in future years as the role of management shifts from direction and control to decision-making and communication. This may cause a reversal of the trend of recent years by making specialist/technical skills more valued than general management skills. The focus of NVQ/SVQs should be more clearly directed at 'acquired' competencies within a balanced framework.

- 'Adapting' competencies should be used as the focus for development activities since this is the accelerator that the person uses to apply his/her natural abilities and knowledge/experience. Adaptation can therefore embrace the full scale from innovation to regulation and include cultural fit, commitment to corporate goals, team working, and decision-making. Since this is the point at which the person 'chooses' whether to apply the 'innate' and 'acquired' competencies, it is the area where development activities can have the greatest leverage in enhancing performance.

- The performance behaviours will form the substance of the general competency framework as the observable behaviours and evidence of performance. These are useful as the basis of evaluating performance – albeit of greater use where measuring output-based activities rather than quality-based activities such as professional advice – and can provide a common language for objective appraisal/feedback. They can also provide the basis for designing organisation and human resource systems such as appraisal and reward.

EXAMPLES OF COMPETENCY DEFINITIONS

The following examples illustrate the way in which competencies are defined. The number of competencies will depend upon the complexity and variety of roles and skills in the organisation but would typically be five or six. It is difficult to maintain practical application if they exceed a dozen or so. The first example is a fairly complex one that differentiates between the competencies required at different levels of the organisation, and includes examples of both 'standard' and 'higher' performance. It is used to drive performance, set levels of pay, and support recruitment and training practices. The second example is a simple approach giving examples that cut across all levels. It is used for performance, development and selection. In both these frameworks there is a specific competency for 'technical skills' that sets out the threshold requirements of knowledge, skill, qualification and experience for selection purposes.

Two Competency Examples

PEOPLE SKILLS	The way we relate to our customers and our colleagues	PEOPLE SKILLS INCLUDES: Communication, Customer Focus/Care, Teamwork, Patience, Empathy, Leadership
LEVELS	**EVERYDAY EXAMPLES OF EXPECTED PERFORMANCE**	**EXAMPLES OF ADVANCED PERFORMANCE**
For Director level	Maintaining effective dialogue with key stakeholders to ensure the vision, strategy and goals of the Community Fund reflect and anticipate changing views, values and demands in the sector. Ensuring that vision, values and strategy of the organisation are clearly and regularly communicated to staff and stakeholders to gain commitment.	Targeting and improving weak external relationships. Promoting and preserving CF's reputation with all contacts, internally and externally, (including those who may hold opposing views), through personal credibility and integrity. Fostering an external network of influential contacts/partnerships able to promote or further CF's interests.
For Senior Manager level	Gaining and giving staff trust, coaching, challenging, developing and supporting them so that they can make a real contribution to the organisation. Creating an environment in which people are clear about, and committed to, their role, and in which there is an opportunity to explore and develop their full potential in order to maximise efficient working. Demonstrating wider knowledge of the organisation's policies and goals in persuading and influencing other to adopt or explore new policies and procedures.	Ensuring that vision, values and strategy of the organisation are clearly and regularly communicated to staff and stakeholders to gain commitment. Taking the bull by the horns to confront difficult situations and dealing with them with integrity. Resolving challenging situations in a professional, adult-to-adult way to enable a win-win solutions with customers and colleagues, e.g. negotiations
For Senior Operations level	Being sensitive to people's needs, aware of where they're coming from and adapting approach to meet the circumstances. Engaging appropriately with a range of people in a range of situations at a variety of levels so that the most appropriate outcome emerges. Automatically consider diversity/range of needs and apply/offer tailored solutions rather than treating everyone in a uniform way.	Developing innovative approaches to diversity and equal opportunity. Turning negative relationships/attitudes into positive ones. Inspiring confidence in all contacts by doing what you say you will do
For Operations level	Adapting style, tone and content of communication to suit the receiver(s). Being open and accessible to existing and potential customers, (both internal and external), showing patience and empathy to achieve a positive perception of Community Fund/A4A. Responding in a positive way to customers even when giving disappointing news to retain their commitment and enhance their chance of success. Anticipating problems and questions	Listening beyond words, so that important, unspoken nuances, needs and feelings are picked up and checked out and responded to appropriately. Identifying what applicants/agencies/colleagues need to know and giving that information in an appropriate way
For Support level	Cooperating with customers and colleagues, taking the time to listen and showing understanding of, and interest in, their views/ideas/project/work. Returning phone calls and responding promptly to correspondence. Demonstrating courtesy, sensitivity, discretion and respect in dealings with everyone and treating people as individuals so that they respond positively. Being open and accessible to existing and potential customers, (both internal and external), showing patience and empathy to achieve a positive perception of Community Fund/A4A.	Understanding, appreciating and respecting the other person's view, even when it is opposing. Dealing calmly and effectively with difficult or angry people Being sensitive to people's needs, aware of where they're coming from and adapting approach to meet the circumstances Working with, respecting and supporting colleagues to promote better team working and internal customer care.
It is not....	☹ Making assumptions about people ☹ Reliant on others ☹ Saying one thing but doing another	

People skills

Covering:

Respect for others, teamworking, communication, confidence

EVERYDAY EXAMPLES OF EXPECTED PERFORMANCE:	PROBABLE OUTCOMES
Taking time to understand others, showing respect, sharing knowledge and ideas, accepting other views and feedback.	A pleasant and productive working environment
Open, outgoing collaborating with others, being receptive to, and willing to volunteer, ideas	Ideas that come forward are realistic and workable
Acting appropriately in managing difficult situations, being prepared to address issues sensitively and unemotionally	Conflict is avoided
Being approachable to others and making time for others in the formal and informal workplace	Better teamwork. Support is available from others when needed
Embracing diversity and adapting to working with people of different skills, outlook, and background, seeing the person as the person	A more interesting workplace where everyone feels valued, and contributes
Other?	

It is not....

☹ Not prepared to listen or take advice
☹ Judgmental or arrogant

9

Role analysis

Since a clear specification will form the foundation for effective recruitment and selection, it is important that the development of the person specification is robust. There are various techniques available to undertake the analysis of roles and to identify the competencies or qualities that drive successful performance in the role.

The choice of technique will depend upon the resources available, including time, and the preference or expertise of the identifier. A traditional approach to developing the person specification is for the selector to meet with the client and identify key requirements of the candidate, paying attention to aspects such as qualification, skill and experience. These may include formal qualifications indicative of general attainment such as a degree, or they may be very specific job-related qualifications such as membership of a professional association. Background information on the kind of experience, perhaps industry sector or work nature, will also be needed together with the profile of the personal qualities which the candidate can bring to the work. Such aspects are covered under the PERSON-specification or the competencies approach that were described earlier in this Part on pages 62 and 68.

Drawing up the specification in this way is useful to ensure that the selector has a clear understanding of the client's requirements, and it provides greater focus for the selector in investigating and making decisions. It is a very quick and easy method and will enable the selection process to get under way without undue delay. The drawback is that it may be very subjective, and there is a danger that the selection will focus on aspects that are not necessarily the key drivers of performance or, at worst, are inappropriate to successful fulfilment of the role. Taking a more measured and structured approach to identifying the profile will pay dividends in delivering a more robust specification, and securing the right candidate. There will however be a delay for this to be undertaken and this is the reason why many organisations undertake general research into the framework of competencies for their organisation, which is then available in readiness for any selection activity – and other human resources actions.

HOW TO ANALYSE ROLES TO IDENTIFY COMPETENCIES

Techniques for analysing roles to identify competencies include activity-based techniques such as:

- focus groups

- inventories or questionnaires

- interviews including critical incident interview

- diaries/work logs.

They may also include people-based techniques such as:

- repertory grids

- observation

- testing.

Focus groups involve bringing together a group of subject matter experts to analyse roles and identify the key competencies underpinning successful performance in those roles. The usual approach is for the group to meet on a periodic basis. The frequency depends on the size of the organisation and the task but usually entails fortnightly meetings over a period of months. The focus group will look at a cross-representation of roles in the organisation. It is customary to define the roles that cover about 80 per cent of the work population. The group will look at the roles, usually through a presentation by a member of the group, and focus on the key elements. This will typically include a statement of the main purpose of the role, the key accountabilities for the role (usually around six to eight) and then the principal activities that flow from those accountabilities. This provides the group with an understanding of the nature of the role and its deliverables. The latter is usually best acquired by seeking performance indicators for the role, such as the measures of how the role is successfully fulfilled attempting to use objective yardsticks. Using the information, the group will then brainstorm the range of qualities needed to perform the role. By looking at each role in turn without reference to the other roles at this stage, the group will develop a pattern of qualities or competencies. When all the roles have been reviewed, the group should list all the qualities that have been identified and then using postcards or post-it notes, sort them into clusters. There is no hard or fast rule on the number of clusters although it is most effective to have as small a number as can be effectively handled and remembered by line managers. This is usually around six to eight. Some organisations use several dozen competencies but the reality is that, in day-to-day work, line managers find such a list far too cumbersome to deal with. The clusters should be of aspects that are similar to each other. Once the clusters have been identified, the focus group will then provide a working title and a definition for each competency, together with 'behavioural indicators' of the competency in action in everyday work.

One of the great advantages of using the focus group is that the titles and the language used in the definitions will be acceptable to the end-users rather than employing the jargon of consultants or psychologists. By using subject-matter experts, i.e. those people who understand and perform the role, the analysis of roles is also thorough. Great care needs to be taken in selecting the focus group to ensure that it is representative of roles across the organisation, both vertically and horizontally, and particular care needs to be taken to ensure that the composition of the group is not distorted on age, race or gender such that the competencies fall in danger of being inherently discriminatory. One of the most significant difficulties with the focus group is securing the release of good quality people for the duration of the project.

Where jobs are well defined and predictable in terms of the tasks and activities required, it is useful to use the **inventory** (sometimes called **questionnaire** or checklist) technique. This approach takes the range of job requirements and breaks them into segments of key tasks that are then sub-divided into day-to-day activities. This breaks the role down into a very significant degree of detail; an activity could for example be described as *checking, coding and registering invoice*. The range of tasks and activities is usually developed by observing the jobs in action and discussions with job holders and managers. There are some proprietary checklists which may form a shortcut in appropriate circumstances. A preliminary range of attributes, or competencies, is developed from the observations and interviews. A questionnaire is then developed to seek information from the job holder on the criticality of the tasks and information from the manager and/or job holder on the link between the competencies and the tasks. This is achieved by asking the job holder to rate, against each of the activities, a score for such elements as:

- the time taken to do the work

- the complexity of the work

- the consequences of error.

The ratings are then multiplied so that the greater the amount of time taken and the greater the complexity and the consequence of error, then the greater the overall rating for that particular task will be. This analysis provides us with the criticality of the tasks. The next stage is to rate, on a matrix, the importance of each competency to the performance of each of the activities. This is most usually undertaken by the manager of the jobholder rather than by the jobholders themselves since it provides a more authoritative view of the required attributes. In practice however it is very useful also to gauge the jobholder's view, preferably in discussion with the line manager, so as to provide a closer-related and balanced assessment. The importance of the competency is then determined by totalling the scores for the competency, against each of the tasks; the rating may cover a scale from 'not required' to 'essential'. Thus for each activity the rater is saying how essential that particular competency is to the performance of the activity.

The activities are weighted according to the criticality score. The sum of the scores then provides the rank order of importance of the competencies. This can be a very useful technique for gauging the views of a large number of jobholders without the cost and inconvenience of focus groups, extended interviews or observation. Although the checklist can look intimidating, a very comprehensive inventory can be completed within about 45 minutes. The greatest time taken is of course in analysis, for which a statistics software programme is essential. The nature of the technique, in looking in detail at the job requirements and involving a large number of jobholders and managers, is very effective as an objective and robust measure. It can also be useful in predicting the competencies for a changing role by re-allocating and re-modelling the frequency or criticality of tasks for the future design of the work. A further advantage of the inventory approach is that it provides a direct linkage between the analysis of the job, and the competencies or attributes of the individual. In many of the other techniques the formulation of the key attributes of the competencies remains a dislocated process.

The **critical incident** technique involves the interviewing of jobholders and/or managers and is focused on identifying specific events which form a critical part of the role. Interviewees are usually asked to describe recent experiences in their work and the interviewer will identify a particular occurrence, usually of some significance, and probe the interviewee on the actions taken and the outcomes. Through the process of structured interviewing of a number of jobholders and managers it becomes possible for the interviewer to infer the attributes or competencies which the job holder draws upon in order to deal successfully with the critical incidents. One of the important considerations here is that the interviewer is not concerned with identifying an exhaustive list of the full range of attributes or competencies required to perform the role, but is more concerned with those aspects which are used in the more demanding or challenging situations and thus likely to be the differentiators between various levels of performance and coping. One of the advantages of this technique is that by focusing directly on the competencies, the normal difficulties of trying to make the transition between the analysis of the work and the identification of the competencies are overcome. Conversely there is less emphasis on an analysis of the work itself and therefore the impact of future changes on the person requirements are more difficult to model and predict. The effectiveness of the critical incident interview is strongly dependent upon the effectiveness of the interviewer and it therefore requires a skilled interviewer, experienced in the application of competencies, and one who is able to draw out the key points successfully.

Diaries or work logs involve the jobholders in maintaining records about themselves over a period of time, from which the appropriate competencies may be deduced. There are two ways in which this approach can be used. The first approach is a diary system in which job holders log the activities they undertake at various periods throughout the day either on a time sampling basis (i.e. at various time points in the day they enter the work on which they are engaged) or on a sequential basis listing down the times they start and complete each of their key activities. The second approach is a factor-based log that lists key criteria – possibly in the form of competencies – and jobholders are asked to record each time these are employed. For example the list could contain perhaps twenty factors, which might include elements such as *decision-making* and *accuracy*. These are listed on a pro-forma and on each occasion the jobholder is required to engage in *decision making* or *accuracy*, they will note down the date, time and the specific example of the work in which they were involved and which required them to use *decision-making* or *accuracy*. In this process it is possible to log a number of factors being employed in one particular activity or time period.

One of the key principles in using competencies is the requirement to differentiate between superior, average, and poor levels of performance. **Repertory grid** is a technique by which the differences between performers is analysed in order to draw out the competencies which cause such performance differences. The repertory grid is undertaken through a series of interviews with managers. In the interview, managers are asked to identify people in various categories of performance, usually poor, average, and superior. To assist in the process the interviewer usually uses a set of cards on which the names of the people are written. It is important in this process that the interview is framed around real people and real examples, even though they need not be current or concurrent. The interviewer prompts the manager to describe some of the examples of performance that differentiate between the superior, average, and poor performers. The interviewer will focus on certain elements, often taking a draft set of competencies, and probe the manager on the differences between the different people.

For example, the manager may be asked to look at the differences in the approach to planning work between different sets of people, and may be asked to identify two people who are excellent at such work, two or three who are average, and two or three who are poor. The interviewer will then start to compare in different permutations and may ask how the 'excellent' people do things that are similar to each other but dissimilar to the 'poor' people. The interviewer may ask what it is that the 'excellent' performers do differently from each other but which one of them does in a similar way to a 'poor' performer. Through this process, constantly re-configuring comparisons and differences, it is possible to isolate and identify the behaviours which accompany performance at different levels and which differentiate performance. It may be, for example, the case that the approach to planning and organising is similar between the high and low performer but different between two high performers, and one would conclude that this is not a key competency in the sense of differentiating or contributing to higher levels of performance. Conversely, if the approach to planning was consistent amongst high-performers and differed from the approach of poor performers, it would be a good indicator of a differentiator of performance, and therefore a key competency.

One of the relatively simple methods of job analysis is to undertake **observation** of jobholders in the normal course of their work, often accompanied by unstructured interviews. In this approach the observer is able to see the work at first hand and witness the behaviours associated with varying levels of performance. Observers will need to be skilled in the analysis of competencies since they will be required to deduce the competencies from the activities being observed. It is however the least disruptive method from the point of view of jobholders and managers, even though there is a certain disruptive element of people standing around observing. The observation may appear to be 'informal', yet it will usually entail the pre-development of a checklist of important or critical behaviours, which the observer will be using as a guide. The observation process can therefore often take the form of two stages: the first stage being the drafting of the various kinds of behaviours into a record form. The second stage is then using the form as the recording mechanism for the observation. The observation may focus on a time series, that is to say noting down the behaviours – now classified into certain key behaviours from the initial observation – being displayed at various times of the day. Alternatively the checklist may take the form of the key behaviours being noted against each of the key activities into which the job has been broken down, in a similar fashion to the inventory approach. Where a large-scale observation study is undertaken using a number of observers, the development, agreement and training in the use of, the observer checklist is very important.

An effective but sensitive approach to identifying the competencies is to use **psychometric tests** on a range of job holders, and correlate the results of the test with job performance, in order to identify differentiating characteristics. In order for this to work it is essential that there are measures of performance available that properly class poor, average, and superior performance. A group of people, spread across the different ranges of performance, are asked to complete a series of tests usually comprising both ability and personality tests. The results of these tests are then compared with the performance rating, and significant correlations will identify the key competencies. Care needs to be taken in choosing the battery of tests and ensuring that there is a sufficiently wide range of tests available to cover the broad spectrum of potential needs. It will not, of course, be possible to know which particular test are of use until the exercise has been completed, since the exercise itself will identify the key correlations. There may be many aspects that the test is able to identify, but which do not differentiate between levels of performance. There is however an extra advantage in that the test battery not only provides the differentiators of performance but also provides some benchmark data on the existing population against which external people can be measured as a guide in selection. Thus, for example, in an exercise of this nature undertaken for bank lenders, the following results were obtained:

- Levels of numerical ability (though not differentiating between the performance of poor, average, and superior lenders) were higher than the average for the general population and subsequently used as an entry benchmark for selection.

- A personality factor was identified which differentiated between levels of performance and which became a key competency.

SUITABILITY

Each of the techniques has its own advantages and disadvantages. One of the great advantages of focus groups, repertory grid, critical incident interviews and checklists is that people are involved in the process. The focus groups in particular involve people in describing the competencies as well as simply identifying them, and this ensures that the language used is appropriate to, and comfortable with, the organisation. The advantages of some of the methodical approaches such as checklist, diaries and critical incident interviews is that they can be easily analysed and therefore both defended and modelled for predicting the outcome of future work changes. The advantage of 'open' approaches such as observation, testing and repertory grid are that they do not predetermine the outcome of the analysis by confining responses to predetermined formats and they may therefore be effective in both picking up unexpected competencies and avoiding existing bias or prejudice. Techniques that differentiate on performance such as repertory grid and testing have the advantage that they have the ability to focus on the key aspects which matter from a performance perspective.

All techniques however have some disadvantages. Techniques such as observation and repertory grid need skilled practitioners to implement, but even then there is an unstructured leap between the activities undertaken and the competencies required. It becomes a matter of judgement, albeit skilled judgement, that is therefore open to the bias of the observer/interviewer. The disadvantage of techniques such as focus group and repertory grid, which rely upon viewpoints of effective performance, is that biases about the way in which jobs should be performed creep into the process. For example in repertory grid a line manager may describe a 'better' way one jobholder handles conflict, whereas the 'poor' way, even if not the style of the manager, may be just as effective. In a similar way, focus groups can highlight competencies that the subject-matter experts 'believe' are important, but may not in fact be key to successful performance. This is particularly pertinent in looking at gender bias where males may give undue emphasis to aggression and females may give undue emphasis to empathy. It is one of the reasons that it is essential to ensure that focus groups have a proper mix of gender, ethnic, disabled, and other groups. Some approaches can be particularly sensitive. This is often the case with testing where people often feel threatened by the process, observation where people sometimes feel uncomfortable with being watched and diaries/work logs, which are seen as an additional burden or intrusion by 'big brother'. Even inventories/checklists, which are likely to take no more than an hour to complete, can be seen as intimidating.

The ideal approach is to use a range of techniques so that the end result is comprehensive and balanced. Equally, thought needs to be given to the outcome of each analytical method. For example, testing can be very effective in identifying potential as part of the selection process: it is very objective and the outcome will provide precise measures against which new candidates can be assessed. It will not however readily provide examples of the competencies in everyday behaviours. Focus groups on the other hand will be able to provide very useful detailed examples of everyday behaviours of the competencies in action but not all of those examples may be useful in identifying potential within people who are being selected. The repertory grid will provide evidence of the key differentiators between the poor, average, and successful performers, but will downplay or overlook the core standards that are essential for all levels of performance.

In looking at the way in which the role analysis can support the selection process, the most important aspect is that it develops a clear specification of the person being sought. This in itself justifies the investment of time and money spent in developing the analysis. It can also extend into direct support for the various selection techniques. An analysis based on testing will of course identify the most appropriate test to identify the differentiating competency and provide norms for benchmarking candidates. Where testing is to become part of the selection process this is therefore a highly valued method of analysis. The information from repertory grid can be very useful in developing the screening process since the application form can be designed to draw out examples of experiences similar to those derived from the grid. The critical incident output and the focus group output provide in particular behavioural indicators which can be very useful in providing examples of experiences to gauge interview answers and frame interview questions.

10

Choosing the labour market

In the UK labour market there have been some very noticeable trends which have impacted recruitment activity. The most important of these trends are the following:

- Labour shortages in the 1980s that accompanied the growth of organisations subsequently turned to a labour surplus in the 1990s following universal trends to downsizing. At the turn of the century however they changed again as the UK retuned to full employment and recorded the highest ever numbers of people employed. This has generally meant a reduction in the workforce but has rarely been accompanied by real improvements in productivity and therefore no additional wealth creation to provide redeployment opportunities for the displaced. Political manipulation of unemployment figures masks the true extent of out-of-work people, but it is clear that that there is a labour surplus which, though slowly declining, will remain for some years to come.

- Skill shortages remain in spite of labour surplus and government intervention (such as Sector Skills Councils and National Vocational Qualifications) and such skill shortages are getting worse in each reported year.

- The age composition of the labour market is changing in line with demographic changes so that there are now fewer young people and a greater number of older people in the population generally.

- The gender composition of the employment market is changing so that growth in employment is in 'female employment' and 'male employment' is either declining or growing less rapidly.

- There is a sectoral shift from manufacturing industry, in which employment is steadily declining, to the leisure and retail sectors where there is growth in employment.

- A significant proportion of the UK workforce is student employment comprising school children, university students and 'gap year' young people.

ACCESSING MARKETS

There are various methods by which employers are able to 'fish in the pool' of labour. Such methods include:

- Employment centres such as careers service or job centres or unemployment offices.

- Agencies, sometimes for temporary positions, sometimes for permanent positions and sometimes as an out-sourced operation in which the agency acts as a provider of services rather than a broker for labour.

- Consultants to undertake search and selection, particularly when searching for high level or more specialised positions where there may be a need to tap into an industry market.

- Advertising through various media whether on a national, local or international basis and whether on a general or specialised focus.

A recent survey by the CIPD showed that the main approaches to the labour market were through the following sources:

- local advertising, used by 87 per cent

- national journals/trade press, used by 75 per cent

- national newspaper, used by 61 per cent

- recruitment agencies, used by 81 per cent

- employment service/job centre, used by 61 per cent

- vacancy board/website, used by 72 per cent

- speculative/unsolicited applications, used by 58 per cent

- links with schools/colleges/university, used by 51 per cent

- employee referral, used by 34 per cent.

There are different models of the labour market. The **economic** market looks at internal (within the organisation or industry) and external (outside the organisation or industry) markets. The **social** market looks at different social classes or socio-economic groups. The **geographic** market considers the availability of labour on a local, regional, national or continental basis. Whichever model of the labour market is chosen, it is important to bear that market in mind when deciding on the approach to it. It may not be, for example, very successful to attempt to tap into the market for chemical engineers using employment centres if there is low unemployment amongst chemical engineers. Nor will local advertising yield results unless there is a high concentration of chemical industry in the locality. It is likely to be more effective to tap into the employment of chemical engineers by regarding them as a national, European or global market and advertising in a trade journal, or using selection consultants specialising in the industry. Thinking about the market to be tapped will help in developing a cost-effective approach to recruitment from that market.

Care needs to be taken at this stage to avoid discrimination. It has been said, for example, that advertising in certain prestige newspapers or journals will be hidden from underprivileged groups; that using newer technology such as the Internet may discriminate against older groups; that cinema advertising may discriminate against the blind, and radio advertising against the deaf; and that some media will discriminate against ethnic groups. The labels used here may not be politically correct but they may help to reinforce the point that care needs to be taken not to perpetuate discrimination indirectly through subconscious use of an approach because of custom or habit.

Psychographics

The fundamental changes to labour markets and to organisations in recent decades necessitates a rethink of the approach to the market. In the 1960s Chris Argyris spoke of the legal and psychological contracts that govern the employment relationship. It is a useful model on which to draw. The traditional view of labour markets as economic, social or geographic models may need to be replaced by a psychological model. So too must the demand side of the equation be reconsidered. Organisations are more frequently moving to a model of core and peripheral workforces and, within the core workforce, looking at career and non-career positions. Consumer marketing has moved from simplistic economic segmentation to the use of psychographics. Originally developed by the Bureau of Applied Research in the United States in the 1930s, psychographics evolved from the proposition that any research aimed at understanding consumer behaviour must 'involve an inter-play among the three broad sets of variables: predisposition, influences and product attributes'. A parallel could be drawn between understanding consumer psychology in relation to product purchase and understanding a labour market psychology in relation to employment seeking. It has been observed that, in consumer product marketing, psychographic research is used to:

- identify target markets

- provide better explanations of consumer behaviour

- improve a company's strategic marketing efforts

- minimise risks for new products and business ventures.

The first three goals will be of great practical value in achieving efficiencies in recruitment advertising or other approaches to the labour market. The fourth goal however is the one of significant interest for recruitment in as much as the major concern for recruiters is to improve the probability of selecting suitable employees and minimise the risks of poor placement. The march of psychographics will not have escaped many people. Readers of this book may have had a recent experience of being asked to complete a form, whether from a supermarket 'special offer' promotion or on the purchase of a new consumer product with the warranty registration, or from the subscriptions department of a magazine. These forms ask for a host of information on hobbies, preferences for types of television programmes, income and many other facets which extend beyond simply the economic or lifestyle classifications.

Countered against the psychological view is the proposition that people are rational, and that they pursue employment for wholly economic terms. Interestingly enough, most studies of labour turnover indicate that economic considerations (i.e. leaving for a better paid job) form a minority, around 3 per cent, of the decisions to leave an employment. Decisions on reasons for joining are rarely if ever researched by organisations, but there is some research evidence around candidates' reactions to the way they were treated during the selection process, which suggests that emotional considerations can often be as significant as rational ones. It is also interesting, from the opposite viewpoint, that a study of the selection of young people by small businesses (employing about a third of the total UK workforce) showed that recruiters regarded the 'emotive' aspects of personality as more important than the 'rational' aspects of ability aptitude or attainment.

It is of course not quite as simple as looking only at the psychological or emotive aspects, to regard the approach to the labour market as a kind of dating agency matching common interests and outlooks. Recruitment of engineers, for example, needs to be undertaken from a pool of engineers and the recruitment of solicitors needs to be undertaken from the pool of legally qualified – disregarding training contracts for the purpose of this illustration. In these cases the consideration of personality and other issues would therefore be a subsidiary consideration. There are however many employment opportunities which are not so constrained by considerations of qualification and, indeed, often the case that flexibility to adapt to changing roles and circumstances is a prime requirement. In such circumstances consideration of the psychographic labour market rather than traditional approaches will be of great practical value. One of the current limitations is that the budget of a marketing department is far greater than that of a human resources department and it is unlikely that many organisations would be able to conduct their own psychographic research. It is also the case that readily available psychographic research such as YCS and SRI International are consumer rather than employment based. There are however many organisation where product market research could be utilised: supermarkets are for example a growth area in employment and at the forefront of psychographic research, often through the medium of their loyalty cards, and coupled with an induction audit of new employees would provide an extremely useful tool for targeting recruitment activity and expenditure.

11

Attracting people

CONSIDERING COSTS

There are some essential costs involved in selecting people. There can be the hidden costs of time and effort involved in sifting through the information on the new person contained in their CV, checking up on their references and preparing for the interview. There may be more visible costs of time spent interviewing the successful candidate, or perhaps the cost of test materials or other ancillaries and the cost of relocating the new person. There will also be the cost of bringing the new person up to speed in terms of training and development. All of these and other costs related to the successful candidate are necessary investments in securing an effective new employee. All other costs are unnecessary. They are incidental to the process. Non-productive costs would include such items as the costs of dealing with unwanted applications, interviewing unsuccessful candidates, advertisements which the successful candidate did not see, or correspondence to unsuccessful candidates. They do not contribute to the successful integration or acquisition of the new person and are therefore unnecessary. Such unnecessary costs are not however always unavoidable. Cost effective selection is concerned with avoiding unnecessary costs, though recognising a realistic target is minimising rather than eliminating unnecessary costs. One of the most effective ways to minimise unnecessary costs and raise the standard of response is an effective approach to marketing the 'employment product'.

EMPLOYMENT BRAND STRATEGY

Selection is of course a two way process: it is about matching people and roles. Selectors know a great deal about the jobs but are disadvantaged in trying to gauge and gather information on the candidate. The candidates know, usually, all about themselves but are disadvantaged in trying to gauge and gather information about the job. Good selectors therefore ensure that there is a high degree of self-selection in the overall process, that is to say the candidates are given plenty of information to help them select in or out of the overall process. This process begins with the strategy for marketing 'employment' in the organisation. In the same way as an organisation will develop a strategy to market its products or 'brands', there should be an 'employment brand' strategy.

There is a view that selectors are buyers; candidates are sellers in that they sell their labour and will continue to be sellers of their labour for so long as the organisation requires. In practice it is more effective if selectors see themselves as sellers rather than buyers and if they view themselves as the agents of an investment company in which people continue to invest their time and effort. By taking the perspective of sellers it is possible to think about 'selling' employment and focus attention on how to market those jobs to aid the selling process. The employment brand strategy is developed in the same way as a classic product marketing strategy through the following means:

- Market research: Instead of 'who buys in what quantity?' we consider the potential source of labour and the types of people who 'buy in' to the company.

- Product research: In this case the 'product' is the jobs on offer, their nature, their suitability and attractiveness to people. It is concerned with the good and bad points of working for the organisation and the particular type of work which is being undertaken.

- Marketing method research: In the same way that marketers would pay attention to the marketing method research to check that the method of communication, the message, and the reach are effective, so too do recruiters need to be concerned that cost effective channels are being used to get the message across.

- Motivational research: In product marketing attention is paid to motivational research to identify the 'emotional purchase' of consumers, asking why people buy the products and what they feel about them. It is interesting that in marketing 'employment', greater attention seems to be paid to winning minds rather than hearts and there is a greater emphasis on logic than on feelings. It is particularly interesting given that research on labour turnover shows that a very small percentage of people leave organisations for logical reasons: the greatest influence being emotive reasons. Greater attention to assessing the motivation of existing and potential employees and a greater emphasis on selling to the heart as much as the mind will increase the cost effectiveness of recruitment marketing.

- Attitude surveys: In the product sense this is the customers' attitudes to the products and the companies who make them. Attitude surveys present an interesting perspective for the recruiter. It is usual to find employee relations staff taking responsibility for employee attitude surveys, or perhaps pay designers or organisation development staff. There is a view that recruiters bring the people in to the organisation and their work ends there. Yet effective recruitment is one that leads to a long-term mutually beneficial relationship between employee and employer. In product marketing it is not unusual for marketers to concentrate effort on reminding existing consumers of the benefits of their purchase in order to retain brand loyalty. It is useful for organisations to continue to remind employees of the value of their 'purchase' in buying in to the company. It is not unrealistic for recruiters to take responsibility for the on-going assessment of internal attitudes and the on-going promotion of the benefits of the 'purchase'.

How to develop an employment brand strategy

The first step is to identify the labour market in which the organisation is going to compete, consider the potential for sources of labour, and identify which groups of people are likely to want to buy into employment with the company. At this stage we should also consider the opportunities and threats. We need to identify other recruiters, and therefore competitors for, external labour. This may seem an obvious point, but all too often organisations compare themselves with others pursuing the same nature of business. In reality however they may be geographically remote and not true competitors for labour, whereas other quite dissimilar organisations in the locality may be competing for the same labour. This stage extends beyond simply looking at competitors and will also be concerned with legislative or other impacts which may pose a threat. Changing demographics, whether a baby boom or pensioner boom, will be obvious aspects for consideration.

The next step is to prepare the marketing objectives and strategy. All too often recruiters attempt to use clever advertising techniques or throw additional money at recruiting people once in 'the eye of the storm', rather than looking ahead to identify the oncoming problem and putting strategies in place to prevent the problem or minimise the adverse consequences. This of course will be more critical for in-house recruiters with long-term perspectives than external consultants who may be undertaking a one-off assignment.

The third step is to formulate the 'marketing mix' to support 'the product' with the use of the following elements:

- the product elements

- the pricing elements

- the promotion elements.

In employment terms this will be an activity beyond the scope of the recruiter alone and will be an aspect which demands the attention of a range of human resources management. It is however something with which the recruiters must be involved. For the **'product elements'** we mean the nature and scope of roles and the structure of the organisation. Since recruiters are attuned to the expectation of people in the external labour market they should have a valid contribution to make in the shaping of the organisation structure. This contribution should cover the careers and opportunities which will exist for people in addition to the way in which roles are designed to make use of the talent available and thereby improve the intrinsic value and attractiveness of such employment. For the **'pricing element'** we mean levels of salary and reward. This is usually the domain of the compensation and benefits people within the organisation and may be the product of collective bargaining arrangements. Since the primary purpose of any pay structure is likely to be concerned with either the recruitment or retention of staff, and since one of the big influences on attracting people to the organisation will be the price tag on their service, it seems obvious that recruiters need to contribute their input into reward decisions. Nowadays it is important to look at the 'total reward strategy' that covers the totality of pay, benefits and work life experience that brings people to the organisation, retains and enthuses them. The **'promotion elements'** cover aspects such as advertising, public relations, direct and indirect promotion. The 'promotion elements' need to be forward looking. It is unlikely that product marketing nowadays will rely only on advertising but will look at a complete range of strategies. This should also be the case with employment marketing. By this stage, there will be a very clear understanding and agreement on the positioning of the employment package in its various forms, the intrinsic (motivational) and extrinsic (salary/reward) features of the package, and a clear understanding, through the research, of the attractiveness of employment with the organisation. The expectations and competitive pressures will combine to give a clear focus to the work needed. This will also enable decisions to be made on the most appropriate support for marketing the product. It is not therefore simply a matter of advertising but of considering the various approaches which will be available to the recruiter.

PRODUCT PROMOTION

The final step in developing an employment brand strategy is to determine the way in which the 'employment product' is to be promoted. The main opportunities are in the following areas:

- public relations

- in-house promotions

- direct mail

- advertising.

It is not generally thought necessary that recruiters should play a pivotal role in the **public relations** of an organisation. In general public relations is handled by specialists either in-house in the case of large organisations or using external consultants in the smaller organisations. In the private sector the focus particularly for share-quoted companies is on the message to investors. In the public sector, if public relations is undertaken, it is generally to ensure an appreciation amongst the 'consumers' of the value of the service being received. It is very rare that public relations specialists consider the impact of a public relations effort on existing employees let alone potential employees. It remains the case however that most potential employees gain more of a feel for the organisation through its public relations effort or product marketing endeavours than through the influence of the HR department. It is important therefore that recruiters use the opportunity to influence the formal public relations and product marketing strategies of the organisation by indicating the messages that they want to convey to the target audience. There are numerous occasions where organisations have deliberately set out to satirize themselves and their staff in an effort to project humour into their product marketing, only to find an adverse reaction from potential employees (and sometimes also from existing employees). In addition to the formal public relations effort, there are many activities which the recruiters can undertake directly, or influence others to undertake with them. Local trade shows, career fairs, liaison with schools and universities and appearances at local associations from Chambers of Commerce to Women's Institutes (depending of course on the target audience/labour market) are all effective. These are however time-consuming activities and need money to be spent if they are to be undertaken professionally. It is also essential that they are undertaken on a planned and regular basis. In recent years for example, blue chip companies have differed in their approach to the graduate recruitment market. Some companies have chosen to scale down their drives but continue them on a regular basis. Others have chosen to adopt a stop-start approach, continuing high visibility in some years and withdrawing completely in others. In the case of the stop-start approach, the absence speaks as loudly against the company in the 'stop' times as the promotional efforts speaks for the company in the 'start' times.

There are often opportunities for **in-house promotion.** Many organisations are involved in providing a product or a service to the public generally and sometimes specifically to a target audience that is their labour market. In such cases it can be very effective to promote the prospect of employment opportunities through this medium. This is nothing new; for example for many years local shops have advertised for staff simply by putting a sign in their window. Given that recruiters need to avoid unnecessary work and expenditure, it is important to ensure that this promotion provides a sufficiently good picture to attract suitable candidates and deter unsuitable candidates. Some organisations have sufficient space to stage a permanent display stand with available information and application forms. Other organisations find it possible to incorporate publicity on careers in their general product and service catalogues. In general, in-house promotion is most often used for lower-level general staff, but curiously there are many occasions where organisations looking for scarce specialist skills fail to promote their career opportunities in sales and other material to their customers, even when the customers are the very specialists the organisation is trying hard to attract.

The age of junk mail is a regret to many. It is however a modern phenomenon and it tends to be only a source of anger or resentment where it is persistent or intrusive and its product or service unwanted. In general it is only junk when people don't want the product. It can be an effective means of selling and those who have bought a wanted item through such a process are not resentful of it. It is also the case that mail which asks the recipient to give something is far less welcome than mail which offers to give something to the recipient. In such terms the interest in **direct mail** to advertise employment is likely to be more cordial than most direct mail aimed at stimulating a purchase. The quality of focus offered by direct mail is unparalleled. It is possible to obtain information on names and addresses categorised in various ways, whether it be social, economic, consumer habits, political persuasion, or financial standing. Good market research will provide information on the target audience for employment which can be matched very precisely with the direct mail campaign. This can either be undertaken in-house by buying-in appropriate mail lists, or can be undertaken by specialist organisations who can arrange the appropriate level of service. This may be something as simple as stuffing and posting envelopes, through to a total campaign in which letters are prepared individually and personalised using computer database and mail-merge facilities, posted, followed up with telephone calls and tracked. The use of the Post Office 'mail sort' facility enables large scale mailings to be pre-sorted (using postcode) by the organisation in order to achieve substantial cost savings on postage.

Advertising tends to be the most popular promotion channel for recruiters. It can take a number of forms including:

- static advertising: newspaper, magazine, and periodical advertising; job centres
- live advertising: radio, cinema and television advertising
- interactive advertising: Internet advertising, recruitment fairs and events.

Static advertising may perhaps be in national newspaper or local newspapers. Nowadays many local newspapers are supplemented by free newspapers which derive income from advertisers rather than readers. The use of the newspaper will depend upon the kind of post to be filled and the target audience. National newspapers generally carry advertisements for more senior positions and although are able to advertise on each day generally give prominence to different types of advertising on different days. It is often the case that job advertisements are carried on a Thursday or a Sunday. The advantage of national newspapers is that they are more frequent and it is possible to place an advertisement at relatively short notice. The advertisements need to be correctly prepared which usually means using a specialist advertising agency and the national newspapers tend to be the most expensive form of advertising costing several thousand pounds. Local newspapers are usually much cheaper, although those serving large areas such as London will be on a par with the cost of national advertising. Where employment is targeted at a specific group such as engineers, IT people or HR staff, but where the target audience is geographically dispersed (perhaps nationally), the use of specialist periodicals and trade journals is often the preferred approach. It is usually (but not always) the case that the specialist journals are far cheaper than national newspaper advertising but more expensive than local newspaper advertising. The benefit of using such media is that it is targeted directly at the appropriate group and therefore minimises response from unsuitable candidates. The downside is that such journals may appear on a monthly basis and it is a number of weeks before an advertisement can be placed which could cause an unwelcome delay in the selection process.

Live advertising such as radio and television advertising is usually the domain of product advertising. Television advertising for employment is very rare and is usually only seen for large recruiters such as the Army. The costs of preparing and screening a television advertisement are on a par with the whole HR budget for many organisations. It also takes a significant period of time to prepare an advertisement and the fees for peak slots are more expensive and generally less available at short notice. All of these aspects conspire to make television advertising generally unsuitable. A lower cost option suitable for a younger general target audience and where time is not a problem (for example pre-planned graduate intakes) is cinema advertising which can be very effective. It also offers the opportunity to localise the advertisement. Radio advertising is generally much cheaper to prepare than television and cinema advertising, is generally cheaper to broadcast, and carries fewer problems of availability or lead times. It can be a very effective means of advertising, although it is more difficult to target particular audiences. It can be particularly effective when used to reinforce other advertising, for example by prompting people to read a newspaper advertisement on a particular evening or to visit an open evening at a particular location. One of the advantages of using live advertising is that it has a very wide coverage, usually far greater than those reading newspapers, and gains attention in ways that the other media cannot. For example newspaper advertising will usually only be read by those who are seeking another job, whereas radio advertising at peak commuting time may catch the attention of a listener driving to or from work and spark their interest to find out more. Care needs to be taken however with the response since it is much easier to respond to written advertisements where there is time to catch all the information on response address etc. whereas television, cinema, and radio advertising is very quick and people may not have the opportunity to take down full details.

Interactive advertising usually takes advantage of new technology. The Internet has revolutionised the world of computing and has spread to advertising. The Internet poses many of the advantages of cinema, television and radio advertising without the disadvantages of cost and speed. Internet advertisements can be prepared in-house and placed on the web almost immediately. The web is in essence a section of the computer network which will hold the 'pages' of the advertisement for users of the Internet to access. Anyone with access to the Internet can have access to the information. This can be particularly effective for international recruitment campaigns. In the same way that live advertising can catch the attention of people not seeking job advertisements, the Internet can catch those who are 'browsing' other information on the service. It also has the added advantage of the potential to link up with other pieces of information about the company. The restrictions of space and cost associated with newspaper and live advertising are not prohibitive with on-line advertising. There is generally little limitation on space and it is possible therefore to put together a few pages of information and, where the organisation has other web sites on its products and services, it can be hyper linked to provide much greater detail. This is comparable to sending out product brochures and the company annual report with every application form. The cost is restricted to the development of the information on the web site. The cost of accessing the information is borne by the 'reader'.

Since the Internet is a multimedia facility, it provides the opportunity to have the best of both worlds in giving written information one would find in static advertising with photographs and video images to supplement the information and thereby achieve the impact of live advertising. A further advantage of this approach is that application forms can be sent through the system either through placing the form on the web or forwarding it by electronic mail. When the electronic mail system is used a candidate can access the form and complete information on themselves and return it. In the same way that the advertiser can include static and live information, the candidate can also return photographs or video images which can be particularly useful when looking at evidence of creative ability. The potential savings in printing and postage on a large-scale campaign can also be beneficial. The Internet can be a very effective means of advertising for certain kinds of staff, particularly those who are likely to be users of the Internet. In the early days of the Internet this was undoubtedly confined to the 'anorak brigade' but the rapid rise in affordability and accessibility of on-line computing is quickly expanding the potential labour market place. The disadvantage is that the Internet may not be suitable for all kinds of positions and is very much a widespread medium, indeed truly global.

A more traditional form of interactive advertising is the use of a recruitment event whether in conjunction with others such as a recruitment fair or dedicated such as an open evening by the company. In this form of advertising, candidates are encouraged to come along and browse the information with the company and this can take the form of written material available, together with static displays and stands and perhaps video cassettes of the company, its products, and employment opportunities. The event can perhaps be supplemented with live presentations or demonstrations. A particular benefit of this approach is that it enables a wide range of information to be fed to potential candidates in helping them to make their choice. It also filters out weak applications in that those who make the effort to attend are more likely to be truly interested. The downside is that it can be expensive to stage events, particularly if third party facilities are being used such as an hotel, and it requires significant resource from the company in terms of staff availability. It also offers the added advantage however of being able to be integrated seamlessly with other parts of the selection process so that it may encompass the completion of application forms during the event and may also include informal interviewing or discussion.

CASE STUDY

Virgin Airways

Virgin is one of the most recognised consumer brands nowadays. Since 1984, Virgin Atlantic has aimed to set new standards of customer service and innovation in air travel, placing its emphasis on value for money, quality, fun and innovation. The brand has become iconic, in part an extension of the personality of founder Sir Richard Branson, conveying entrepreneurial spirit and his role as customer champion. As a brand, it is seen as distinctive, fun loving, friendly and innovative, but with an intelligence and integrity that ensures quality standards.

Virgin promotes this singular personality through wit, charm and straight talking, and is never afraid to push boundaries. There is a keen appreciation of the power of publicity and the role of the employer brand is both recognised and encouraged within the organisation. Although budgets are very carefully managed, creative ideas and innovations are not only encouraged: they are positively expected.

The advertising agency aia is responsible for all of Virgin Atlantic Airway's external recruitment marketing They have placed an emphasis on developing a close working relationship with their client and have worked closely with Virgin's recruitment team with frequent access to them, their colleagues and their business plans to ensure an understanding of VAA's short, medium and long-term resourcing challenges. By understanding their people, their culture and their aspirations, they have sought to translate the 'what's it like?' message through recruitment materials to ensure that VAA are attracting the right candidates – candidates who fulfil the cultural as well as technical requirements.

Cabin crew recruitment is understandably a massive exercise for VAA, with a rolling drive throughout the year aiming to fill regular training courses. Crew are often the most immediate 'face' of the Virgin brand for customers and so it is essential that crew live and breathe the brand and can deliver that experience to customers who are expecting the best.

The advertising agency aia supports VAA in setting six-month attraction strategies, targeting the right candidates via the right media: on and off-line, outdoor and ambient, live and static. The creative message is built on detailed research including internal focus groups, conducted with existing staff, as well as regular statistical analysis and research. The agency also conducts external qualitative and quantitative research into VAA's ideal candidates and how to communicate with them. The combination of planning and research has provided a strategic platform that allows them to measure results and continually refine the approach to improve results against key performance indicators such as cost-per-hire and attrition.

Using the market research the agency has been able to develop the marketing mix and a promotion strategy that includes both campaigns and one-off creative advertisements for cabin crew. Their aim is 'to keep our ads 'impactful' and interesting enough to ensure our messages stand out, but at the same time honest and clear enough to ensure that candidates are getting the real picture and not one that is entirely focused on the glamour. Virgin look to attract candidates who not only fit the bill in terms of living the brand values and image, but also have the personal maturity, energy and tenacity to withstand some of the tougher elements of the job.'

An example of the importance of using the visual image to target the 'emotional buy-in' of potential candidates and using market research to understand the candidates' emotions, was the Snowman campaign that won the CIPD Recruitment Marketing Award. The agency and client were both very pleased with the outcome. The agency's comments on the campaign are worth quoting in full:

'While many organisations are reluctant to advertise in December, due to perceived poor responses levels across the festive season, VAA's constant demand for talent means they're as happy to recruit over Christmas as any other time of year. Plus, of course, a seasonal message provides the perfect opportunity to showcase that all-important Virgin brand. Snowman delivered on both counts. Unquestionably festive and unmistakably Virgin, its charm made a real connection with the target audience. This had to do with the media strategy as well as the wit and style of the ad itself. Running in the London Evening Standard the week before Christmas (a quiet time for advertising), Snowman commanded huge impact in the publication.'

'Crucially, the messages within the ad were also designed to deter the unsuitable candidate; the role of cabin crew with VAA offers fantastic and exciting opportunities to travel, experience new cultures and learn a multitude of transferable skills, but there is a price to pay and working on Christmas Day is just one of these. By being brave enough to be honest, we are ensuring an initial filtering by the candidates themselves, thus saving the resourcing teams at VAA time and therefore money assessing candidates who ultimately are not up to the more challenging aspects of the role.'

'Response levels to the ad not only belied the supposed seasonal slump with a good volume or response, but also delivered the calibre of candidates VAA needed. Particularly gratifying, for an ad that appeared just once, Snowman was referred to consistently and with great affection by a large number of applicants throughout the early 2004 interviews and training courses.'

Part 4

Choosing people

12

Screening

A well-developed method of attracting people to apply to the organisation, whether it is a carefully drafted and comprehensive advertisement or any of the other methods mentioned in earlier chapters on attracting candidates, will be effective in improving the response quality. That is to say, the proportion of potentially suitable candidates will be increased, and unsuitable candidates will be deterred or will select themselves out, thereby reducing the overall number of candidates. The thrust of the attraction process should therefore be to bring in a smaller total number of applications with a higher proportion of suitable applicants.

However good the attraction process, it is probable that there will be more candidates than positions to be filled and often (but not always) the case that there will be more candidates than can be realistically taken on to the next stage of more time-consuming selection processes such as interviewing or testing. A screening process will therefore be needed to distil the full response of applicants to a manageable number of candidates for further, more detailed, consideration.

It is not always the case that there is a need for a screening process. In some instances there may be a very small number of candidates for positions and the use of a screening technique needs to be fully questioned. This may seem an obvious point, yet it frequently occurs that speculative applicants for a hard-to-fill vacancy are asked to complete an application form which might delay or even deter progress of the application. In practice, the application form is often a less useful method of selection than an interview, test, or other assessment process which can be immediately set up. Screening techniques should therefore not usually be considered as a means of improving the selection decision but rather as a means of refining application volume into a manageable quantity.

There are two main approaches to screening: those who approach it as a means of screening out and those who approach it as a means of screening in. The screening-out school of thought is to look for any aspects within the application form which will provide an 'excuse' to reject the candidate. The screening-in school of thought will review the application and attempt to draw conclusions, however preliminary, on the candidate's suitability for the post. This may seem a subtle variation but in practice it is a very important and fundamental difference in approach, which will impact greatly on the efficacy of the selection process. In general the screening-out approach will prove far less effective and more damaging than the screening-in approach. The screening-in approach will be to use key criteria – usually competencies – derived from the role analysis and related to the person specification. The application form will be assessed to identify whether there is any evidence that the applicant matches the criteria. There are various degrees of sophistication to this process which are described under the techniques below. The screening-out approach is less person oriented and more process oriented. It is concerned with reducing the number of forms rather than the number of people. Typically the screening out-approach is likely to be the selector discarding an application because it is completed in blue ink when the instructions said black, or typed when the instructions said hand-written. These may of course be perfectly valid objections if the organisation is looking for people who are not innovators, not risk takers and have neat handwriting, and where the organisation does not want to embark on the not-so-complex task of training people to use black ink ('this is a black pen, use it') or has a legally defensible requirement to discriminate against colour-blind people. Assuming these things are valid however it may be that they have been allowed to override more important criteria and otherwise suitable candidates may be rejected before there is an opportunity to fully consider and evaluate some of their other criteria. It is of course easy to criticise such approaches, but it should not be overlooked that they often occur when there is a very high number of applications, perhaps several thousand, a pressing time deadline and very limited resources to handle the task. In such circumstances care needs to be given to improving the attraction techniques, automating the selection process, or increasing the availability of resources. The importance of the screening process cannot be over emphasised because later selection techniques can only help to identify the potential of the candidates in the available pool, they will not improve the quality of the pool itself.

The main techniques for screening are:

- application forms/curricula vitae
- telephone screening
- biodata.

In recent years some organisations have also resorted to random techniques for screening such as the use of computer generated random selection of candidate numbers or pulling names out of a hat. Incredulous though it may seem, such techniques have found favour with a number of responsible organisations, including some public sector organisations, as a means of handling high volumes of applications. They are however lotteries rather than selection techniques and not deserving of attention in any serious consideration of recruitment and selection.

APPLICATION FORMS/CURRICULA VITAE

One of the most popular tools in recruitment and selection is the written (or printed) application. Some studies have shown that it is used in 98 per cent of selection projects. It has become so much a part of recruitment custom that it is wholly expected by candidates and taken for granted by most recruiters. The written application can either take the form of a standard application form or curriculum vitae (CV).

The CV approach allows the candidate to develop their own format and send the information they consider appropriate in the way in which they feel appropriate. It is generally used for more senior positions where the use of a standard form is frowned upon as a somewhat clerical activity for senior people to be engaged in. One of the advantages of the CV approach is that it is speedier and less costly in that there is no delay in sending out an application form and the cost of its postage is avoided. Some recruiters prefer to use the CV because it demonstrates the ability of the candidate to martial their thoughts and put together a clear piece of communication. The disadvantage of a CV is that it enables the candidate to construct the application to inflate their strong points and obscure any weakness or concerns. It is also the case that some 'professional applicants' can print off many copies and send them indiscriminately to organisations whereas the work involved in completing the application form would test their resolve and therefore their seriousness.

The standard application form is the most common technique for screening applications. Ideally each application form should be designed around the role to be recruited. In practice this is unlikely to be feasible and, depending on the size of the organisation and diversity of roles, there may be a single uniform application or a small number of applications for different kinds of job families. The application form is probably one of the most maligned and misused recruitment tools. With careful design and proper attention it can become an extremely effective part of the overall selection process. In designing the application form it should be considered as an investigative tool rather than a piece of protocol. It should be designed to elicit information in the way that an interview or any other recruitment tool provides a vehicle for candidates to provide answers in response to questions. It should therefore be designed very much with the questions in view. Thought also needs to be given to both ergonomics of the form, in the sense of ease of completion by candidates, and to the visual impact since it may be one of the first impressions of the company that the candidate receives. It is generally better to martial the questions into homogenous blocks. So, for example, personal information such as name, address or contact number will be in one section; information on work record and experience will be in another section; educational qualifications or professional qualifications will be in another section, and so on. Within each section it is more sensible for the information to be constructed in chronological order since it becomes much easier to assess the application.

The written application needs of course to fulfil a number of purposes. On one hand it will be the reference document used for the contact address and phone number of the candidate and become an integral part of the administration of the selection process. It will also form a guide for vetting the candidates prior to appointment, so that qualifications can be checked, work records confirmed, medical conditions verified, and references taken up. The form will also be used in preparation for the interview and as a means of framing interview questions around key points of information in the form. Finally the key purpose of the form will be to provide information on which decisions can be made on whether or not to take people forward to the next stage of the selection process. It is worth bearing in mind these different uses in designing the form since different people will be accessing different parts of the form, and efficiencies of processing can be particularly important in dealing with large volumes of recruitment applications.

In order to ease administrative burdens on the management of recruitment and selection, many organisations have now automated the administrative process. There are many computer software packages which combine a word-processing and database mail-merge facility so that the name and contact address of the candidate can be entered on to the system once only and then called up from the database to produce acknowledgement letters, invitations to interview, or rejection letters at the appropriate stage without the need to re-enter the data, giving a personalised letter to all candidates even though the computer may generate hundreds or thousands of identical letters. In order to use automated processes it is necessary to allocate a number or other identifier to candidates and some organisations have taken this a stage further in using bar codes to identify candidates and 'assemble' information from a range of sources including the test results, application form or interview results by using the bar code system.

A more recent form of automation is the use of the Internet. In its early days it may have been the domain of 'computer nerds', but its general use and acceptability has become commonplace in the UK. It is, of course, less novel to younger people and very suitable therefore for graduate recruitment. A review of traditional application-response times by Hewlett-Packard in the USA showed that 'good' job-seekers could obtain a new post within a week, but the cycle time for recruitment was over 50 days; which meant that 'good' candidates were not caught in time. The Internet allows a radical reduction in candidate-response time, immediate screener access and faster employer-response time. The improved cycle time enabled the quality of response to be improved. The Internet can work by allowing the candidate to submit their electronic CV or complete an electronic application form.

It may seem an obvious point that the form should be 'road tested' to ensure that there is sufficient space for people to complete the information requested of them and that the instructions are clear. This point is often missed, judging by the design of some application forms. Forms are never easy to complete by those who are not involved in the design, and the use of correct simple terminology, boxes, lines and shading all help the candidate. Colour is an important consideration particularly where large volume of forms will need to be read. Black ink on a yellow background is the most legible of all colour combinations and professional form designers will be able to advise on these and other aspects. Many application forms still use headings rather than questions to seek information. For some roles, such as blue collar work where form filling may be more unusual and perhaps intimidating, some organisations have found it successful to use the approach of a questionnaire rather than a form so that the headings are phrased as questions for candidates to answer.

How to screen applications effectively

Although the screening of applications is an important part of the process, for many organisations it is an unstructured part. It is also a part of the process which selectors often feel can be delegated to junior staff. It is the case however that the unstructured approach is also the hit and miss approach. For some reason it is common in organisations to overlook the time needed to review application forms and there are many occasions where recruiters find themselves sifting through large volumes of applications on their lap in front of the evening television. For some it is difficult to delegate this aspect of the work if junior staff do not have sufficient experience to make selection decisions. There are however techniques which can considerably help to improve the screening process. It is of course a necessary prerequisite to have a very clear person specification and this is more helpful if it is in the form of competencies. Taking the framework outlined in Part 3, the application should focus on the acquired skills and adapting behaviours. The 'acquired' would be the knowledge and experience. Knowledge can be specified in terms of qualifications and these can be checked through the application form, experience can similarly be specified by reference to a number of years, perhaps a type of industry or organisation or company, and nature of role. The 'adapting' elements will look at the way in which the individual has applied their talent to different circumstances or situations, and the more senior the appointment the more the screener will look for evidence of achievement in different settings. Very often some of these competencies are very easy to specify, as with the requirement for a driving licence, or a typing qualification, or an accountancy qualification or experience of shift working, or of dealing with members of the public. As part of the screening process the competencies that are to be assessed at this stage should be identified and prioritised as appropriate. This is likely to be a small number of competencies – perhaps not more than six. These should then be given a weighting so that the total score of the competencies comes to a hundred. A simple rating system, perhaps four scale, should be used which will, for example, identify whether the applicant falls into one of the following categories:

- Shows no evidence of the competency.

- Shows some evidence of the competency.

- Shows full evidence of the competency.

- Shows evidence of the competency displayed at higher levels than this role.

Examples are then provided to the screener of what is meant by the competency at each of these levels.

Taking a hypothetical example, one of the competencies may be *technical knowledge* which may have been defined as '*human resource management*' and described as '*provides guidance to line management in the application of existing procedures for the management of staff including selection, discipline, grievance and performance management procedures...*' which would be further qualified in the person specification as '*evidenced by three to four years at HR/Personnel Officer...*' This would then be anchored as the third level in the example rating so that:

- A candidate who worked as HR Officer giving general advice would go into rating 2 because there is some evidence but it does not indicate that they were involved in all the aspects such as selection or discipline.

- A candidate giving the specified examples would go into rating 3.

- A candidate showing they were responsible for designing, developing. implementing and advising on some of those policies would go into rating 4.

- A candidate with no experience in HR would be on rating 1.

Thus the competencies are derived from the competency framework and the screener simply applies a rating scale that can have as many ratings as desired. Given that competencies in organisations are usually described in a way which lend themselves to observation and such observation will of course be denied when it comes to screening, it is important to add those additional descriptors such as '*three to four years experience at...*'. Continuing to use this example, if the technical knowledge had been weighted at twenty points and the candidate had been rated at 3 they would have scored 60 points. The process is repeated for the remainder of the competencies to be screened and a total score obtained. The degree to which this screening process is simple or complex is governed by the number of competencies chosen and the number of ratings used. It does mean however that there is a consistency to the screening process.

In many organisations where an unstructured approach is used there is very little consistency in the screening process. It is often the case that the selection is based upon the perceptions and values of the screener, who may not be representative of the values and aspirations of the kind of person being sought. A simple test organisations can use, to check consistency of screenings, is to provide the same set of applications to a range of different people who are asked (without conferring) to create a shortlist. In the unstructured process it is highly likely that the shortlists will be different. The use of a structured scoring system may appear at first to be more complex but it can significantly simplify and speed up the process in addition to improving consistency and defensibility. Additionally the use of such scoring enables the cut-off point to be adjusted to allow for greater or fewer numbers to proceed to the next stage in accordance with the specific circumstances of each selection assignment. See Figure 12.1.

*Figure 12.1 / **Rating an application through weighted competencies***

Competency	Weight	Rating	Score
Technical knowledge	40	3	120
Business knowledge	30	4	120
Results	20	4	80
People experience	10	2	20
TOTAL			340

The structured screening process can be used with any application form but it is particularly suitable where the application form has been designed with this process in mind. Some organisations therefore construct the application form so that there are sections on the screened competency. In these sections the applicant is given the definition of the competency and perhaps some examples to help them understand and they then have a free text box in which to complete information which would help the screener identify their level of competency in that regard. This system is not only fairer to candidates but is much easier for selectors since it prompts the candidates to provide the information which is essential for undertaking effective screening of their application. It is in some ways a significant move towards self-screening.

JOB QUESTIONNAIRES

A technique, although not screening in the strict sense, which can assist in the objective of reducing the numbers at this stage, is the use of job questionnaires (JQs). It has been shown that information given to applicants is not always read. In one case study of graduate recruits it was found that the company brochure (rather glossy and expensive) was not read by applicants until the night before their interview as a means of 'revision'. It did not influence their decision to submit or withhold their application for employment. It was therefore an unnecessary cost for the organisation not only in terms of the cost of the brochure itself but also of the additional cost of postage and administration. Conversely, job questionnaires have been shown to be influential to people in forming their decision to submit or withhold their application. The job questionnaire takes the form of a number of questions which are a self-scored quiz similar in form to the light-hearted questionnaires found in popular leisure magazines. The applicant answers the question, scores in accordance with the instructions, and then proceeds to read the answer and check against the scoring key. Thus the questionnaire may be along the lines of the following question:

Q1 The job of the Sales Clerk means frequent contact with potential and existing customers. True or False?

The applicant is then faced with a range of these questions, perhaps 15 or 20, to which they must answer true or false. They will go to the scoring key which will tell them that the answer to Q1 is false, and to score 1 if they answered 'false', score 0 if they answered 'true'. There then follows a short statement which gives information about that answer. For example, '*False. The key contact from the company for customers is the sales representative through whom all relationships should be conducted. The sales clerk will mainly be working with the sales representatives and routing all queries through them although there may be occasions when a customer query has to be handled directly. The thrust of this role is not on relationships but on making sure that the sales documentation is properly processed, that the information on the customers accounts is properly maintained, and linked through to the invoicing procedures...*'. Similar information is provided for each of the questions and because the applicants have bothered to do the test, they are likely to be interested in seeing the result. They then total all the scores and look at a ready reckoner which will say something along the lines of:

Score 8 or less.
This role may not be right for you, it may not offer the challenges or opportunities you were looking for and you should think very carefully before proceeding any further with the application.

Score 8 to 13.
This role may be different from the way in which you originally envisaged it. Think carefully before you proceed and read further information in the job description attached or contact the recruitment selection helpline on ......, before proceeding with your application.

Score 14 to 20.
This role could be just what you are looking for. Take a look through the enclosed job description and information, and complete and return the form within the next week so that we have the opportunity to give your application full consideration.

In this way applicants are helped to screen themselves out of the process without the adverse consequences of rejection and without the cost of dealing with the returned application. In times of high unemployment there will always be 'desperation applications', but JQs are still a very valuable tool for reducing unsuitable applications.

TELEPHONE SCREENING

One of the modern approaches to screening is the use of telephone screening. This is particularly suitable for those roles that will involve telephone contact such as helpline positions. It works through advertising the job and inviting applicants to telephone – usually a specific number during a certain time or within a defined period of perhaps days or weeks. Applicants ring to find out more about the job but they are answered by an operator who is provided with a script incorporating a set of questions and a scoring system similar to that described in the screening process above. This system may be a manual system but is more often a computer-based scoring which also operates a response log. The response log is particularly appropriate where a number of operators are assigned to handle a large volume of telephone calls. This means the scoring is performed on screen by the operator during the telephone call, the system will undertake the calculation but, more importantly, will provide the operator with information on whether that candidate's score puts them amongst the top respondents, the middle, or the bottom and therefore helps to direct the next stage. The next stage is for the operator to place the applicant on the fast or slow track. A 'fast track' applicant will be asked to proceed to the next stage which may be either a face-to-face interview or being asked to telephone again at a set time and date to engage in a more lengthy discussion which will form a telephone interview. The computer-based logging system will help the operator to give the appropriate slot to the applicant. Information may simultaneously be sent to the applicant, which will include a standard application form or other company details, although this process may render some or all of that activity unnecessary. A 'slow track' applicant will be advised that a pack will be sent to them in the post, which will contain further information and an application form. It can be, but rarely is, the case that the applicant is advised that their application will not be suitable. This is rare because of the adverse reaction to being rejected 'over the phone'. Sending out information to the applicants therefore enables them to believe that their application will still be considered and overcomes the potential adverse reactions but does not disrupt the selection process, which is continuing for the 'fast track' applicants. Furthermore, there is the opportunity of a safety net to consider submitted applications further if required using the structured screening approach.

The telephone screening approach has many advantages. It is particularly useful where the positions being considered involve a high level of telephone activity and where it is extremely difficult to assess such skills from an application form but where such skills may be so fundamental as to rule out the candidate. It is a very speedy process and controls the rate at which applicants respond in a way which written applications cannot, given the timing of the postal system. It also has the advantage of building a personal bond with the organisation; a telephone call of even the most clinical nature tends to be seen as far more personal than the most carefully drafted and warm letter. The disadvantages are primarily logistics and cost. It may not be possible to predict fully and accurately the scale of response and put sufficient operators on duty to answer the calls. It will of course need dedicated telephone lines and a number of operators to answer and this usually means manning such lines outside normal office hours. There is also the requirement to create an effective script and scoring mechanism and this can be quite costly when an automated scoring mechanism and logging or diary system is used. It is likely to be beyond the scope and resources of most HR departments to mount such an operation internally, but it is quite feasible to use third-party resources successfully for such an exercise. Whilst there may be some cost savings in the avoidance of postage and printing costs for sending out applications and other information, these cannot be entirely avoided and, even if they could, may still be less than the cost of mounting the operation. Cost considerations will therefore remain the key constraint on widespread use of this approach. There are few other problems with this approach, most people nowadays have access to telephones and providing the opportunity to call at out-of-hours times avoids further difficulties. There are some hidden advantages in that it avoids some of the problems of race and disability discrimination, since the telephone call may give no indication of these.

As yet there has been no indication that organisations will be taking this a stage further into 'cold calling' by targeting people, using labour market data such as psychographics, and persuading them to apply. Sandwiched between the early-evening phone calls, from the bank calling to offer its latest insurance scheme and the ubiquitous double glazing salesmen, there may yet be organisations phoning about their employment offerings, but to date this kind of activity has been limited to executive search consultants.

BIODATA

Biodata is a technique which is rarely used in selection, yet does well on all measures of effectiveness. Biodata is an abbreviation of biographical data and is the process by which the story of people's lives can contain keys to their future. It uses the simple assumption that past actions and behaviours will be the best predictor of future behaviours and patterns. Biodata as a concept is not new nor is it particularly unfamiliar outside of the selection process. Most people are accustomed to being asked to complete questions about themselves when they apply for bank loans, credit cards or car insurance. Furthermore, most people are aware that the premium they pay for their car insurance will be linked to their history of incident-free driving and their age, and the make and model of car. It is well known that a 20 year-old male driver of a two seater sports car with a recent history of accidents and claims will pay a higher premium than a 50 year-old driver with a clean record and driving a family saloon. Similarly, most people are aware that the postcode of their home will have a significant bearing on the amount of home contents premium they pay and will be used by insurance companies to gauge the probability of burglary at their homes. In the information age, our address, age and occupation can be used in a variety of situations: by political parties to predict our affiliations, by supermarkets to plan location of their new stores, marketers to decide which products to inform us about, and by financial institutions to decide the degree of risk we may pose. It is not surprising therefore that the history of biodata began with insurance companies who are accustomed to using biographical information for decision making.

The earliest recorded use of biodata was with Chicago underwriters in 1894 when Colonel Thomas Peters of the Washington Life Insurance Company used biodata to improve the selection of life insurance agents. In the same way that Peters used biodata for insurance calculations so he took data on successful and unsuccessful insurance salesmen to attempt to predict the likelihood of them succeeding and staying in their particular role. The process was taken a stage further in the 1920s when another insurance company looked at 500 people selling life insurance and focused on 50 good, 50 poor, and 50 'middling' salesmen from the sample and analysed their application forms. The researcher looked at all the basic information on the form such as age, marital status, education and experience, together with the response to the question *'what amount of insurance are you confident of placing each month?'* The researcher looked at whether the candidate replied to the question, not to the reply itself. By careful correlation it was possible to see what items distinguished good from 'middling' and 'middling' from bad. Each of these factors was then assigned a set of scores to be used in weighting the rating of their response. This was turned into a 'weighted application blank' (WAB). This is in some way similar to the structured screening format for application forms, but differs in that the form itself is structured solely around these aspects, is not based on any analysis of roles but on the 'coincidences' of successful people, and adopts a fairly complex scoring process.

There are two main approaches used in modern biodata methods:

- weighted application blanks (WAB) and

- rational biodata.

Weighted application blanks are used more extensively in recruitment in the USA than they are in the UK. They are particularly prevalent for military service, being used by both the US Navy and the US Army, in department stores and manufacturers. The WAB has been called 'mindlessly empirical' by its critics, since it takes the significant differences, applies a weighting and uses it regardless of any understanding of why it should exist. It may say that 23-year-old employees with dark hair living in post codes X and Y who play tennis and enjoy going to the cinema and live at home with their parents and own a certain make of car are more effective at serving on the sales counter, or whatever, than those who do not fit that description.

It is, in essence, coincidence that determines and predicts suitability rather than any understandable criteria. Because it is derived from the existing differences in performance it cannot be constructed from the ground up, but can only be constructed by looking at the differences which exist.

It can be argued that this approach is absolutely fair in the sense that it concerns itself only with those factors which differentiate between different levels of performance and uses them to drive selection decisions. In practice people tend to feel uncomfortable with the unexplained factors and feel somehow that it is 'unfair'. This has perhaps been one of the most important barriers to the further growth of weighted application blanks in general use. In some ways it is not an altogether new process: many seasoned recruiters will have set preferences in looking through application forms from certain schools or universities and may maintain that previous people recruited from those institutions perhaps performed better or stayed longer than those from other institutions. The same is often said about certain neighbourhoods. Interestingly enough the danger of prejudice and subjectivity creeping in to such judgements should make them more uncomfortable than the mechanistic approach of the WABs, yet it does not seem to be so in practice.

To take a specific example, during World War II the United States Air Force used comprehensive selection techniques to predict success in flight training for pilots. The techniques included a complete battery of psychological tests, interviews, and assessment exercises together with a biodata which contained the question '*Did you ever build a model aeroplane that flew?*' At first sight it seems rather strange to be asking grown men – and it was exclusively men at that time – questions about their boyhood activities especially given the seriousness of the task for which they were being selected. Yet it was the case that this single question was almost as good a predictor of success for flight training as the entire test battery.

The rational biodata is to the untrained eye little different from the empirical biodata of the weighted application blank. It differs however in its approach and is therefore a fundamental shift. In principle it attempts to avoid mindlessly using coincidences, but instead identifies the factors, seeks some explanation of them, and then constructs questions designed to identify those factors. Thus in this approach, using a competency framework in which one of the competencies is perhaps decision-making, the biodata would set out to ask questions which correlated with the levels of decision-making in high-performing, average, and low performing employees. Using this approach, the biographical information which diagnosed the decision-making in applicants would form the question to be incorporated in the biodata. In practice this would mean incorporating a number of questions around decision-making in the same way as a psychological test would be constructed to avoid over-reliance on one question alone. As a consequence the biodata would be able to identify whether the patterns of the applicant's life matched the patterns in the life of those people who were good at decision-making in the organisation. It would not however be able to identify whether they would be able to make different types of decision from those people; whether they would be significantly better, slightly better or slightly worse; whether they would be consistent in their decision making; or the style in which they would go about their decision-making. It would simply say that they are likely to be decision-makers in the same mould as those whom the organisation currently regards as good at decision-making. It therefore goes some way towards providing a rationale for the process, but it still remains a largely inexplicable process.

How to design a biodata process

The design of biodata using **weighted application blanks** proceeds according to the following stages:

The first stage is to develop a set of questions to be put to applicants with the application form. These are open-ended questions which may for example have one question saying *'what are your interests or hobbies?'* This is given on a trial basis to applicants along with the existing application form or whatever other method is used. When a sufficiently large enough response has been received, the forms can be analysed to identify the most frequent responses thus under the question on interests. It may be that football, hockey, netball, cinema, gardening, reading, television and stamp collecting are the most frequent responses.

The next stage is to turn the open questions into closed questions and create a modified form which would now ask the question *'please indicate which hobbies you have: gardening, swimming etc.'*. It is of course essential that the open question form should have encompassed a whole raft of issues of every conceivable biographical kind in order to get to the closed questions. The closed questionnaire is then used alongside existing selection methods but the responses are stored and tracked over a period of time to identify which people stayed with the organisation and which people were more likely to be short listed or which were more likely to succeed. This needs to be undertaken over a period of time, usually about three to five years.

At the end of the study period it may, for example, be shown that the hobbies and interests of people bore no correlation to whether they were short listed, did well on the interview, stayed longer or performed better. In that case it would be removed from the final biodata form. It may be the case however that swimming, watching television and netball correlated highly with those who stayed or with those who performed. In that case the interest question would remain on the form and those three responses would receive a plus score to identify a correlation. It may be that one of the responses, perhaps football, correlated strongly with those people who did not last long in the job or who did not perform, and it would then receive a negative score. The remaining interests can either be removed from the form and subsumed under 'other' or remain on the form and receive a neutral i.e. zero score. The final form will therefore be not only a form but a scoring mechanism and scores will be allocated to the different responses which people make. The final scores will then determine whether people will be brought forward in the selection process.

Some organisations are not prepared to wait a number of years to develop biodata and therefore issue the form to existing staff, correlate it with their performance ratings and make assumptions on that basis. There are some dangers in this approach because the response to these questions will change after people have joined the organisation, but it can nevertheless be a useful shortcut to developing the biodata form.

The development of the **rational biodata** differs slightly in that the initial form would not be a scatter-gun approach to identifying every conceivable biographical element. Instead it would begin by taking the competencies identified in the organisation and frame a set of questions linked to identifying responses indicative of those competencies. The correlation and scoring aspects would however be the same for both WAB and the rational biodata. It is implicit in this process of course that correlations need to be statistically significant in order to be useful and that the population size on which the research is based should also be statistically significant.

The development of biodata can be a slow process and it can be an expensive process. Once completed it offers a number of advantages in improving the selection process. As could be seen in the chapter on choosing techniques, it is an effective predictor of success, higher in some studies than personality tests, interviewing, or traditional methods of screening applications. As such it could therefore obviate existing processes. It could for example be used alone, eliminating application forms, testing, and interviewing. Alternatively it could be used simply as a screening process, as an effective means of reducing applications into a manageable number. There is however a difficulty with the biodata in this approach: an interviewer may see person A as far more suitable than person B, but biodata measures person B to be far more suitable than person A. Since the interview is entirely rational – it is hoped – and the biodata is entirely empirical, it is impossible to explain or reconcile the differences. The biodata will be proven to be more effective than the interview as a means of predicting performance, but in practice the interviewer may dismiss person B in favour of person A and in so doing also dismiss the biodata as a short listing mechanism because it is out of tune with their rational judgements. In this case of course the biodata is not only more effective but also more objective than the interview.

One of the limitations of biodata is its shelf life, as it will only be a matter of time before word gets around that '*to get a job in that organisation you need to be good at tennis*'. Biodata can therefore be capable of manipulation and will need to be re-visited every few years and amended, which is of course a cost implication. Biodata provides the opportunity to automate the process fully using the biodata as an alternative to the application form and can be designed to be read through an optical character recognition machine which can score in a second or less. This in turn can be linked to a computer selection software package to trigger rejection letters, or invitations to interview. At first sight it may seem a discomforting scenario, but it is fair to the candidates (and also effective for the organisation) when compared to random selection or subjective vagaries.

One of the greatest difficulties facing biodata is the perception of applicants. Although we may be accustomed to insurance premium and junk mail being determined on biographical data, we are less happy about job prospects being so determined. Where it is used it should therefore be used as an appendix to a traditional-looking application form and its use carefully explained as a means of matching the preference and expectations of the applicant with the organisation and the teams in which they will be working.

The six conditions for successful use of biodata have been established by Gunter, Furnham and Drakely in their book on biodata. They are as follows:

- *The criteria for job success or acceptability must be defined clearly.*
  Some people will use biodata to predict whether people are likely to stay with the organisation, others use it to predict whether they are likely to be successful in performance. Some may use it for both. When it comes to performance there must be a very clear idea of what is actually meant by performance. On paper it seems a simple matter, in practice it is anything but. It is not easy to gain agreement among sales managers of who is the most successful sales person, among bank managers of who is a successful lender, or among universities of who is the most successful academic. Performance ratings are notorious as a reliable indicator of performance. These criteria need to be accurately established if reliance is to be placed on the biodata to identify them.

- *The target jobs should be relatively homogenous.*
  In large or complex organisations a range of job roles may cover for example sales, manufacturing, clerical and professional or advisery roles, and it is unlikely that a common set of criteria can be established to cover all those roles. In such circumstances it may be possible to use the same biodata form, but the defining criteria and the scoring mechanism underlying the form will be different for each of the groups.

- *The likely candidates for the job should be of broadly similar age and background.*
  This is not so much a prerequisite for successful development of biodata as an observation on the experiences of those who have developed biodata thus far. It flows from the concern that if asking questions framed around for example university degrees, such questions will have a different connotation for different age groups. Younger people will provide different interpretations where access to higher education has been more available than for an older population where such access was constrained by social background. Similarly care needs to be taken in developing the biodata to avoid building in any cultural discriminators, particularly where they may be racially discriminatory. Framing questions around party-going would for example be difficult for Muslim women to answer in the same way as others.

- *Researchers should have access to large development and cross validation samples.*
  The recommendation from Gunter, Furnham and Drakeley is that a sample size should be around 500 people for development purposes and, assuming 50 to 70 per cent of the original items are valid in the development sample, a further 250 to 350 for cross validation. This underlines the potential complexity and cost of biodata development.

- *If part of an application blank (form), a biodata must be in a format acceptable to candidates.*
  This point was made earlier but Gunter, Furnham and Drakeley point out that not all candidates are hostile to the biodata appearance and that in one organisation, engineering graduates found a multiple choice biodata a refreshing change from the 'burden of writing florid prose in response to the usual open ended questions'.

- *People must be aware of what constitutes success in using biodata.*
  This is key to the acceptability of biodata as a selection tool by recruiters. It is not easy for recruiters to accept the 'black box' principle of biodata and they feel uncomfortable in accepting decisions which are not accompanied by any rational explanation or theory. It is necessary to understand that biodata will not predict interview performance or test performance: it will however predict job performance and it therefore sits as a competitor to other techniques rather than a complement.

Given the nature of biodata it is probably most likely to be used as an alternative to applications in large-volume frequent recruitment rather than as an alternative to aspects such as interviewing and testing. Furthermore although it can be seen as a selection tool, its attractiveness is more likely to be as a screening tool. It is also worth remembering that biodata can be used as a predictor of various measures which include performance but also absenteeism, job tenure, cultural fit, work satisfaction, and honesty. Perhaps one of the key points which limits the more extensive use of biodata is that it has to be developed for each organisation based on the criteria and biographical indicators linked to those criteria which surface for that particular organisation. A biodata developed for one group or one company cannot be easily transported to another and therefore proprietary models are almost impossible to develop. Finally biodata cannot be built up from some general assumptions or pet notions: it has to be built on hard factual data which necessitates a significant amount of 'investment' before any return can be made.

CASE STUDY

Ladbrokes Telebetting

The Occupational Psychologists CGR collaborated with the leading gaming company Ladbrokes in the design of the Telebetting biodata for selecting call centre agents. The biodata was in a multiple choice format. The scoring system was developed empirically, using a concurrent design strategy.

Data collection
The first stage in designing the biodata was to collect job performance data to develop the scoring system. Three kinds of data were collected:

- supervisors' ratings: using a specially designed validation form (based on competencies identified through job analysis).

- customer service ratings (based on actual call performance and putting the 'Customer First'),

- productivity data (number of calls taken per hour).

These data were collected to represent actual performance as measured on the job and for all of the Agents who volunteered to take part in the study.

Next, a draft biographical questionnaire was distributed to all agents who were asked, again on a voluntary basis, to fill in the form as if they were applying to Ladbrokes for the first time. This form contained multiple choice biodata items designed to be related to the selection criteria, job performance measures, and certain demographic variables necessary to ensure that the scoring key complied with the equal opportunities legislation. Arrangements were made to ensure that both the biographical questionnaires and the supervisors' validation forms could be completed and returned in confidence. In all, 100 completed pairs of forms were returned.

Criterion development

With most empirical methods of scoring biodata it is necessary to identify 'high performers' and 'low performers' in terms of some overall criterion of success. For example, where supervisors' ratings of job performance are used it is usual to calculate a composite rating by computing some kind of average and then splitting the group into high and low performers around the median. Since there were three possible ways of identifying high and low performers, it was initially envisaged that three separate scoring keys would be developed: one each for the validation form, the customer first ratings and the productivity data (calls per hour). In the event, it proved possible to develop a single scoring key to predict all three job performance measures.

The following sections of this paper describe the general approach used to develop this scoring key, using hypothetical examples to preserve the confidentiality of the actual scoring system developed.

Weighted Application Blank Approach

Weights for the biodata were developed on an item-by-item basis according to a method developed by George England. This can be illustrated using the example question shown below, and a hypothetical distribution of responses that might be made by high and low performers (see table shown overleaf).

In this hypothetical example, four people left the question blank and their responses therefore do not count towards the valid total. While 18 of the remaining 47 high performers answered 'A', only 13 of the 49 low performers made this same response; i.e. 38 per cent of high performers, versus 27 per cent of low performers answered 'A', a difference (high minus low) of 11 per cent.

Using England's method, the weight for any given answer would be based on the statistical significance of this difference in per cents, and is obtained from look-up tables (the so-called 'Strong's tables'). England's method was followed except that no item was given a weight of more than ±3 points – a more conservative approach than the original method. An 11 per cent difference would be worth 3 points in England's system, therefore response 'A' would receive the maximum 3 points in this example.

The item responses B to D would be weighted in the same way. In the case of responses where the percentage of low performers is greater than the percentage of high performers the weight is, of course, negative. Negative weights are generally thought to be undesirable as the minus sign can be left off when checking scores by hand, and they lead to total scores that are less than zero. It is therefore usual to add a constant, which is equal to the lowest negative weight within an item, to all of the item weights to produce the final score for each response (the last column in the table).

Which one of the following gives you the greatest personal satisfaction?

A   Knowing that you have done a good job
B   Helping others to sort out their problems
C   Solving a difficult problem on your own
D   Being with family or close friends
E   None of the above

Answer	Number High	Number Low	% High	% Low Low	% Diff.	Weight	Score
A	18	13	38	27	11	3	4
B	4	8	9	16	−3	−1	0
C	15	14	32	29	3	1	2
D	8	11	17	22	−5	−1	0
E	2	3	4	6	−2	→	1
Valid total	47	49	100%	100%	weights above based on 96 valid responses		
Blank	3	1	→	→	→	→	1
Grand	50	50	Grand total = 100 but questions left blank not included in development of weights				

Adding a constant to all of the weights means that the 'neutral' score (where the difference in the percentage high and percentage low is less than ±3 per cent and the weight is zero) is equal to the value of the constant. In the example, the neutral score is therefore '1'. The neutral score, rather than the lowest score (zero) is given to people who leave the question blank, giving them the 'benefit of the doubt'. The neutral score is also given to the response 'E' for the reasons noted above.

The biodata were weighted on an item-by-item basis using the above method for each of the three performance criteria. Items that did not discriminate between high and low performing agents on any criterion were set to one side and excluded from further consideration.

Final item selection
Up until this point in the analysis, there were three possible ways of scoring the biodata. However, a single score would have been preferable from a practical point

of view. The most valid items from each of the three scoring keys were therefore combined into a single composite scoring key. Before validating this key, the inter-item, part-whole and item-criterion correlations were to be checked for any unusual relationships that might indicate the presence of chance effects or selection bias in the weights. In the event, four items were dropped because they were positively correlated with both the gender and ethnic origin. Four further items were dropped in consultation with Ladbrokes so as not to over emphasise attitudes to schoolwork and to reduce duplication with other parts of the selection procedure.

Composite Scoring Key Validity
In order to determine the validity of the biodata, the composite weighting system was applied to the draft biographical questionnaire to produce a total score for every Agent in the sample. The correlations between the biodata scores and the performance criteria were as shown below:

Composite Biodata Scoring with:	*Validity*
Job performance (versus full rating scale)	
Validation form	.47
Customer first	.29
Calls per hour	.34
Job performance (above versus below median)	
Validation form	.52
Customer first	.34
Calls per hour	.40

Typical validity coefficients for biodata in the published literature are around .35 to .40, but these are sometimes corrected for various statistical artefacts that can increase the size of obtained correlations. Typical uncorrected validities for single ability tests are around .30, and it is safe to assume that studies which show validities much lower than this probably do not find a publisher very often. The obtained validities range from .29 to .52, which seems both reasonable and consistent with the literature.

There were no statistically significant differences attributable to either of the demographic variables: gender and ethnicity. This result, and the results of the concurrent study suggest that the biodata provides both a job-related and fair method of selecting agents for the call centre.

Implementation

The final application form was designed so that it could be completed on a laptop (at recruitment fairs), on-line, or more conventionally. In practice, most applicants complete the form by hand and post it to Ladbrokes for processing. This involves entering the applicants' data into a PC which scores the biodata. See the Figure below for an illustration of the on-line and data entry software.

The biodata score is used in order to make the decision to 'reject', or to advance the applicant to the next stage of the selection procedure, using applicant-norm-referenced cut-offs.

In the longer term the intention is to conduct a predictive follow-up study on the biodata. In this respect, some 'shrinkage' in the validity of the biodata is anticipated. The boundary of the validity of the scoring key is more likely to be in the usual .35 to .40 range rather than the .52 obtained in the development sample.

13

Interviewing

The interview is the most popular selection technique. It is the most popular in two senses: it is the technique most frequently used in selection decisions and it is the technique upon which most reliance is placed in formulating the selection decision. It can also be one of the least effective and most ill-used of selection tools.

Recent studies in the UK by the CIPD and others have shown that the interview is used in more than 90 per cent of selection assignments. This is not a phenomenon particularly limited to the UK, as the same conclusions arise from studies in various countries around the world. It is also popular from a candidate's viewpoint. If the first aspiration of candidates is to get the job, then the second is certainly to get an interview. A selection decision made without any interview taking place will be one viewed with suspicion, if not hostility, by many candidates. It is of course one of the few parts of the selection process, and one of the few techniques, which is truly a two-way process. The reason for the popularity of interviews may be the fact that it is a very natural process: being able to sit and talk to others is a skill that is not confined to the professional recruiter and is shared by the candidate and the line manager/client. It may also be a cause of the downfall of many interviews that are designed as an opportunity to talk rather than a technique for gathering data on a candidate in order to make a decision. Even in the most sophisticated selection assignments, it can nevertheless be the case that candidates are called to a number of interviews sometimes even with the same interviewer. An IRS study revealed that one in six employers asked managerial candidates to face three or more interviews; which casts serious doubt on the efficacy of the first two interviews or the decisiveness of the selectors. This is perhaps the crux of the problem with interviews, and the opportunity. The interview can be a very effective technique if properly focused, used and analysed.

USES OF THE INTERVIEW

The interview is a versatile tool in that it can be used for a number of purposes. One is as an **information exchange** which enables the candidate to find out more about the role, the organisation, and other factors which will be important in helping the candidate to make a decision whether to apply to the organisation or accept the job. In a scarce labour market therefore where many organisations are chasing a few candidates, the interview can be an especially effective technique for 'hooking' candidates and helping them to make decisions about the organisation based on a feel for it and its people without having to make hard decisions on brochures or other impersonal data. It can therefore serve as an attracting process, and one in which the preparation of the selector is more geared to responding to candidates' potential questions than preparing questions to ask the candidate. Although not overtly interviewing the candidate, the selector should nevertheless be in a position to apply subtle techniques of gathering data from the candidate so that a two-way interview is taking place. Many 'open days', career fairs and trade shows are useful opportunities for interviews to take place. Similarly even the humble job vacancy notice in the shop window provides an opportunity for an interview to take place when potential candidates make an enquiry, even if that enquiry is simply asking for an application form.

The second use of an interview may be for **screening** purposes. Although it is a costly technique, in that it takes valuable resource of selectors to undertake, it can be very effective particularly if there is not a very large volume of response in the first place. A short 10 to 15 minute interview can cover more than sufficient information to make decisions on whether to proceed with the candidate's application. It has the advantage of the personal touch and the opportunity to give candidates information about the organisation, and provides them with a feel whether they wish to continue with their application. Using the interview as a screening process needs to be a clear decision however and not by default. Some organisations ask candidates to complete an application form and proceed to a 'first interview' without undertaking more than a cursory glance at the application form. In such circumstances it is better to decide whether to place reliance on the form for screening or disregard the form and use the interview as a screening process. Being half-hearted about both means being productive on neither.

The third use of interviewing is a **selection** tool, which may be undertaken in tandem with other techniques, such as testing or assessment exercises, or as the sole decision point. Using the interview as the final selection tool requires a greater degree of sophistication and preparation. It remains the case that whatever use is made of the interview it will be more effective if it is properly prepared, has a clear focus, and is undertaken by skilled people. There has been criticism of the interview as an effective selection technique, but much of the criticism has been about the way in which it has been used rather than the technique itself. If for example a junior member of staff sits down with a candidate for an unprepared 'chat' and without a clear specification for the role being sought or time taken to research the candidate's biography, this may not yield a particularly good result. It becomes more of a reflection on the selector than it is on the value of the interview process itself. It is the case that all too often the interview has been criticised as an ineffective technique when it is the people undertaking it and the circumstances in which it is undertaken that are at fault.

INTERVIEW PANELS

There is no golden rule about the number of interviewers appropriate to the interview: it is a matter of organisation preference. Some research has indicated that panel interviews are more effective than one-to-one interviews. Many organisations prefer to do a series of one-to-one interviews; others prefer to use a panel approach, and some are more formal than others. It is the usual practice for search and selection consultants to undertake a one-to-one interview to prepare a shortlist that is then submitted to the client for final interview.

The modern practice inclines towards an interviewing duo. This consists of a skilled interviewer, usually a member of the HR department, and the 'client', i.e. the person who has requested the selection process and for whom the successful candidate will be directly or ultimately working. The importance of involving the client cannot be over emphasised. However objective the interview and other selection tools may be, it remains an important element in selection that the chemistry between the new hire and their boss is right. This is a two-way process and it is as much in the interest of the candidate as it is in the interest of the organisation. There are many cases where a technically sound appointment has gone wrong and the new hire failed to optimise their contribution simply because of a personality difference. This is a simple fact of working life and it is important that the selection process recognises it. It is also the case that, however effective the techniques are, and however sound the decision may be, selecting people is still a very personal issue and it is all too easy for clients to criticise the selectors for their decision. Agreeing a clear specification is one of the most important ways of avoiding this problem but equally, involving the client manager in the decision and judgement is also important.

Although there is no golden rule on the number of interviewers, it is obvious that it needs to be a small enough number to facilitate decision-making and avoid intimidating the candidate. Some organisations have engaged in some absurd practices, notably some local authorities that involve the full council in the selection interview. This may be useful as an opportunity for the candidate to undertake a selling presentation but it is stretching a point to call it an interview.

The constitution of the interview panel will depend upon the purpose of the interview. Any skilled interviewer without detailed knowledge of the work that the candidate will be performing can undertake an interview designed to investigate personal qualities. An interview designed to investigate technical capability or experience will of course necessitate someone with such knowledge and expertise in order to judge the response. There may be occasions where a regulatory requirement exists for an independent assessor to be present or for a particular specialist; this is particularly the case in many NHS professional appointments. In organisations where team working is of great importance it may be appropriate to involve peers in the process of selection. There is an academic argument which supports the notion that subordinates should be involved in the selection of their boss – because effective leadership is determined by the acceptance of the group being lead – but there are very few reported examples of this although the use of 360 degree assessment as a selection tool is gaining popularity in the USA.

Types of interview

Interviews can be either structured or unstructured. **Unstructured interviews** follow a natural process of dialogue and, although unstructured, may involve the interviewer in asking some 'favourite' questions. The unstructured interview may also probe some questions around the application form and CV or a set of questions around aspects such as work history, aspirations, and personal circumstances. It is unstructured in the sense that the candidate is encouraged to lead the interview and talk freely in response to the set of questions or even just one opening question. The advantage of the unstructured interview is that candidates may feel comfortable with the process and are able to cover the aspects that they would wish to see covered. It also enables the interviewer to concentrate on listening, recording and assessing the response. Some unstructured interviews take the form of an informal dialogue but again with the interviewer placing less reliance on the framing of the question and more reliance on listening to the answers. A further 'advantage' of the unstructured interview is that it requires little in the way of preparation particularly in terms of reviewing the application or CV. The disadvantages of the unstructured interview are that it relies heavily on the ability of the interviewer particularly in terms of assessment skills; it is inconsistent and provides little basis for comparison between candidates; is difficult to control particularly from a time element; and is generally less effective than a structured interview. All research has shown that unstructured interviews are significantly less effective than structured interviews.

Structured interviews although more effective are generally less common. They fall into two main types:

- situational interviews
- behavioural interviews.

In simple terms the difference between the two is that the situational interview asks the candidate to put themselves into some hypothetical future situation and describe how they would handle it, whereas in the behavioural interview the candidate is asked to recall specific examples from their past experience and describe what they did. Research has shown that the behavioural interview is more effective than the situational interview and less likely to lead to unfair discrimination, but both types are far more effective than unstructured interviews.

The **situational interview** is almost like a verbal role play. The candidate is presented with a potential future scenario and asked how they would be likely to handle it. For example, an interviewee for a supervisory position in a packaging department may be asked:

'You are at the start of the day's operations, a third of your shift has failed to appear because of a flu epidemic, you have two lines of product which need to be packed today. Product A is the company's main product and is particularly profitable. Product B is a new product on which the company is still recovering development costs. The reduced labour availability means you will not be able to meet the targets for packaging both product A and product B. All the product and packing materials for product B have been delivered to your packing hall, the product and inner boxes for product A have been delivered but not the outer boxes into which the inner boxes have to be packed. What do you do next?'

Such a question may be designed to assess how the candidate will cope with pressure, how they will undertake their planning and organising, or how they will approach problem solving. The benefit of this kind of situational interview is that it is work-related; it provides the candidate with a flavour of the kinds of things with which they will be faced; it focuses judgement on work-related rather than peripheral or abstract qualities; and it is often welcomed by the candidates as a more thorough and realistic interview than a general unstructured 'chit chat'. The weakness is that knowing what to do is no guarantee that they will do it.

The **behavioural interview** works on the premise that the best indicator of future behaviour is past behaviour, that the way in which a person responded to a situation in the past is the most likely indication of how they will respond in the future. The situational interview may indicate that the candidate knows how to handle a particular situation, but knowing what to do does not necessarily indicate the propensity to do it when the time comes. The behavioural interview is however focused on the behaviours or competencies that underpin job performance. Interview questions are then framed with a view to eliciting information about those behaviours or competencies. The question is of course only an opening question and enables the interviewer to probe the responses of the interviewee. The question is framed by reference to the candidate's own history so that the example can be anchored in past history rather than future speculation. Thus taking the example above, looking to assess the problem-solving capabilities of the candidate for the packaging supervisor position, the interviewer may for example ask the question:

'What's the most difficult problem you've encountered in the last six months in your role?'

The same question could be adapted to school life, home life, studies, or hobbies. The candidate is allowed to provide examples of past behaviour which will give an indication of their future behaviour. Thus the candidate may answer:

'Dealing with the insurance claims for lost luggage of people while they were still on holiday'.

Note that this has nothing to do with working in a packing hall. Yet it is an opportunity to explore problem solving in an entirely different context but which will reveal the problem solving capabilities of the candidate that they would be likely to apply in the role of supervisor in the packaging department. The answer above is of course too superficial to facilitate judgement. In order to assess the behaviour it would be necessary for the interviewer to further explore the answer and ask for a specific recent example and then start to probe through follow-up questions for further detail. It provides concrete examples, and the interviewer would then be in a position to assess whether the candidate was proficient or not in their past attempts at problem solving. The past success or failure would be a reliable indication of their effectiveness at future problem solving.

The use of a competency based approach to selection allows the structured behavioural interview technique to be adopted, allowing the interviewer to structure questions around the key competencies identified for the role. This provides a clear focus for the interview and allows a consistent approach for interviewers to adopt. If different interviewers are engaged in the process they can distribute the interviewing tasks effectively by concentrating on different competencies. Alternatively where the recruiter and the client are interviewing separately on the same competency, they can have a common basis on which to compare the response. Furthermore the competency framework will usually include descriptions of behaviours of the competency in action in everyday use. These can act as a guide to identify 'good' or 'poor' answers. It is often the case that interviewers know how to frame the question but may have more difficulty in evaluating the answers given and determining whether candidates are demonstrating the required level of ability, or a higher or lower level. Research has shown that using behavioural examples of the competencies as a guide to evaluating candidates' answers can increase the efficiency of the interview process. In practical terms it is also a very welcome benefit for clients and colleagues who may be involved in recruitment as an adjunct to, rather than the mainstream of, their work.

A well constructed behaviourally-based structured interview will enable an interviewer to explore four to six competencies in a period of around 45 minutes, less for a well skilled interviewer. This is a particularly efficient use of interview time and, since it is focused on a certain number of competencies, means that attention is paid to using other techniques to measure the other competencies. This makes for a more efficient use of the overall selection process rather than duplicating interviews with screening and testing, and attempting to reconcile a hotchpotch of information.

CHOICE

There are advantages and disadvantages to the various types of interview.

The unstructured interview can be undertaken with a minimum of training, requires less preparation, and allows candidates a great degree of flexibility. The disadvantages are that it is less effective at predicting performance than structured interviews; can be uncomfortable for occasional interviewers such as line colleagues or clients; and is difficult to fit systematically within the overall selection process. The lack of compartmentalisation often means that interview assessments are inconsistent between candidates, and can be at odds with other parts of the selection process such as testing. It is often the case that different interviewers reach different conclusions about the candidate, and often over non-specific generalisations.

The advantage of the structured interview – whether it is situational or behavioural – is that it is a more effective predictor of performance than the unstructured interview. In general, structured interviews are better perceived by candidates who feel that the interview has been relevant and thorough. The focus also makes it easier to prepare meaningful reports on candidates. The disadvantage of the structured interview is that it is not a natural process and requires training and experience to raise the skill of the interviewer. A particular disadvantage of the situational interview is that it has the potential to be discriminatory, since it requires candidates to hypothesise about future situations and use indirect formal language in an unfamiliar artificial context. For ethnic minority applicants whose first language may not be that of the interviewer, this may create a disadvantage. It may also make the interview unnecessarily difficult for people working in a shop-floor environment where a more direct and colourful language may be the norm. There is the danger therefore that the interviews are more of a test of language fluency than an investigation into the particular competency. The behavioural interview does not suffer this disadvantage and indeed has an added advantage in that transporting people back to their past experiences, and asking them to talk about it, makes it much easier for them to answer the questions by relating to specific issues.

How to conduct an effective interview

Interviewing is not a natural activity. It is a task requiring the application of skill and planning to undertake successfully. It is not unusual for an interviewer to be as nervous as the candidate, particularly where the interviewer is new to the experience. Even experienced interviewers sometime suffer some of the downsides such as the inability to keep from making a snap judgement in the first few minutes, trying to control candidates, maintaining concentration in the middle part of the interview, and remembering all the candidates who are interviewed. The list goes on. Yet a good interview is not too difficult to conduct: it can be pleasant, meaningful, and need not take more than thirty minutes to provide sound

---

data on which to make a good judgement, particularly where it is used as part of an overall selection process involving other techniques. Following some key principles and adopting them as good habits will help improve interviewing effectiveness.

Prepare: Before the interview the interviewer should ensure that they are fully prepared to conduct the interview and that all arrangements have been made to provide a professional image to the candidate. This involves a proper reading of the application form, making sure there will be no interruptions during the interview, and preparing the interview questions.

Welcome: A proper welcome creates the right atmosphere for mutual confidence throughout the interview. The relationship between the candidate and the interviewer should be friendly, supportive and non-threatening. By building rapport and putting the candidate at ease the interviewer will be more likely to get spontaneous, and therefore honest, answers to questions. Care needs to be taken with the interview surroundings. It is, sadly, not unusual to find 'confidential' interviews being undertaken in the midst of a busy hotel lounge with hapless candidates balancing coffee and papers whilst attempting to answer questions in a confident and up-beat way without the conversation being overheard by others in the lounge – many of whom are nonchalantly drinking their coffee and straining to hear every word. The most effective interviewing environment is a quiet office, with telephones diverted, and interruptions barred, and with seating in a semi-formal arrangement.

Control: most interviews are designed to last a scheduled time. The interviewer will need to ensure that information on the key criteria is collected in that time. It is important that the interviewer maintains control of the interview and may need to encourage reticent candidates to provide more detail in their answers or restrict more garrulous candidates to offering less detail. Candidates need cues to help them know what is expected. Some interviews they will have attended may have consisted of only one question and they were be expected to keep the rest of the interview going, whereas other interviews may have been a continuous stream of interrogatory questions. It is important therefore to help the candidate understand how the interview will be structured, that there will be time for the candidate to ask questions either at the beginning or the end, and that the interviewer may ask a few or many questions. In maintaining control it is important that the candidate is treated properly and allowed to maintain self-esteem and confidence.

Probe: The purpose of an interview is to gain evidence to show whether the candidate does or does not have the appropriate qualities to undertake the role. Interviewers must therefore expect to go beyond the platitudes and find real answers and be prepared to 'interrogate' in a way which does not seem overtly so. During the interview it is possible to keep the candidates focused on the right issue by using certain questioning techniques. Interviewers should ask simple open-ended questions which try to avoid leading the candidate or suggest the answer required. Examples of this type of question may be '*how do your organise your work?*' or '*what sort of problem did you have to tackle?*' The question should be indirect using phrases such as '*how, when, where, why, who, what, which, tell me more, in what way, explain, describe*' . Indirect and open-ended questions will generally yield a better response from candidates. Direct questions and closed questions will not. A direct question will invite a yes or no response and close down the dialogue. For example asking the question '*how is your health?*' will almost certainly produce the reply '*good*'. Asking specifically '*how much sickness absence have you lost in the last six months?*' or '*when was your most recent illness?*' will lead to an answer which is capable of being further explored. Similarly, leading questions are to be avoided. Asking '*I imagine you are accomplished at delegating?*' will have a predictable answer.

Clarify: It is important to pin down specific examples in the candidate's answers if they are to be relied upon. All too often interviewers will be pleased to receive an answer and move to the next question even though that answer does not provide the information required. Very often interview questions need to be followed up with several probing questions before being able to clarify the information needed. It is also important to seek balanced information, searching for 'contrary evidence'. In the event that the candidate provides an answer that appears to demonstrate that they have high levels of problem solving, the interviewer should pose questions aimed at uncovering the problems with problem solving. The interviewer is then able to assess whether the frequency or severity of poor problem solving examples is greater or lesser than the good examples, and can judge the candidate's ability in problem solving.

Note: No one has a perfect memory and note taking is therefore important. This is not easy and needs practice but candidates do not consider it rude for interviewers to take notes. The notes should however only be brief memory joggers and should not be an attempt to evaluate the candidate during the course of the interview.

Close: Interviewers need to bring interviews to a firm but clear close, consulting their checklist to make sure that there are no major gaps in the information that has been provided. Candidates should be invited to offer any other information that has not been covered in the main part of the interview and that they think important. The candidate should receive clear guidance on what is to happen next and when they should be expected to hear from the organisation.

> **Review:** Judging the candidate should not take place until the interview has been completed. As soon as the interview has finished, the interviewer should take time to conduct an evaluation rather than stepping straight into the next interview. A scoring system, particularly linked to competencies, will help significantly. It is important to avoid making an assessment of the candidate during the course of the interview.

PITFALLS

Research into the effectiveness of interviews has shown a number of pitfalls that are all too common.

Snap Judgements are often formed about the candidate within the first few seconds of meeting them. It has been shown that judgements are formed quickly, usually in the first two minutes, and the interview process then becomes the means by which evidence is gathered to reinforce that judgement.

The **concentration span** of many interviews follows a distinct pattern of a sharp downward dip in the main part of the interview with peaks of concentration in the first five minutes and the last five minutes of the interview. This is one of the reasons for note taking during the interview, not only to refresh the memory at a later stage but also as a prompt to continued concentration.

Interviewers can often **ignore the context** or environment in which the candidate is working, when forming judgements. It is easy to attribute dynamism to a candidate performing well in a high-achievement organisation or culture when they may be swept away in the tide of performance rather than necessarily directly contributing to it. Equally, candidates working in a risk-averse culture may not be assessed as entrepreneurial or innovative in comparison with other candidates. It is important to seek information on the environment in which they are working and to judge answers in context.

There is a danger in **stereotyping** both good and bad groups. This can be a particular problem for discriminating against ethnic minorities. Every candidate deserves to be regarded as unique and individual, and assessed as such.

Mirroring, in which subjectivity creeps into the assessment of an interview so that people are rated positively or negatively according to whether they are similar or dissimilar to the interviewer. This is often a subconscious process and is a particular risk in an unstructured interview. There have been many unfortunate examples of people in roles who bear an uncannily similar outlook to the interviewer but occupying roles that the interviewer would not choose to perform. There are of course more obvious cases of where the candidate bears an uncanny similarity to the interviewer and an identical surname.

14

Psychological testing

Psychological testing is one of the oldest, and perhaps most contentious, selection tools. As long ago as 500 BC, the Chinese were using a battery of psychological tests to aid the selection of government officials. Yet today they are still regarded by many as a new and unproved fad. Psychological tests are sometimes described as Psychometrics to denote that they are concerned with identifying the mental characteristics of people (psycho-) and putting a measurement (-metric) against such characteristics. Psychometric tests fall into two main types:

- ability tests
- personality tests.

ABILITY TESTS

Ability tests are sometimes known as aptitude tests and they are designed to simulate the work requirements so that a consistent sample of work is required to be undertaken by a range of candidates and their relative performance can then be measured.

A bricklayer being assessed for a job may be asked to lay a course of bricks as a means of demonstrating competence. That would in its simplest sense be an ability test. In order to make meaningful comparisons between a range of applicants, however, it may be necessary to specify how many bricks are to be laid, in whatever pattern over a specific period of time. There may be additional requirements or measures for the stability of the structure or wastage of materials, or tidiness of the job. Furthermore it may be necessary to establish that, for true comparison, it needs to be undertaken in the same weather conditions and therefore may become an indoor rather than an outdoor activity. In its crudest sense therefore the laying of the brick wall has become an ability test, and specifying the type of bricks, the number of courses to be laid, the pattern of laying and the timing, (using standard instructions and a consistent environment). It should be possible to compare and contrast the performance of different bricklayers (at different times in different places and by different testers) in order to determine their relative abilities.

This may tell us something about the candidates relative to each other, but it may not necessarily tell us whether they would become proficient bricklayers. Thus a number of proficient bricklayers would have to be asked to undertake the test so that we can establish a comparative measure. This benchmark would be known as a normative sample and would perhaps determine that they could lay X bricks in Y minutes. For completeness it would be useful to have poor or incompetent bricklayers to complete the test so that we can identify the minimal amount of time in which the test is to be completed. This then becomes the normative data against which the candidates are measured to see whether or not they are up to the job. This is the simple and basic premise that underlies the development and application of ability tests. It is the attempt to identify whether someone has the ability to be able to undertake the tasks for which they are being selected. It is therefore a test in the true sense of the word in that candidates may do well, do badly, or fail altogether.

A wide range of ability tests exist, and familiar ones include:

- Typing tests based on work samples which ask candidates to type a set amount of text in a certain period of time.

- Tests of manual dexterity which would require operators to slot pegs into holes in a certain sequence and pattern over a period of time.

- Tests of spatial ability to see whether candidates are capable of operating machinery.

The driving test is probably the best known example of a widely-used ability test.

There are some tests that are not based on work samples but are tests of an ability that is deemed to contribute to job performance. For example, tests around verbal skills, mental reasoning, and numeracy are common examples of tests used in clerical work situations. Some tests are designed to identify the extent to which the individual is able to acquire and apply learning. These are called cognitive tests and work on the principle that job performance is a reflection of people's ability to acquire the knowledge needed to perform the job and apply that knowledge to new or unusual situations. An example often used, of cognitive ability, is that of a police officer dealing with crowds. Being taught the principles of crowd control is the skill to be learned but it will need to be applied in different situations, such as dealing with a crowd of onlookers at a car accident; dealing with a crowd of demonstrators where a protest demonstration is just getting out of hand; or dealing with a street crowd in the middle of an armed robbery. These are all aspects of crowd control but a police officer will be required to adapt their knowledge effectively to each of those situations. Cognitive tests attempt to identify this ability. Generally speaking, ability tests are divided into three main categories:

- **Achievement tests:** These measure the knowledge and skill which the person has acquired. The tests mentioned above for bricklayers and typists would be seen as achievement tests. They are also sometimes known as trade tests.

- **Aptitude tests:** These may either be based on an occupational aptitude such as computer programming or sales ability, or related to 'primary mental abilities' such as verbal reasoning, numerical ability, abstract reasoning, clerical speed and accuracy, mechanical reasoning, spatial ability, spelling and language usage. There are some tests that specifically measure one of the aptitudes, and others that form a battery of measurement for a range of aptitudes and are known as 'differential aptitude batteries'.

- **Intelligence tests:** These attempt to measure intelligence albeit that there is some disagreement over the content of intelligence. In order to derive a measure of intelligence the tests may look at numerical aspects such as '*complete the missing number 2,4,7,11,..,22*' or verbal aspects, posing questions such as '*man is to woman as bicycle is to ...*'. (A spurious example to which hard-line feminists will know the answer is '*fish*'.)

There has been some argument over the value of intelligence tests. Until the 1980s they were not generally regarded as predictive of work performance but a re-evaluation of research data in recent years has led to a new movement in support of their use. It remains the case however, that intelligence, however measured, is not a predictor of performance in high-level roles such as managerial positions. It has been argued that the popularity of IQ as a measure is a means of social discrimination rather than a determinant of potential performance – ensuring that class structures remain the determinant of workplace hierarchies. It is certainly the case that IQ tests discriminate against the under-privileged, which may potentially cause them to be indirect unlawful discrimination.

PERSONALITY TESTS

Although ability tests are tests in the true sense of levels of performance and of pass or fail, the same is not true of personality tests that aim to gauge the innate traits and characteristics of people, codify them, and compare them with others. In that sense the measures are comparisons rather than absolute values. Although ability tests have been in existence for several thousand years, personality tests are a more recent phenomenon and have existed for less than a century. They evolved from the development of intelligence tests, and there is still some blurring of boundaries between intelligence and personality in some of the tests that are marketed as personality tests. The greatest boost to development came in the 1940s with the requirement to select people for war duty, and to consider how different personalities would cope with different and extreme conditions. In particular it was noted that fighter pilots could be in command of an aeroplane representing a substantial piece of investment and could be taught to fly and tested in that proficiency. However, the moment of truth would come in aerial combat and some process was needed for predicting whether the individual would be able to cope with such stress or 'crack up'. It was thus in military usage that psychological testing became established and is still relied upon by many of the leading military forces in today's world. It is also interesting that the use of psychometric testing in the Second World War marked the cross over of testing from clinical into occupational purposes. In the first half of the century a focus of activity had been on psychological measurements in the context of mental ill health and mental illness. Many tests used psychiatric patients as their benchmark. The First World War of course showed that the 'occupational' factor of soldiering could contribute to psychological damage. Hence the attention to tests supplied to 'normal' people that would have hitherto been the domain of practitioners in clinics. Even beyond the Second World War, as occupational testing became more acceptable, many of the leading tests still held their origins or emphasis on clinical diagnosis rather than occupational guidance.

One of the most influential tests in the development of testing was the Minnesota Multiphasic Personality Inventory (MMPI). It was developed in the 1930s and was significant in comparing the answers against criterion groups, and measured nine psychiatric criteria. The MMPI has been used for occupational testing purposes but because of its psychiatric connotations has been regarded as offensive. In the 1950s Cattell produced a theory of sixteen factors constituting 'personality' and a test to measure those sixteen factors called the 16PF. It became widely used and has probably been the single greatest influence on the development of occupational testing in the UK. One of the reasons for its popularity is the read-across of personality factors into occupational suitability. There were however some questions which had a clinical feel and made people apprehensive about completion. The sixteen factors used were:

- cool – warm
- concrete-thinking – abstract-thinking
- affected by feelings – emotionally stable
- submissive – dominant
- sober – enthusiastic
- expedient – conscientious
- shy – bold
- tough-minded – tender-minded
- trusting – suspicious
- forthright – shrewd
- self-assured – apprehensive
- conservative – experimenting
- practical – imaginative

- group-oriented – self-sufficient
- undisciplined/self-conflict – following self-image
- relaxed – tense.

Of less popular note in the UK but of significant interest in the USA and in the world of testing generally has been the California Psychological Inventory (CPI) against which many occupational tests are benchmarked. The CPI measured 22 personality traits:

- dominance
- capacity for status
- sociability
- social presence
- self-acceptance
- sense of well-being (absence of worries)
- responsibility
- socialisation (social maturity/integrity)
- self-control
- tolerance
- good impression (concerned with others' opinions)
- communality
- achievement via conformance
- achievement via independence
- intellectual efficiency
- psychological mindedness
- flexibility
- femininity
- empathy
- independence
- managerial potential
- work orientation (strong work ethic).

The 16 PF and CPI, although used for occupational purposes such as selection, continue to be used for clinical diagnosis and counselling.

The importance of both the 16 PF and the CPI is that they attempt to sub-divide personality into distinguishable factors which are separate and describable. Although the tests are popular and effective, it has been difficult for others to correlate their research on personality with the 16 or 22 factors. In the 1930s McDougall (1932) wrote that *'personality may to advantage be broadly analysed into five distinguishable but separate factors, maybe intellect, character, temperament, disposition, and temper'*. Researchers attempting to correlate their findings with the 16 PF and CPI found that there was more evidence of a smaller number, rather than a greater number, of personality factors. In the 1950s Eysenck developed the theory that personality could be broken down into the 'big two' factors of extraversion and emotional stability in order to support his theories on 'intelligence'. Eysenck was largely responsible for popularising the myth that extraversion is a pre-requisite of high performance and was particularly successful at predicting pilot suitability through his work. In the 1960s a number of studies served to support the view that personality could be divided into five factors. These have come to be known as the 'Big Five'. In the 1970s, 1980s and 1990s, numerous studies have served to reinforce the validity of the Big Five. In 1987 McCrae & Costa published research, followed in 1991 by Barrick & Mount, into the meta-analysis of studies of the Big Five and predictions of job performance, measured against such aspects as productivity, tenure, status change, salary and performance rating. The study showed that the Big Five factors were valid predictors of work performance and that one factor in particular, 'conscientiousness', was a particularly effective predictor of all aspects of job performance.

The five factors cover the following aspects of human nature:

- **Extroversion/introversion**: traits such as being gregarious, assertive, talkative and active, together with ambition, expressiveness and impetuousness;

- **Emotional stability**: aspects such as anxiety, anger, worry, insecurity, together with resilience and independent thought;

- **Agreeableness,** sometimes also labelled 'likeability': social conformity, being courteous, flexible, co-operative, forgiving, soft-hearted, tolerant, trusting or cynical;

- **Conscientiousness**: hard-working, persevering, careful, organised, and preferences for rules and procedures as against spontaneity and creativity;

- **Openness to experience**: curious, imaginative, broad-minded traits as well as 'intelligence' – however defined.

It is important to realise that the personality factors are in themselves neither good nor bad, nor have they good or bad ends to their scales. They are merely differences which make some personalities more suitable for certain activities than others. The combination of factors is a very important consideration. For example, someone high on extroversion and low in another factor such as agreeableness will act very differently from someone who is also high on extroversion, but high on agreeableness. The volume and mix determines the final cocktail. It may seem uncomfortable to divide the vast range of personalities into five criteria, but they are five sub-sections rather than five types. In the same way that the six balls in the lottery create imponderable permutations, so too do the permutations of the five factors create the rich tapestry of human behaviour.

The emergence of the big five theory has enabled psychologists to develop occupational tests concerned with predicting job performance and which are used purely for selection rather than spin-offs from clinical diagnosis. This has enabled tests to be developed without using contentious questions such as '*do you feel suicidal?*' and has made them more acceptable to candidates as part of the selection process. In the UK, the emergence of a small number of active and highly visible test developers and suppliers, committed to energetic marketing, has served to increase the acceptability, usage and reliability of occupational tests.

Tests and Horoscopes

Tests are often said to be objective. They are not. They simply absorb the test-taker's views of themselves, record them, codify and regurgitate them in a set of standard responses. In that sense therefore they are not a 'black box' but a process similar to an interview, less transparent and more controlled. Research has shown that people's self perception as evidenced by test results is remarkably consistent and impartial. Test publishers often sell their tests by asking the purchaser to sample, and offer the opportunity to provide a test result on the purchaser. Who, after all, is best able to assess the description of the purchaser than the purchaser? The purchaser then completes the test and, surprise surprise, is provided with an '*uncannily accurate picture*' of themselves. A good test will do this, but a nonsense test with a carefully crafted narrative will do the same. Take for, example, the statement '*you feel less comfortable making decisions and resolving problems in the absence of feedback from your boss*'. Such a narrative is likely to lead to nodding heads and sageful sighs if given in response to the personality test for most managers in today's climate. A psychologist charted such an effect by asking a conference of human resource managers to complete a (valid) psychometric test and instead of providing the proper result gave them bogus feedback in the form of thirteen statements taken from horoscopes. When asked about the accuracy, none of the test-takers thought the results were wrong, 40 per cent thought them 'rather good' and over 50 per cent viewed them as 'amazingly accurate'. Unscrupulous test publishers will ensure that their narrative is suitably vague and horoscope-like to make the test results acceptable. A good test will gave the test-taker feedback which includes information that gives 'a glow' together with some uncomfortable 'home truths'.

TEST QUALITY AND CHOICE

To ensure that tests are able to do the things that they ought to do, some standards of quality are applied. These standards are concerned with the **validity** and **reliability** of tests.

Validity is expressed in different ways:

- Face validity

- Content validity

- Construct validity

- Criterion related validity.

Face validity is concerned with the question *'does the test look like it measures what it is supposed to measure?'* This depends on the nature of the test and the context in which it would be used. Face validity is concerned with people's perceptions on what a test measures. Therefore it is not a true kind of validity, and is usually played down by psychologists, but is of great practical importance for selectors wishing to avoid offence to candidates and ridicule by line colleagues.

Content validity relates to the question *'do the items in the test adequately cover every aspect of what the test is supposed to measure?'* If, for example, the 'analytical reasoning' was identified as a test subject and defined as a general mental ability involved in both numerical and verbal components, any test designed to measure 'analytical reasoning' would need to include both numerical and verbal items. The absence of one or other would reduce the content validity of the test.

Construct validity is the most theoretically interesting type because it relates to the issue of whether the idea behind the test is valid or not. For practical purposes it is concerned with the question *'does the test really measure what it is supposed to measure and not something else?'* If, for example, we established a test for a sixth dimension of personality, then we would need to demonstrate that there was this additional sixth dimension and that the test measured it rather than it measuring one of the Big Five and naming them in a different way. Equally if the test is supposed to be measuring full personality, then it will need to be seen to be measuring all five factors, not just some of them. Most modern occupational tests are constructed on the basis of the Big Five and therefore the focus of attention is usually on the effectiveness of the test in measuring those dimensions, rather than on the theory behind the test.

Criterion related validity has the most practical significance for selectors as it is concerned with the question *'do the scores on the test relate to anything important in the world of work?'* In occupational testing 'anything important' is usually some measure of job performance like supervisors' ratings, sales achieved, absence, turnover or achievement.

Reliability is looked at in three ways:

- Test-retest reliability
- Internal consistency
- Parallel forms reliability.

Test-retest is concerned with the stability of test scores over time. It involves administering the test to the same individuals on two or more separate occasions, normally a few weeks or months apart. The test-retest reliability is for correlation between the scores obtained on the two occasions. Whereas in theory there is concern about people rehearsing by re-taking tests, in practice the results of the two or more occasions will need to be consistent since different results will tend to show that it is the test that is inconsistent rather than the people taking it.

Internal consistency is concerned with the idea that all of the items within a test should be measuring the same thing and therefore should be correlated with each other. For example, if a test question asked whether '*do you prefer going to parties or learning a new skill?*', it would be an inconsistent question because the first part of the question will be linked to 'extroversion' and the second part of the question will be linked to 'openness to experience'.

Parallel forms reliability is the ability of a test to measure the same way as another test designed to measure the same construct. It is particularly important if the publisher produces two versions of the same test since they should then be highly correlated.

Reliability and validity are both important in deciding whether a test is of sufficient quality. Reliability is however generally more important than validity, since a test cannot measure anything at all if it does not at least measure it consistently. Measures are usually expressed as a 'correlation co-efficient'. This is an index of the strength of the relationship between two variables (for example the test result and a supervisor's rating) which varies from a 'perfect negative relationship' of -1 (as the test scores go up, the supervisor's rating scores go down), through 'no relationship' of 0, to a 'perfect positive relationship' of +1 (scores for the test and supervisor's rating go up and down together). Generally speaking, 0.7 is regarded as the minimum score for reliability and 0.3 is regarded as useful for criterion-related validity.

Quality is of course defined as meeting the specification. One of the difficulties faced when looking for suitable tests is being clear of what it is to be used for. To say a Rolls-Royce is a good car is not a point of argument, but if the car needed is a cheap run-around and easy to park, then it is not particularly suitable. There is a great danger in being coaxed into buying tests from test publishers because they have been proven as suitable for a particular organisation, when the real starting point ought to be the recruiter's own organisation's needs. The first stage should therefore be determining what it is the test is going to measure. Using the framework outlined in the chapter on defining requirements, the following statements could be made:

- Acquired skills or knowledge would lend themselves to ability testing.

- Innate/natural qualities and adapting behaviours would lend themselves to personality testing.

In looking at the overall selection process, it is also worth considering whether other techniques would be more suitable than the selection test. For the adapting behaviours, assessment centre and work sampling would be appropriate. For the 'acquired' aspects, the evidence of educational certificates or professional qualifications or appropriate experience could be gained through the application form or biodata. The adapting behaviours could also be probed through interview, as could some of the innate/natural qualities. It is however in the 'innate/natural' cluster that testing will offer an advantage over other techniques. Many personality characteristics are subtle nuances rather than stereotypes. In adulthood most people have learned to acquire behaviours that mask or enhance, as appropriate, their personality dimensions. Observation and interview may not reveal the hidden depths. There are, for example, many cases of film stars and musicians whose ebullient and charismatic public persona masked an anxious and introverted personality. In such cases the sad price of career achievement is the high cost of personal failure and perhaps reliance on alcohol or drugs. So too in the work place it may be difficult to gauge accurately the personality and probable behaviours of people without the use of personality testing. It is highly likely that the collapse of Barings Bank would have been avoidable if personality testing had been used for the selection of its management team and its dealers.

Before using a test we therefore need to be quite clear what it is we are testing for. This is equally important whether choosing an ability test or a personality test. There have been high-profile discrimination cases in the UK in recent years concerning the use of testing and these have usually been ability tests. One notable case was that of train drivers being required to undergo a test that measured their competence in the English language. The case was settled before being heard but the argument was made that language proficiency was unrelated to the skill of driving a railway engine. It was directly discriminatory to those whose first language was not English.

How to choose a psychological test

The two approaches for choosing tests are the rational approach and the empirical approach. The rational approach is to undertake an analysis of the person's requirements, preferably using a competencies approach, based on role analysis. This identifies the key criteria to be tested. The next stage is to identify tests that will accurately measure such criteria.

The empirical approach is to pilot a wide battery of tests on the existing population and undertake a statistical correlation with factors of job performance. This will identify the key criteria and competencies and, simultaneously, show which test is most appropriate for identifying them. Further guidance on these approaches is contained in the chapter on role analysis in Part 3. Whichever approach is used, it is important to ensure good quality advice and if an organisation does not have an in-house psychologist, then the services of an independent psychologist would be a worthwhile investment. Reliance on test publishers' recommendations or the suitability of the test for other organisations is a risky approach.

In choosing a test, selectors may decide whether:

- They should buy a proprietary test.

- They should adopt a free test.

- They should develop their own test.

The most popular approach is to buy proprietary tests. This may in part be due to the fact that much of the growth in test usage in the UK is attributable to the marketing efforts of test publishers. In general, buying a proprietary test means that the hard work on development has already been undertaken, that there will usually be a good level of support for further development and that copies of the test and other materials and validation studies will have correctly been undertaken, and that proper training and technical support will be available. These are the advantages that would accrue from buying a proprietary test, but they do not necessarily flow in all cases and care should be taken to check out all of these selling points. The validity and reliability aspects discussed above should be checked.

Using a free test may seem an option too good to be true. There are however thousands of tests available which have been developed by researchers as part of wider studies, perhaps on theories of personality type. It is often the case that such researchers do not want their academic rigour sullied by commercial consideration, and their lack of entrepreneurial opportunism should not therefore be deduced as any lack of faith in their own test. It is also the case that very often such tests have much greater evidence of validity and reliability studies than proprietary tests where commercial pressures may have necessitated some shortcuts in development. The great advantage of the free tests is that they carry no fees for use, no licence charges, and no obligation to undertake supplier training. The downside is that training will be unlikely to be available, technical support will not be forthcoming and no reliance can be made on any further developments. There is also a greater opportunity – but usually no greater likelihood – that candidates will also be able to get hold of the test beforehand.

The third option of 'Do-It-Yourself ' test development is feasible and has the advantage that it can be specifically geared to the needs of the organisation, and that control of costs, further development, training and support are all within the organisation's domain. The time and cost of development however are likely to be significant and, where the organisation does not have its own psychologists, will mean sub-contracting to external psychologists. This could involve reliance on the third party for further development training and support. It may be however far more cost effective for the organisation to undertake this approach than to buy-in proprietary tests, where there is likely to be a large-scale recruitment activity over a sustained period.

TEST APPEARANCE

Ability tests look like the tests that most people would have encountered in childhood, although the ability being tested will dictate the final appearance of the test. Ability tests are often 'power' tests which means that It is highly unlikely that test takers will be able to complete the test within the period allocated. Results are driven by the speed of the test taker and the accuracy of answers. Because they are tests in the strict sense of the word, test conditions need to be applied and specific instructions given to candidates; the timing carefully controlled through the use of a stopwatch; and 'examination room' conditions set up. The tests will usually be supplied with a scoring key, frequently in the form of a template, which is often computerised. The scores are compared with the scores of the benchmark population – referred to as the 'population norm' – to determine whether the results are high or low. The population norm is usually the group that the test publisher used in developing the test, and are invariably school children or university students. This can be a particular problem for placing reliance on some ability tests where such test-takers will generally be more 'rehearsed' through their environment and therefore more adept than an older working population.

Personality tests do not look like tests as such, but are really questionnaires. They usually, but not always, take the form of:

- statements

- choices

- adjectives.

The statement type are usually open-ended questions to which the candidate replies true or false or may have a range of responses from '*very much like me*' to '*not at all like me*', or similar. These tests are usually constructed in such a way that the question will be asked in many different ways on a number of occasions as a means of gauging a typical answer. In an omnibus test (full personality) this means the test can cover over a hundred questions.

The 'choice' type, sometimes called *ipsative*, is one in which the test maker is required to make a choice between two statements or adjectives. Sometimes it is a straight choice, and sometimes there is a scale of response. There is some concern about the use of such tests. To illustrate, if we provide a test taker with a choice '*I often beat my spouse and family*' or '*I often steal from shops or my employer*' we will be able to deduce from the answer that the test taker either has violent tendencies or dishonest tendencies. In practice the respondent could be either violent or dishonest or both or neither of them. Deducing answers from forced choices are therefore fraught with difficulties. Nevertheless it remains a feature of some dubious tests, but also of some very valid and well-constructed tests.

The adjective test has become more popular in recent years, partly because of improvements in its development and partly because it generally offers a quicker and more cost effective route to testing. In this approach test takers are required to respond to an adjective as '*like me*' or '*not like me*' or respond to a choice of adjectives as to which is most appropriate for them.

Whatever the style of the personality test, it is not a test in the strict sense, and therefore timing is not important other than in keeping to the schedule of the selector. There is often a guide and these will vary according to the test from 15 minutes to 90 minutes or more. It is often the case that personality tests are available in either paper and pencil format, or on computer screen. It is also the norm nowadays for the test results to be calculated by the computer and output either as a set of raw scores, or a set of sten scores (a standard ten point scale derived from the range of responses in the population norm) and often with a narrative report which is derived from logarithms of test results and candidate profiles. Although personality tests are not strictly tests, it is usually the case however that administration is undertaken in test examination conditions.

ADMINISTRATION

The use and administration of psychological tests in the UK is carefully controlled. The British Psychological Society grants a licence to undertake the administration and scoring of ability tests (level A) and the administration, scoring and interpretation of personality tests (level B). The level A qualification is a prerequisite of level B training. Training is provided by psychologists, who are approved by the BPS. In many cases the test publishers provide the training. Test publishers restrict supplies of tests to licensed people (individuals not organisations). The costs of training are substantial: approximately six days of training for each level. Although publishers provide general training at level B, it is often the case that they require users to undertake further specific training in their own tests. There is some concern over whether the licence system is a safety precaution or a closed shop. Given the opportunity to apply computer-based administration, scoring, interpretation and report-generation, the on-going validity of the current approach is subject to question.

BUYING A TEST?

- Be clear as to why the test is needed and what it is going to measure.

- Look for evidence of reliability (0.70 or greater).

- Look for evidence of validity (0.30 or greater). If it is a personality test, does it relate to the 'big five' factors? And does it predict job performance?

- Expect to see a manual giving all the above data, plus development background and administration instructions.

- Confirm the availability of benchmark comparisons (normative data).

- Ensure that the test is not discriminatory in design or application.

- Check availability of training and support.

- Clarify cost arrangements and any hidden 'licence fees'.

- See whether it is used elsewhere but avoid taking other's views on its suitability for you and also avoid an over-used test with which your candidates may be too familiar.

WHAT DO TESTS LOOK LIKE?

This is an example of an ability test. The 'Following Instructions Test' (FIT) was developed by Knight Chapman Psychological Ltd to measure verbal comprehension in administrative/clerical staff.

Following Instructions Test

Instructions

This is a test of your ability to read and understand instructions.

On each page of this booklet, you will find some written instructions followed by a number of statements.

For each statement, you must fill in your answer on the Answer Sheet using these rules:

FILL IN CIRCLE A if the statement is **TRUE** from the information given.

FILL IN CIRCLE B if the statement is **FALSE** from the information given.

FILL IN CIRCLE C if it is **IMPOSSIBLE** to say for certain whether the statement is true or false from the information given.

These rules are given on each page of the test.

Before you start the test there are some example questions below. Please do these now in your own time, giving your answers in the Example Section on your Answer Sheet.

Using your Mobile Phone Addressbook

You can store up to 500 entries, each with 3 phone numbers and one fax number, and additional address information in the Addressbook. These entries are managed separately from those in the Phonebook. However you can exchange data between the Addressbook and the Phonebook.

To Add a New Entry
Press Menu
Press Office
Press Addressbook **or** to use the Phonebook see Page 9
Select New Entry
Enter the first or last name and a phone number
Make further entries field by field
Press Save to store the entry

Examples

1. Addressbook entries are managed separately from Phonebook entries.

2. The Addressbook stores more numbers than the Phonebook.

3. To use the Phonebook you have to refer to Page 19.

Remember:
You will have 13 minutes for the 30 questions in this test so you will need to work quickly but accurately.

Use the pencils provided to fill in your answers on the Answer Sheet, so that you can erase and change your answers if you want to.

If you are not sure of an answer, give your best choice but avoid simply guessing.

PLEASE DO NOT TURN OVER THE PAGE UNTIL ASKED TO DO SO

This is an extract from a personality test. The Managerial and Professional Profiler (MAPP) was developed by Knight Chapman Psychological Ltd as a personality and motivational questionnaire for graduate, managerial and professional staff.

Managerial and Professional Profiler

PLEASE READ THESE INSTRUCTIONS

MAPP is a self-report questionnaire. You are asked to rate yourself on a number of statements that make up the questionnaire.

After reading each statement, give your answer by marking the answer sheet as shown below:

Fill in circle A if you **strongly disagree** with the statement.

Fill in circle B if you **disagree** with the statement.

Fill in circle C if you are **in between** or you neither agree nor disagree with the statement.

Fill in circle D if you **agree** with the statement.

Fill in circle E if you **strongly agree** with the statement.

Examples

A Strongly disagree	B Disagree	C In between	D Agree	E Strongly agree

1.   I am often the person with most to say in a group.

2.   Rules are made to be broken.

In Example 1, the respondent has indicated that they **strongly disagree** that the statement, "**I am often the person with most to say in a group**" applies to them. In Example 2, the person has indicated that they **agree** with the statement, "**Rules are made to be broken**".

There are two parts to this questionnaire. There are 228 questions in Part 1 and 168 questions in Part 2. There are separate answer sheets for Part 1 and Part 2. If you are being asked to complete both parts, continue to Part 2 as soon as you have finished Part 1, giving ratings for all of the statements in this booklet.

When giving your ratings, please remember:

● Be as honest as you can.

● There are no right answers or wrong answers.

● Sometimes you might think that your answer depends on the situation. If so, try to give the answer that is most **typical** of you.

● The questionnaire is primarily concerned with you in the work context.

● Answer as you think you really are, not how you would like to be.

● Try to avoid giving the "In between" rating wherever possible.

● Rub out any answer you wish to change.

● Make sure that the number on the answer sheet where you are giving your rating is the same as the number of the question you are answering.

● Although there is no time limit, please work as quickly as you can.

CASE STUDY

Knight Chapman Psychological was asked to assist a major catering organisation with many branches at motorway service stations across the UK. The client had two distinct requirements. First, to identify internal and external candidates for Section Manager (supervisory) and Operations Manager positions, and second to select above average catering and retail staff.

In both cases, the company was concerned to appoint candidates who were results-oriented, proactive and strongly concerned to deliver outstanding customer service.

For the Section and Operations Manager positions, KCP administered one of their psychological tests, the Customer Service Inventory (CSI), to a large sample of existing employees. Independently, they obtained job performance ratings, and were thus able to identify excellent, average and below average performers. By correlating the CSI results with performance ratings, KCP were able to produce success profiles, enabling the company to administer the Customer Service Inventory (CSI) to all internal and external candidates and quickly identify those who were most likely to succeed and deliver above average customer service.

For catering and retail staff, KCP conducted a similar study and then developed a short, concentrated version of the CSI which enabled line personnel staff to match candidates swiftly with known profiles of successful and unsuccessful performers.

KCP was able to additionally develop the norms from similar studies they have conducted in the leisure and retail sector and for pub bar, kitchen and waiting staff. By adopting this approach the client has been able to gain a very clear profile of the kind of people who will succeed in their business and is able to apply an objective measurable assessment of candidates to compare their profile with the desired profile.

15

Graphology

Graphology is the study of handwriting to identify the character and motives of people, and is used in support of selection decisions.

Interest in the study of handwriting as a guide to character has existed for over six centuries and the earliest recorded reflection on the value of handwriting for analysis was by Aristotle who gave as much weight to the individuality of writing as to the individuality of speech. The earliest recorded scientific approach to the analysis of handwriting was in 1625 by the Italian physician, Camillo Baldi, who published a 'Treaties on a method to recognise the nature and quality of a writer from his letters'. Baldi categorised writing into a number of elements capable of analysis. In the 1870s Abbé Louis Flandrin conducted extensive research into handwriting and his assistant Jean-Hyppolite Michon coined the term 'graphology'. Over a period of 40 years Flandrin and Michon developed a system that gave specific meaning to individual 'signs' within handwriting. The studies were undertaken by clergymen with their humanistic interest in personality, but Michon's disciple Crépieux-Jamin recognised the implications and value for business when publishing his book 'Handwriting and character' in 1921. Crépieux-Jamin differed slightly from Flandrin and Michon in that he advocated a concept of evaluation based on the wider analysis of the writing, and moved away from assigning specific meanings to individual signs. In the 1920s, the study of handwriting achieved significant momentum particularly in Germany, Switzerland and the USA. Wilhelm Preyer undertook experiments at the University of Berlin which caused him to conclude that handwriting was 'brain writing' and therefore reflected individual personality and character. Similarly Max Pulver in Switzerland demonstrated how conscious and unconscious drives are projected into the writing pattern. In Germany, Ludwig Klages coined the term 'expressive movement' to refer to all motor activities performed habitually and automatically without conscious thought, and provided the momentum for more systematic and scientific study of the analysis of handwriting. In the United States, the Harvard psychologists Gordon Allport and Philip Vernon supported the brain-writing theory stating that writing is 'not merely handwriting, but also 'brain-writing' influenced by all manner of expression of neural impulses giving individual flavour to the coping movements of the hand'. They made three basic assumptions that personality is consistent, the movement is expressive of the personality, and the gestures and other expressive movement of an individual are consistent with one another. Also in the United States, Milton Bunker undertook extensive research into handwriting analysis, motivated by Crépieux-Jamin's work, and coined the term 'graphoanalysis'.

There are two main schools of graphology:

- Gestalt graphology and

- Graphoanalysis.

It has been said that the United States approach is graphoanalysis and the European approach is Gestalt. In practice, the Gestalt approach is more prevalent in Germany and Switzerland, due to its links with psychiatry and psychoanalysis, whereas graphoanalysis is prevalent in the United States and France due to the influence of Crépieux-Jamin. There is no definitive research into use in the UK to shed light on the most prevalent approach, but the greater influence of the United States, rather than mainland Europe, on UK management practices would tend to suggest that, where graphology is used, it is more likely to be graphoanalysis.

GESTALT GRAPHOLOGY

The gestalt school of graphology developed in Germany alongside psychiatry and psychoanalysis, strongly influenced by both Freud and Jung, and developed by Klages and Pulver. The gestalt graphologist evaluates the writing to uncover the pattern or 'gestalt' that indicates various aspects of the writer's personality. The gestalt graphologist will ascribe meaning to the writing by looking at the following characteristics:

- the repetition of strokes and incorporation into total writing

- the location and orientation of the writing on the page

- how the writing is connected and other aspects of letter formation relating to the expressive whole of the writing pattern

- form, movement, and use of space.

The gestalt is the image that develops from these interacting elements and is used to assess the writer's character and underlying personality traits. It has been said that gestalt analysts regard the page as representing the writer's world and attempt to analyse how the writer sees himself or herself in that world.

In undertaking the analysis the graphologist does not look at the content of the writing, but the shape and manner of the writing and uses it to link with theories of personality grounded in psychiatry and psychoanalysis. Using Aristotle's parallel of the written word to the spoken word, this approach can be likened to a 'written interview' by a psychologist.

GRAPHOANALYSIS

Graphoanalysis was developed by Milton Bunker in the United States and is the study of the individual strokes in the handwriting to determine character and personality. In common with gestalt graphologists, graphoanalysts pay regard to the location and orientation of the writing on the page but, unlike the gestalt approach, they break the writing down into individual strokes and ascribe meaning to each of those strokes. The strokes are however not looked at in isolation but as components of the whole picture of the piece of writing.

In looking at writing, graphoanalysis breaks the character of the writing into five main factors:

- **Slant:** Slant is used to assess the emotional responsiveness of a writer and is measured from the upstrokes of the writing on an assumed base line. The upstrokes are used because they are the ones produced unconsciously by the relaxed extensor muscles, whereas the downstrokes are consciously produced by contraction.

- **Depth:** Depth reflects mental and physical energy and denotes how an individual absorbs emotional experiences, and the strength and endurance of the emotions felt.

- **Imagination:** This is primarily indicated by loops and looks at the ability to form mental pictures and ideas.

- **Size:** Size of writing relates to intensity and concentration.

- **Rhythm:** Rhythm is the regularity of the writing and denotes stability of personality.

In addition to these aspects the signature is also – as in gestalt graphology – an important element. Each of these aspects is measured and marked in relation to character. The marks are based on comparisons with a study of population norms.

The differences between the gestalt graphologist and the graphoanalyst are that the gestalt graphologist will imply meaning directly from the writing, whereas the graphoanalyst will break down the writing into measurable components. On the face of it therefore the former is more art than science, but of course uses a scientist's perceptions. However both approaches converge in the final part of the analysis that is to draw conclusions on the nature of the writer from the writing. These conclusions will form the analyst's perception of the writer's personality together with some other aspects such as fears and vocational aptitudes. It has been claimed that graphologists can detect an individual's disposition to dishonesty and theft. An isolated study by Alfred Kanfer in Vienna and New York indicated the ability to detect the likelihood of cancer from handwriting some time before it becomes clinically detectable.

How to use graphology

In order to obtain a sample of handwriting for assessment purposes, it is necessary to ask the candidate to complete two pages of handwriting together with a signature. The writing should be free-flowing, that is to say it should not be copied from another text since copying distorts the natural process of individual handwriting. The content of the writing is irrelevant, but it should be undertaken when the writer is relaxed and will need to be completed in either a fountain pen or a biro. Pencil and felt tip pen are known to distort the evaluation. A trained graphologist then assesses the writing.

Graphology, like all other selection techniques, is not legally controlled but subject to voluntary regulation. In theory it is possible therefore to buy a book on graphology, and undertake analysis on a DIY basis. In practice however it is a skill that needs to be properly acquired. Gestalt graphologists will have undertaken training in gestalt psychology as well as graphology, and graphoanalysts will have undertaken a prescribed course of study. Although not subject to legal regulation, the International Graphology Association in the UK promotes professional standards through research, the adoption of a code of ethics, and a structured course of study over 18 months leading to recognised qualifications. It may be possible, using the principles of graphoanalysis, to develop optical character recognition programmes as a computer based approach to screening but to all intent and purposes the main application of graphology in its current form will be the use of trained graphologists to assess handwriting and provide recommendations on employment. It is therefore more likely to be used as an aid in selection decisions rather than screening.

ADVANTAGES AND DISADVANTAGES

One of the key advantages of graphology is that it is easy to set up in that no special forms or preparation are required and the level of literacy in the UK is high enough to enable it to be incorporated easily into the selection procedures. It is a very flexible instrument in that the graphologists can be given a clear indication of the person specification or the competencies for the role and asked to produce a report tailored to the information required. Since handwriting is a poor indicator of gender or ethnicity, and given that the content of the writing is disregarded, it is perhaps the least discriminatory selection technique available. Although there is a significant body of antagonism towards graphology in the UK, there is sufficient evidence to support its usefulness in selection decisions particularly if used as part of a wider battery of selection techniques rather than a single indicator.

One of the greatest disadvantages to the use of graphology in the UK is its novelty. Although it is widely used in mainland Europe – with one study suggesting that 85 per cent of French companies used it – and is not uncommon in selection practices in the USA, it does not have a high visibility in the UK. In part this is because it may not have high usage, but also in part because some companies using it are for some reason nervous of publicly acknowledging their use of the technique. Although it may seem to candidates to be no more awkward or offensive than ability tests, personality questionnaires, or bio-data questions, there can be some unease about its use. Furthermore attacks on its validity, most vociferously by some psychologists, cause potential users to be nervous about its application. A significant practical drawback is the requirement for a trained graphologist to undertake the analysis which adds to the cost and slows down the process. It is therefore more likely to be used for senior level appointments where the cost of a consultant to interpret the handwriting will not necessarily be out of proportion to other selection costs and some graphologists offer a full selection service. The use of graphology for screening would necessitate expensive use of trained personnel or investment in computer technology, both of which are likely to render practical application unlikely.

16

Assessment Centres

The Assessment Centre is a process that involves a number of techniques and a number of assessors, breaking down the assessment of candidates into a number of components and then re-assembling for a complete picture on which a decision is based. There are two main purposes for assessment centres:

- development
- selection.

The distinction between the two is sometimes blurred but, in essence, the development type will aim to assess the strengths and weaknesses of the candidate and provides a framework for utilising the strengths and addressing the weaknesses through developmental programmes and training. The focus of the assessment centre is often on the provision of information to the 'candidate' with great emphasis on feedback.

The selection based assessment centre may be used for external selection or internal promotion or both. Its focus is on identifying the suitability of the candidate for the current or future planned position.

The distinction between the two types of assessment centre is not always so clear-cut. Sometimes the purpose of the centre is to fill current or future positions, but considerable time is taken to provide feedback and development guidance to candidates. Sometimes assessment centres influence 'separate' decisions on selection for certain positions. The focus of this chapter is on the use of assessment centres for making selection decisions.

The origin of assessment centres can be traced to the Second World War when it was used by the War Office Selection Board to select officers. The First World War had cruelly exposed the incompetence of some officers and in so doing condemned a history of selection that owed more to social status than leadership. The move, in the early part of the century, from bought commissions to proper selection techniques, had begun a focus on capability, but the process was compromised by the reliance on the judgement of selectors who suffered prejudices of old. The War Office Selection Board devised a system of selection techniques that included exercises, tests and interviews. The system also placed the selection decision in the hands of a number of assessors, including a psychiatrist. The new system led to a significant improvement in the success rate of selection and was subsequently adopted by the United States for the selection of its Intelligence staff.

Based on its wartime success, the assessment centre was adopted in different forms in the Civil Service and the Public Sector. In the United States, some private sector organisations saw the potential of the assessment centre for use in identifying management potential, and AT & T and Standard Oil were at the forefront of its use. The 1980s saw a significant growth in the use of assessment centres in both the UK and the USA, with emphasis on their use for management selection and graduate recruitment.

It is difficult to define an assessment centre, as its nature and content may differ significantly from one organisation to another. It is probably fair to say however that the key aspects are the following:

- The assessment centre uses multiple selection techniques with each technique being only one piece of the jigsaw building up to the complete picture of the candidate.

- The assessment centre uses a group of assessors with selection decisions usually being made on a group basis.

A 'typical' assessment centre is likely to involve one or more interviews (sometimes one to one and sometimes panel interviews), a set of exercises, and ability or personality testing (or both). The assessment centre will involve a number of assessors who are usually trained in the specific assessment centre methodology being applied, and the assessors will usually be a mix of HR staff and line managers. The assessors will undertake active roles within the assessment centre process, usually interviewing and observing during exercises. In some assessment centres the assessors are assigned specific candidates whom they follow throughout the process and rate. In others the assessor may be assigned to a part of the process and rate candidates for that particular part. In both cases it is customary for all assessors to be involved in the final decision on candidates, which usually takes the form of a selection conference.

How to design an Assessment Centre

Assessment centres are usually bespoke systems. It is very rare that an assessment centre is imported from one organisation to another or made available on a proprietary basis. There are four stages involved in the process:

Step 1 is to identify the key criteria upon which the assessment will be based. In practice this usually means that assessment centres are competency based and, where a competency framework does not already exist, work will be undertaken

---

through role analysis to identify the success criteria. This is covered in Chapter 9 on role analysis.

Step 2 will be the choice of techniques to incorporate in the assessment centre, identifying the most suitable technique for each competency. Cost and time constraints may of course influence these decisions.

Step 3 is the development of the techniques which may involve 'buying in' or developing 'in-house'. For the interview this will mean the preparation of interview questions of either the situational type based on the projected work for which the candidate is being assessed, or a behavioural type to identify the experiences of the candidate. It is of course possible for the assessment centre to use unstructured interviews but a well-designed assessment centre will inevitably use a well-designed and structured interview technique. For the test, whether bought-in or designed in-house, it will mean ensuring the availability of suitably trained test administrators and ensuring test conditions. For the exercises it will be a case of buying in or developing and testing any bespoke exercises. Although there is a ready availability of interview material, psychological tests, and assessment exercises, it is usual to find that most assessment centres only buy in psychological tests and design their own interview structure and exercises.

Step 4 The final stage involved is the selection and training of assessors. In so doing consideration is given not only to the resourcing of the assessment centre – in having sufficient assessors available to support the process – but also to the involvement of line managers in the selection process. This adds realism to the assessment process as well as commitment and support to those chosen through it. Since the selection decisions will usually be group decisions involving all the assessors it is important that they are fully trained in its use and in reaching conclusions from it. This invariably means the development of a rating system within the design of the exercises. It may however entail training in specific techniques, perhaps in test administration, or in interviewing skills, or in the process and skills of observation.

The design of an assessment centre is rarely a one-person job and is usually undertaken as a project that involves a steering group on which the client will sit and which will determine policy aspects such as the budget for the assessment centre and the nomination of assessors. The size of the project team undertaking the design will depend upon the degree of original design needed, in particular whether or not success criteria such as competencies already exist in the organisation and whether an emphasis is to be placed on buying in or developing in-house. It is frequently the case that external consultants are used to advise and assist in the design process

COMPONENTS

The components of the assessment centre will include the interview, testing and exercises. Interviewing and testing are covered in the earlier chapters. The range of exercises can have their basis in either work simulations or competencies. Furthermore they are characterised as either **group exercises** or **individual exercises**, and it is usual to find more than one exercise involved in an assessment centre.

Work simulation exercises are designed to provide a realistic flavour of the scope and nature of the work that the candidate will be undertaking. On an individual basis this could mean an in-tray exercise in which a range of documents are given to the individual over a timed period and they are expected to clear the work and in so doing some of their competencies can be assessed. The point is not necessarily to clear the tray at all costs so that the propensity to delegate may be only one factor in consideration: each of the pieces of paper would be designed to elicit information on certain competencies. There may for example be a complaint letter aimed at identifying service orientation, empathy or diplomacy. There may be another piece of paper as an internal request for additional budgets or resources aimed at measuring decision-making. Thus the in-tray will comprise a number of mini assessments. Carefully designed it will replicate many of the occurrences in the work for which the candidate is being selected. An individual work simulation could also be a role play in which the assessor or an actor plays the role of a customer or a disgruntled foreman or a demanding boss, and the candidate is given a briefing which includes objectives to be achieved from their meeting. This is a particularly useful technique for assessing interpersonal skills. The individual exercises do not however have to be work simulated. They can be abstract so that a written exercise which contains puzzles of a non-work kind may be given to the candidate to gauge problem solving, or they may be asked to write a summary of the day's news in order to assess report-writing abilities and analytical skills. The advantage of individual exercises is that they can in certain circumstances be more administratively convenient and they help to filter out 'disturbance' from competing candidates that could interfere with individual assessment as part of a group exercise. The abstract exercises provide a level playing field in that they do not demand prior knowledge or experience, but they can appear as school tests rather than serious selection. The simulations may favour candidates with the relevant experience, but they have the advantage of giving the candidate a feel for the nature of the work in which they will be involved.

Work simulations can be directed at a group and include role plays in which the group is given a work-related project to consider and plan. This may be designed to assess leadership qualities or team-working or problem-solving or some other competency. There are some other exercises in which the assessed group is subsumed within a larger group. Thus for example the group may be subjected to 'trial by sausage roll' in which they are invited to an 'informal' buffet to meet with current employees to find out more about the work. In so doing they are observed by assessors who will gauge their skill in identifying key influencers, instigating discussions, handling dialogue, and 'working the room'. This is a particularly effective technique for selecting political candidates, but it also has much to commend it for 'social' roles such as sales representatives or project managers where the role will involve dealing with people in a variety of settings and maintaining control and purpose in establishing dialogue. It is good practice to advise the candidates that the 'informal' gathering is an exercise to be formally assessed.

Some assessment centres use group exercises in an abstract setting asking teams for example to play out desert survival games or build log bridges or Lego castles. They may be asked to enter into general discussions or to make a presentation to the rest of the group with the observers assessing either the presentation skills of the presenter or the team skills of the 'audience'.

Regardless of whether the exercises are set at group or individual level or whether they are work simulations or abstract, the purpose of the exercise should be clearly defined and the competencies to be measured by it should be kept firmly in view. In general terms, the more abstract the exercise the more uncomfortable the participants tend to be with it. Thus the abstract exercises tend to be found more frequently where the target group are school leavers or graduates. Of course the cost and resource availability will dictate the scale of the exercises. Some organisations are able to use sophisticated exercises such as flight simulators for pilots or simulated call centres for tele-sales staff, and these can provide very effective and realistic assessments. Where abstract exercises are being used care must be taken to ensure that the competencies which they seek to measure are relevant to the work. One high street bank used to conduct three-week assessment centres at their staff college and the assessment included observation of dining skills, including correct use of the cutlery and the direction in which they passed the port!

Whatever exercises are designed it is essential to pilot and test them to check that the timings are appropriate, that the instructions are clear and unambiguous, and that they achieve the balance of giving enough direction to ensure that the candidates can undertake them but without prompting them in any direction. In designing the exercises, the rating form is also designed so that the assessors are clear on the particular competencies that they are attempting to rate.

ADVANTAGES AND DISADVANTAGES

There are many advantages to using assessment centres.

- They focus on the key elements of the role and are therefore very specific in measuring the suitability of candidates.

- They are thorough, avoiding over reliance on a single technique but ensuring that a range of techniques is used to gather a full picture and a range of assessors employed to gather a balanced picture. By using a variety of techniques the overall validity of the process is enhanced.

- The assessment centres can be interesting for the candidates since they provide a variety of activities and often the opportunity to meet with other candidates and, through the involvement of assessors, a greater number of people from the organisation than is usually available through other techniques.

- The assessment exercises in particular can provide a useful glimpse into and the flavour of the work, which can be important in ensuring that the candidate is making the right choice.

- Some studies have shown that assessment centres are more effective at predicting successful candidates than other techniques. However, care needs to be taken with this conclusion since assessment centres are most frequently used for the selection of high fliers and there is therefore a self-fulfilling prophecy in operation).

There are some disadvantages to using assessment centres.

- The process can feel uncomfortable with some candidates, particularly at a senior level, and particularly where abstract exercises are involved. Candidates can be offended by being asked to build Lego blocks when decisions about their career are on the line.

- Assessment centres are sometimes transparent and it is all too easy for candidates to 'act' in group exercises and other aspects which may be sustained for a few days or weeks in the assessment centre but is not fulfilled in the real world.

- The centres can be time consuming for the organisation and the candidates. While school leavers and graduates may be able to devote time to assessment centres, those currently in employment will have difficulty devoting more than half a day. Where exercises are involved the high proportion of observers to candidates makes it time-consuming and therefore costly for the organisation. Added to the active involvement there is also the time needed to be trained (and up-dated) and take part in the decision-making.

- One of the prerequisites of assessment centre exercises is that they should be appropriate to the general level of intellect and experience of the candidates. This therefore means that some stereotyping has already taken place and the danger of discrimination is present but not easily recognised. More easily recognised is the discrimination of exercises that involve physical activities that cannot be performed by people with disability.

CASE STUDY

Assessment Centre for Sales Representatives

A confectionery company was experiencing difficulties in recruiting sales representatives for its London Region. Despite the fact that the company had world-leading brands and a competitive reward package, repeated efforts to recruit had resulted in a poor response rate and a poor quality of candidates. The company had attempted direct recruitment and used specialist recruitment agencies. The newly appointed HR director, taking account of the continued loss of sales income and the growing number of vacancies, decided that investment in an assessment centre would be appropriate.

The first step was to identify the person specification. It became very quickly apparent that the existing specification was based on generalised assumptions without any empirical evidence. The general sales manager and regional sales managers met to review the performance of every individual in the sales force against 'hard data' criteria such as sales achieved, number of calls, and quality of documentation. Using the data, and making allowance for qualitative judgements on aspects such as the socio-economic status of the sales territory and its geographical and communication difficulties together with customer profile, a consensus ranking of sales representatives was agreed. An analysis of the ranking failed to identify any obvious selection criteria. All appropriate and inappropriate criteria such as experience, qualifications, age and gender, failed to establish any meaningful correlation with performance. All sales representatives agreed to undertake a battery of psychometric tests to identify any specific skills or personality traits that correlated with performance. An occupational psychologist correlated the performance ranking with the test outputs. In return for participation, the individuals received feedback on their profile – the results were anonymised for the company. A number of personality traits, together with verbal reasoning and numerical skills, were shown to have a positive correlation with performance and were used as the starting point for the specification.

The next step was to provide the psychologist's report to an advertising agency and ask them to convert it into simple language and prepare a marketing strategy. The Agency devised an advertising campaign that said ' *We've taken a long hard look at our sales people. They are... (description of the competencies). If these are the qualities you have, why not think about joining us ...*' The competencies identified in the analysis were presented in clear, understandable descriptions. A 'drive time' radio advertisement alerted potential candidates to look in the following day's London Evening Standard that carried the advertisement. The response, from over 200 candidates, resulted in a shortlist of 90 candidates invited to attend an assessment centre arranged at a London hotel for a Saturday. The assessment centre consisted of a warm welcome and explanation of the day, a series of ability and personality tests to identify the key competencies, an exercise in the form of a presentation to a small group of fellow candidates – to assess the listening and interpersonal skills of both presenter and 'audience' rather than the presenter's presentation skills, a structured panel interview, a formal presentation by the company, and informal discussions with sales representatives. Candidates were given a 'goody bag' of company products (confectionery) and literature.

Following the centre, each candidate was assessed by a panel, giving weight to each of the centre components, and a 'whole profile' decision taken against the specification. Four appointments were made and a further four people agreed to join a waiting list in readiness for appointment to vacancies occurring over the next year. Six of the new people joined the top 25 per cent of performers in the national sales force within six months of joining, with consequential improvements to company sales performance in the London Region.

Part 5

Getting it right

17

Decision-making

The key purpose of selection activity is, of course, to match the candidate or candidates to the position or positions. At the end of the day a decision needs to be made – no matter how complex or simple and no matter how long or short the procedure. Even where there is only one candidate, a decision still needs to be made on whether or not to offer the position to that candidate, and such 'Hobson's Choice' can often be the most difficult. In some cases it may be possible to defer the decision by offering the candidate a temporary position or work trial to provide more time and evidence. In most cases, however, a decision needs to be taken on the evidence available and however good the technique, it usually means a degree of judgement.

The two key elements in making the final selection are: gathering the evidence and making the decision. This may seem obvious; however, selection is not unlike other aspects of managerial decision-making where the practice sometimes becomes 'ready, fire, aim' and evidence is gathered to justify decisions rather than shape them.

GATHERING THE EVIDENCE

The development of the specification at the beginning of the selection process should form the framework for making the decision and therefore the checklist for ensuring that all data has been gathered.

In using a non-competency based approach the PERSON specification will be checked to ensure that there is evidence of the **P**ersonal qualities, the **E**xperience required, the **R**ecord of achievement desired, the **S**kills and qualifications needed, the fit with the **O**rganisation, and whether the **N**eeds of the candidate are likely to be fulfilled in this position.

Using the competency-based approach the process is slightly easier because there is a logical structure. Each of the competencies being sought is clear, and the framework for the choice of selection tools will provide a map of where the evidence can be found. Figure 17.1 shows how a specification can be compared directly with an 'audit trail' to show where evidence of each competency can be found.

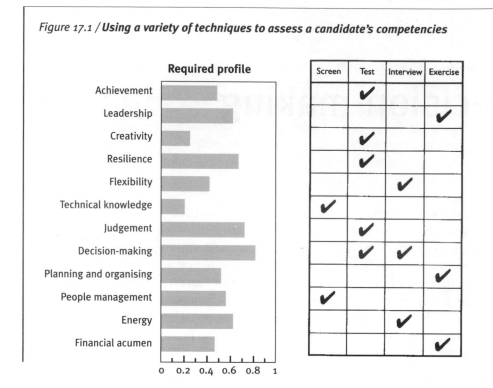

Figure 17.1 / *Using a variety of techniques to assess a candidate's competencies*

Required profile

	Screen	Test	Interview	Exercise
Achievement		✔		
Leadership				✔
Creativity		✔		
Resilience		✔		
Flexibility			✔	
Technical knowledge	✔			
Judgement		✔		
Decision-making		✔	✔	
Planning and organising				✔
People management	✔			
Energy			✔	
Financial acumen				✔

0   0.2   0.4   0.6   0.8   1

Both the PERSON method and the competency-based method follow the 'whole picture' approach rather than the 'hurdle' approach.

In the 'hurdle' approach, each part of the selection process is regarded as an entity in its own right. Thus, for example, the application screen, once completed, will progress shortlisted candidates to the next stage, but the information gathered in making the shortlisting decision will be jettisoned. The next stage may perhaps be a test and initial interview that will allow some candidates to come forward to a final interview, which will then be the sole decision point. The final interview will determine whether the candidate is offered the position, and all earlier stages will have been steps along the way or 'hurdles' which the candidate needs to negotiate successfully in order to be eligible for the final selection.

In the 'whole picture' approach, there may still be a 'whittling-down' activity in the same way as the 'hurdle' approach with fewer candidates at the final stage than at the first screening. The difference however is that the information from all parts of the selection process is assembled and the decision formed on the basis of the 'whole picture'. Thus the 'whole picture' would include the assessment and rating of the application form, the results of the test and the outcome of all the interviews; a balanced view is then taken based on the complete range of information.

The terms adopted by psychologists for the two approaches are non-compensatory (hurdle) and compensatory (whole picture). Research into the two approaches shows that the 'whole picture' approach provides significantly greater success in making selection decisions than using the 'hurdle' approach. It is particularly useful when used with a competency-based selection structure, because the components do not overlap or duplicate each other, thereby avoiding potential conflict and unnecessary cost.

It is a useful discipline to use an evidence organiser for candidate information throughout the selection process. The organiser maintains records for scores or assessments at each stage of the process so that a single form can be used instead of trying to collect the information from different documents. The use of computer software packages to support the selection process can help significantly in presenting information, by for example providing an analysis across candidates at each stage or across all stages for each candidate.

Consideration will need to be given to whether the information from each of the selection stages will be assessed on a common scale. For example, should the application screen be subdivided into five scales of acceptability, the interview rating in a similar format and the test sten scores clustered into five standard scores? This aspect will be most significant if the actuarial approach to decision-making, discussed below, is used.

How to make the selection decision

There are two main approaches to selection decisions: actuarial and interpretative.

The **actuarial** approach is very mechanistic and objective. The scores for each stage of the selection process are added together and the position(s) offered to the candidate(s) with the highest score(s). It may be the case that certain stages are weighted to give greater emphasis. For example, using a non-weighted approach, candidates A and B may be assessed on a five point scale as follows:

	A	B
Application	3	3
Test	4	3
First Interview	4	5
Exercise	4	4
Second Interview	4	5
Total Scores	19	20

and candidate B would be offered the job. A similar approach can be used where each competency is assessed and scored, again using a five point scale for illustration:

	A	B
Planning & Organising	3	4
Relationships	4	5
Knowledge	3	3
Judgement	4	3
Adaptability	4	5
Total Scores	18	20

In the second example each of the competencies would be assessed from different stages and techniques, but with some perhaps being measured by more than one technique. Assume, for example, that judgement is measured by a test and an interview. In that event, the final score would be the average of the two ratings.

Both the above examples assume that equal importance would be attached to each stage (in the first example) or each competency (in the second example). It may of course be the case that greater importance is to be attached to one or another, and a weighting system would be applied. Using the above examples, if the test in the first example received a weighting of 2.0 and the exercise received a weighting of 1.5, then both candidates would have equal scores. In the second example, weighting competencies of 'relationships' and 'adaptability' by 1.5 would increase the advantage of B over A.

There are some considerations with the actuarial approach. First, weightings need to be determined at the start of the process rather than 'modelled' at the end to fit the desired outcome. Secondly, the greater the scale the more meaningful the differences and usefulness of final scores, and a 10 point scale is particularly useful. Thirdly, when weighting is attached to stages it can either be used to underline the importance of that stage or to 'balance' it if there are concerns – about the validity or consistency or whatever – around that stage.

The advantage of the actuarial approach is that it is transparent and consistent. It is easy to see 'fairness' of the outcome and, even with weightings, it ensures a balanced reliance on all elements of the selection process. The disadvantages are firstly that it can 'dilute' significant failings at any one stage – for example a poor 'fit' between the organisation and candidate – which though only part of the process may be a fundamental flaw. Secondly, it tends not to work too well in practice in that it feels overly mechanistic, and successful candidates may be those of a 'middle-ground' character rather than the noticeable candidates. For the second reason it can be unpopular with selectors.

The **interpretative** approach is similar in some ways to the actuarial in that all stages are considered and, usually, scored. The difference however is that the decision is not automatic: the evidence is analysed and a judgement made. In so doing, the selector may decide to downplay lack of experience gleaned from the application form, due to a good grasp of the issues displayed in the interview. More importantly perhaps the interpretative approach, when used for competency-based selection, allows for finer judgement. Thus, for example, while marginal scores in relationships and adaptability may not in themselves detract from overall scores, their combined significance may cause the selector to reject the candidate. In this way, the interpretative approach allows for the interplay of competencies to be considered and therefore provide a more refined decision.

It is frequently the case in the interpretative approach that a graphical representation of scores, such as a bar chart, is used instead of plain scores since it helps decision-makers in gaining a clearer overview of the candidate. This is illustrated in Figure 17.2.

Figure 17.2 / **Comparing the candidate's profile with the person specification**

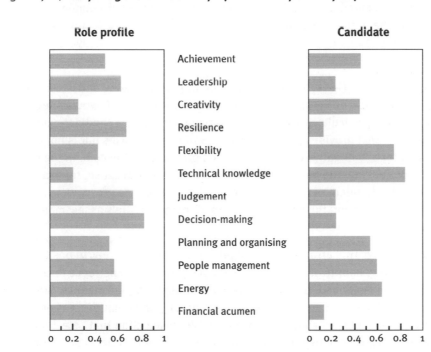

MISTAKES

Selection is not a perfect science. Mistakes occur, and from time to time there are serious errors of judgement. Sometimes such errors may lead to the most suitable candidate not being selected; sometimes it leads to a poor candidate being selected, and sometimes it leads to discrimination against candidates. The following are some common errors in decision-making that need to be guarded against:

- **Ignoring the specification:** This may seem an obvious mistake but one that is not always so easily avoided, since there can be a danger of the selection assignment becoming a competition rather than a search, and candidates are compared with each other rather than compared with the specification. In the same way that an auction bidder sets bid limits and negotiators predetermine remits, so too must selectors ensure that the parameters they set, through the specification, are adhered to in the final decision-making. Where no candidates match the specification, and there is no opportunity to redesign the role to accommodate shortfalls, appointments should not be made.

- **Over-reliance on a single element** : This can sometimes lead to mistakes where for example a first-class interview performance is allowed to eclipse concerns around past experience or test results. There may, of course, be occasions where a reasoned decision is made to 'allow' for some shortcomings but, in general, the purpose of a multiple-technique approach to selection is to gain a balanced picture and over-reliance on any single element will give a distorted view.

- **The halo effect:** This error is a variation on the above theme and occurs where a particular virtue of the candidate is allowed to obscure or downplay negative factors. It is particularly prevalent in interviewing where a candidate may give an answer that provides positive indicators of competencies but is not then probed for any negative examples, to see both sides of the coin. In the overall decision-making, the halo effect can sometimes occur because, for example, the university attended, or a specific company experience, can carry weight with the decision-maker and the negative aspects of the candidate's assessment are downplayed or ignored.

- **Stereotyping:** This error occurs both positively and negatively. In positive stereotyping, people of a certain age or background or experience in common with others employed, but of no causal relationship to performance, are deemed to be suitable candidates. In negative stereotyping a similar process occurs to the detriment of the candidate. It is inevitable in selection that selectors will drift to categories of people, but to lump people together because of their physical attributes, social background or skin colour is a generalisation that is so widely inaccurate that it turns selection into a lottery. A carefully drafted specification should help ensure that proper selection penetrates such superficial categorisation.

- **Mirroring or similarity-identity bias**: This error occurs where the selector favours a candidate, usually subconsciously, because the candidate matches the selector's own outlook or experience. It is a particularly prevalent mistake in interviewing where the interviewer 'gets on well' with the candidate and establishes rapport because of common interests. This is a very common problem where a specification has not been properly drafted or agreed with the client, and it has not been uncommon for some recruiters to select candidates 'in their own image' for positions for which they (the recruiter) would be neither suitable nor motivated.

- **Prejudice**: This error occurs both consciously and unconsciously. There are still sadly incidents of people being rejected because of physical disabilities, age, social background or ethnicity. The moral (and legal) perspective is condemnatory, but equally lamentable is the harsh truth that organisations are denied suitable (and sometimes the most suitable) candidates because of the personal failings of selectors. Prejudice is not always obvious; in one study female interviewees suffered gender bias in interviews, but the bias did not come from male interviewers (who displayed no bias to either gender in the interview and subsequent decision-making), but from female interviewers who identified themselves with successful males and were gender-biased against female candidates.

- **Non-involvement of clients**: This error in the selection process and in decision-making may adversely affect the successful integration of the new appointee and therefore retrospectively corrupt the decision. It would be rare indeed for an external selection consultant not to involve his or her client in an interview and to go further than making a recommendation for the client's final decision. In the case of internal recruiters, it may still be the case that decisions are occasionally made on behalf of internal 'clients', or the 'client' is bullied or blinded into decisions. The interpersonal rapport between a new hire and their new boss is important to success and such 'chemistry' should not be ignored. Equally, the involvement of line managers (and future colleagues) in the selection decision will make them more committed to the success of the new person.

18

Checks and offers

CHECKING

While it is the case that more than half UK employers declare that they take up references before a job offer is made, it is very rarely the case that references and other checks are undertaken before a decision is made on the candidate. This chapter is therefore concerned with the steps that need to be undertaken to verify claims by the candidate being offered a position, whether or not the offer is made before, after, or subject to, the checks. There are three main areas for checking: document checks, statutory checks and references.

DOCUMENTS

Document checking is concerned with verifying that the qualifications, certificates etc., claimed by the candidate can be substantiated. Documents may include personal certificates such as birth certificates and marriage certificates, which may be relevant to the job in terms of minimum age, but are more frequently a requirement for satisfying pension scheme eligibility. Since qualifications ought only to be sought and mentioned where they are pertinent to job performance, it follows that any claims ought to be verified and the original documents checked. This should be an obvious point, and a simple practice, but the author's own experience and anecdotal evidence of others, suggests that it is a frequent flaw in recruitment practices. The incidence of bogus professionals operating in even the most regulated professions may be more common-place than generally thought. Any licences claimed by the applicant, and pertinent to the role, should also be checked, not least because the employer will be vicariously liable for any accidents arising in the course of employment. This applies particularly for driving licences, LGV licences, fork-lift truck licences, and pilots' licence. Where membership of professional associations is claimed, they should also be checked. Most professional organisations provide a certificate of membership and some publish a register or yearbook, but exercise care with omissions which may be printer's error or lapsed subscriptions rather than non-membership. It is a question of convenience whether these checks are undertaken during the course of the selection process, such as interview, or whether the checks are undertaken before employment is started or on the day it is started. It is, however, good practice to advise all applicants that any qualifications and licences claimed will be checked. It is prudent to keep a record of the check and/or a photocopy of the certificates on the employee's file, in the event of any future legal action being taken by a third party against the employer, who may be vicariously liable for the employee.

STATUTORY

There are certain statutory obligations that must be fulfilled by an employer. Employees must be registered for National Insurance contributions and it is the duty of an employer to ensure that there is such registration for National Insurance purposes. At one time, employees were provided with National Insurance cards which an employer could obtain, but nowadays the only 'proof' is a National Insurance number which the employee should quote when taking up work. There is still some leeway for employers to allow the employment to begin, and to make payments to the employee, but this can only be a short-term arrangement and if the employee cannot provide a National Insurance number within fourteen days of beginning employment, the employment must be suspended until such time as a number can be obtained. The Department of Work and Pensions will help in the provision of temporary National Insurance numbers where there are particular difficulties.

The Asylum and Immigration Act 1996 makes it a criminal offence to employ a person over 16 who is subject to immigration control unless the following conditions apply:

- The person has current and valid permission to be in the UK – such as a work permit.

- The permission does not prevent him or her from taking the job in question.

- The person comes into a category where the employment is otherwise allowed – for example au pair.

There is no small measure of difficulty with this requirement. It is an offence of strict liability which means that it is irrelevant whether the employer knew the law, or whether the employer was unaware, or did not suspect, that the employee needed such a document. Citizens of member states of the European community are entitled to move freely within it and are not required to provide any form of certificate. Similarly, Commonwealth citizens may be exempt from immigration controls. It is an offence to deny someone employment because of their nationality (under the Race Relations Act 1976) and there may be a presumption of racial discrimination if a non-white is asked questions about work permits or immigration restrictions at interview (unless all applicants are asked the question). The different aims of different pieces of separately drafted legislation can therefore 'cause a headache' for the employer trying to work within them.

The employer can mount a defence to prosecution under the Asylum and Immigration Act by showing that eligibility for employment was correctly checked through National Insurance number, passport, or work permit (if there is a copy for proof) and it would seem prudent therefore to ensure that 'start to work' information is properly secured and separated from the application form or other selection documents. The Asylum and Immigration Act only applies where there is a direct employment relationship.

REFERENCES

References seem to be an almost universal requirement and nearly all employers seek them. References are sometimes taken up before an offer is made, sometimes after an offer is made, and sometimes an offer is made 'subject to satisfactory references'. Some employers will not provide references, and some will not provide references where an offer has already been made 'subject to' satisfactory ones being received. Even where employers operate such policies, they do not appear to be embarrassed about seeking references for their own candidates. References may take a number of forms:

- References from schools or universities – often focusing on academic achievement: Some Head Teachers decline to provide such references because of the sheer workload and the availability of records of achievement which should provide the evidence employers require.

- Personal or character references which generally show that the new employee is a decent sort of person (whatever that may be) and may be sought from friends, colleagues, acquaintances or, more frequently, 'reputable' people in professional positions. The local JP, GP, and vicar have not been spared such burdens by other advances in selection methods.

- Work references may be the most sought after. Sometimes such references are simply an open request for information about the candidate, sometimes they may be a closed questionnaire seeking specific information to verify claims made, asking specific questions on employment dates, attendance record, work performance, relationships with people, and other pertinent information from their past. Sometimes the reference seeks the views of the current or former employer on the suitability of the candidate to undertake the post for which they have applied, in which case it is important to provide information about the role and the qualities and competencies needed to perform it.

- Specialist references such as credit history, medical history and criminal record: Credit checks are more frequently undertaken for positions where cash-handling or other financial transactions are important, and therefore commonplace in financial institutions which are characterised by such work, and where access to the information is more readily available. Medical history may be sought in an over-zealous concern for attendance or because it has a significant bearing on the employment (e.g. flying or sea-diving) and may be accompanied by a requirement to undergo a medical examination. There is a requirement for the individual to consent to the release of such information. Access to criminal history is through the Criminal Records Bureau which provides Criminal Record Certificates (called Disclosures) to employers in occupations that are exceptions under the Rehabilitation of Offenders Act, together with Enhanced Criminal Record Disclosures (for those working on a regular unsupervised basis with children) giving information on convictions and non-conviction information. Fees are payable for the disclosures.

There are variations in the timing of references. Some employers choose to take up references for candidates at one of the stages in the selection process, usually the interview. Some take up references when they have decided to select the candidate, but before an offer is made. Some seek references after the offer is made, sometimes making such an offer 'subject to receipt of satisfactory references'. Some will be happy to receive references after the employee has started. Seeking references during the selection process should only be undertaken where they are needed to contribute to the selection decision, otherwise it is administratively inefficient and also a waste of time for the referees. Where references are taken up in this way, it is essential that candidates be advised beforehand that it is the practice and their consent is obtained. It is particularly important that, whatever the stage at which they are sought, references from current employers are not sought without the clear knowledge of the candidate for it would not be unusual for such requests to put the employee's current or future job prospects at risk. Some referees take offence at being asked to provide a reference for someone who has been offered a job 'subject to receipt of satisfactory references', and some companies adopt a policy of refusing to provide references in such circumstances.

There is great unease about references, both in the giving and the taking. Referees must ensure that they provide truthful, accurate and reliable information, and hold a legal liability, to take care, to those to whom they supply a reference (*Hedley Byrne v Heller* 1964) and to those who are the subject of the reference (*Spring v Guardian Assurance* 1994). Failure to disclose relevant information will create as much liability as providing false information. There is a view that employers are under a legal obligation to their employees to provide references on their behalf where future work is dependent upon them; as yet this has not been established in case law. Given that referees are rarely paid for the service they provide, it is interesting to understand why they provide it. This may be because they are concerned that, if everyone 'drops out of the game', they will be denied access to information in times when they themselves need it.

It is all the more curious therefore to note that many employers are cynical of the value of information they receive in references. This is particularly the case in 'open' references where reading between the lines is often more important than reading what is on them. Thus, statements such as 'he left us fired with enthusiasm' or 'you will be lucky to get her to work for you' may be capable of more than one meaning. It is worthwhile decoding with care such expressions as 'attentive to detail' (nit picking), 'co-operative' (follows the herd), 'independent' (stubborn), 'supportive' (sucks up to the boss) and 'flexible' (indecisive). There has been little research into the effectiveness of references but those few studies that have been undertaken in the UK have indicated a positive correlation in that 'good reference' predicted 'good performer'. Most employers however approach references as a safety net, as a means of checking that the information given to them by the candidate is factual. To this end, references can be more reliable when they are sought as a questionnaire that elicits specific answers to specific questions such as:

- the period of employment

- work performance, usually providing a simple scale from poor through acceptable, good and very good to excellent

- time lost due to sickness or other absence

- reason for leaving (if already left)

- a question of whether the employer would re-employ

- a catch-all question seeking any other relevant information and/or reasons why he or she should not be employed.

Referees generally find it easier to complete pre-formatted questionnaires and the information tends to be more reliable and more speedily returned. See Figure 18.1. It is not always the case that references are written: often they are sought by telephone and, even when a written reference is obtained, a follow-up phone call may be used or offered. It is often felt that a more accurate picture will be obtained over the telephone than in writing, but it should be noted that liability for false or misleading information applies as much to verbal representations as to written information.

REFERENCE AGENCIES

A more recent trend in the United States, and beginning to grow in the UK, has been the use of reference-checking agencies. For a fixed fee the agency will undertake to obtain references from former employers, and check out any specific aspects such as credit, health and criminal history. The benefit of using such an agency is that by specialising they develop expertise in procuring the information; they know how to abide by all the appropriate legal and ethical standards; and by focusing on the task they can devote time to chasing the information and thereby free selectors from the chore.

Figure 18.1 / *Example of a reference request*

```
REQUEST FOR REFERENCE

Mr/Ms ...........................................................................................................
has applied for the post of ........................................................................
and has advised that you are prepared to provide a reference on his/her behalf.

How long have you known him/her? ........................................................
In what capacity? ........................................................................................
Please assess the following:
                            Poor    Acceptable    Good    Excellent

Attitude to work
Abilities
Productivity
Working with people
Honesty
Attendance

Do you know any reason why we should not employ? ..............................

If employed by you, please state        date joined ...................................
                                        date left ......................................
                                        would you re-employ? .......................


Signature ............................................................ Date ............................

Please return in the envelope provided or telephone ..........................
```

CRIMINAL RECORD

The Rehabilitation of Offenders Act (1974) permits a convicted person to become 'rehabilitated' after a certain period which in effect means the conviction becomes 'spent' and gives the person certain rights. The person will not be required to disclose the conviction and is entitled to say, in response to any request for information on criminal convictions, that they have none. Furthermore the conviction, once 'spent', cannot be used as a reason for rejecting the applicant. The length of 'rehabilitation' varies from six months to 10 years dependent upon the penalty imposed, but convictions resulting in imprisonment for more than 30 months are never spent.

There are exceptions to the Rehabilitation of Offenders Act, particularly in professions such as doctors, nurses, midwives, dentists, barristers, solicitors, accountants, teachers, policemen and directors of building societies. The Act is excluded from any office or employment concerned with the provision of accommodation, care, leisure and recreational facilities, schooling and social services, or supervision or training of persons under 18 which would involve access to such minors in the ordinary course of employment.

MAKING AN OFFER

Offers of employment may be conditional or unconditional. An unconditional offer is one where the post is offered to the candidate without 'any strings' attached, and it is left to the candidate to determine whether or not to accept. Conditional offers fall into two main types: pre-conditions and post-conditions.

Typical pre-conditions include making the offer 'subject to receipt of satisfactory references' or subject to attainment of certain qualifications or educational grades. Such pre-conditions should be treated by both the employer and potential employee as a deferment of the appointment to the new role until the conditions have been met. They should also signal that failure to achieve the conditions will mean that the offer is withdrawn. Post-conditional offers may include an appointment 'subject to completion of a satisfactory probationary period' or (less common nowadays) taking up residence within a certain time period, or staying for a minimum period. It should be clear that where such conditions are not subsequently met, the employment will terminate. In practice such clarity does not always follow, and while pre-conditions are often regarded by both parties as essential prerequisites, post-conditions somehow come to be regarded, by either or both parties, as a mere formality. Even where formal processes exist for the review of probationary periods, termination seems to occur less frequently than 'duff' appointments.

Whatever conditions are attached to the appointment, they must be clearly communicated and acknowledged. Similarly the terms of any offer should be clear and unequivocal. There may be positions where the appointment is subject to some flexibility on pay and some negotiation may take place between the employer and the candidate. Where such negotiation is likely to take place, employers will find themselves in a stronger position if they discuss pay during the selection process (for example at interview) rather than at the point of offer, when the candidate knows that they are in a stronger negotiating position. At this point they know that they are the preferred or only suitable candidate and refusal will involve the employer in further costs of re-advertising. Negotiations ought however to take place in good faith and any indications of employment conditions during the recruitment assignment should be realistic. Advertisements, for example, should carry a figure approximate to the amount the new hire will earn rather than some hypothetical long-term salary. It is, of course, quite in order to put forward long-term earnings or on-target earnings but, in so doing, the figures should be clearly described as such. This is not simply good manners, but prudently avoids the disappointment of candidates rejecting offers, or new employees leaving prematurely. In constructing the offer, it should be borne in mind that many candidates falsely inflate current earning in an attempt to improve their future prospects.

LEGAL CONSIDERATIONS

It needs to be remembered that employment is a legal contract. While the new recruit may not become an employee until the employment begins, the contract itself is legally enforceable as soon as it is formed. It is formed when:

- There is an offer and acceptance of the offer.

- Both parties intend it to be a legally binding arrangement.

- There is 'consideration' (something of value attached to the contract).

- There is sufficient certainty of terms.

With the exception of apprentices and merchant seafarers, there is no requirement that an employment contract must be in writing to be legally enforceable. An offer made and accepted at interview or over the phone, will therefore be legally enforceable, and provide the candidate with the right to claim for breach of contract if the accepted offer is withdrawn. It used to be thought that such an action would need to be pursued through the courts, but the Employment Appeal Tribunal, in *Sarker v South Tees Acute Hospitals NHS Trust (1997)*, held that Employment Tribunals are able to adjudicate on a breach of contract, prior to commencement of 'employment', in accordance with the Industrial Tribunals Extension of Jurisdiction Order 1994.

There is however a statutory requirement on employers to provide new employees with a written statement of the main terms and conditions of employment either before the employment begins or within two months of commencing work. Although the statement may be issued in instalments, and reference made to other documents such as handbooks or staff codes, certain terms must be in a single document known as 'the principal statement' or set out in the contract of employment. The principal statement will need to include:

- the name of the employer and employee

- the date employment began

- whether any previous period of employment counts as part of the employee's continuous employment

- any terms about holidays

- job title or job description and place of work or mobility clause

- the scale or rate of remuneration, the method of calculation of the remuneration, and the intervals at which paid

- hours of work, including any rules on overtime

- sick pay and pension arrangements (if any)

- the length of notice to be given on either side

- disciplinary and grievance procedures

- details of any collective bargaining agreements affecting the contract.

The last point is important to illustrate that the terms of an employment contract may be express, implied or incorporated.

- 'Express terms' are those which are directly agreed between the employer and the employee, but 'express' does not necessarily mean written; a term offered orally will bind the employer regardless of any subsequent attempt to substitute inferior terms in writing (unless the employee accepts). It is therefore important that any offers made at the interview, over the phone or any other low-key mode are clear, unambiguous and made with full authority, for they will form the binding contract – even if the person making the offer was not fully authorised to do so.

- 'Implied terms' come in to play when there are no express or incorporated terms to cover them. They are 'read into' the contract and come about either through custom and practice or by common law or statute. Common Law is the body of cases that set out legal precedent, such as the duty to provide work for the employee, the duty to provide mutual respect, etc. The statutes provide a significant source of implied terms, particularly Health & Safety at Work legislation providing duties of care, and the various discrimination acts that provide that less favourable terms may not be offered to candidates on grounds of gender, race, disability, sexual orientation and religion. People covered by such legislation can either accept the employment and then use the law to enforce terms that are equally favourable, or reject the offer and pursue a claim for discrimination.

- 'Incorporated terms' mean those which are 'imported' from elsewhere. Thus, if the employee is employed on terms which are negotiated locally or centrally with the employer, or perhaps with the employer's federation, then any changes which the Trade Union negotiates will 'automatically' form part of the employee's contract.

In practice, most employers have an established set of terms and conditions of employment, and employment is clearly and explicitly offered within such terms. A leading New Zealand lawyer once noted 'the paradoxical truth is that a lengthy agreement in writing which sets out the terms relating to all conceivable contingencies produces a less complex contract than the one created by the word and the nod'.

19

Equal opportunities and discrimination

DISCRIMINATION

Discrimination is the essence of recruitment; it is about trying to discriminate and segregate the suitable from the unsuitable and it is not always 'fair' in that employment invariably is given to those suitable to perform the task, rather than the most needy. It may not be 'fair' to offer the job to the candidate who is already in employment, and who may have a number of alternative offers, over the candidate who is unemployed and thus has no work alternative. The duty of selectors is to ensure the most appropriate selection rather than to redistribute social justice. There are however certain groups in society facing unfair disadvantages and prejudices, and whom the law seeks to protect. The law does not attempt to provide such groups with an unfair advantage, rather it attempts to ensure that there is an equal playing field so that they may receive proper consideration in applying for positions. The law directly precludes unfair discrimination against people based on their gender, race, disability, criminal history, trade union situation, religion or belief, sexual orientation, and (from 2006) age. From a legal perspective there are three main ways in which discrimination can take place: direct discrimination, indirect discrimination and victimisation.

Direct discrimination, as the phrase implies, is where someone is discriminated against directly because of one of the unlawful factors. Thus, it would discriminate directly against non-whites and women to permit only white males to be considered for a particular role. Indirect discrimination occurs where an act, though not discriminatory in itself, has the effect of discriminating against key groups. Thus, it would most probably be indirect discrimination against non-whites and women to reserve employment for people with blonde hair and a beard because, by virtue of their race or gender, they would be far less likely to fulfil the criteria than others. It would not be indirect discrimination against men because dark-haired, clean-shaven males are excluded: they will not be excluded because of their gender since a significant proportion of men will still be able to fulfil the criteria. Discrimination by victimisation occurs where someone is treated less favourably because they have committed a protected act, such as brought proceedings or assisted in bringing proceedings or complaints under equal opportunities laws. The significance of whether the discrimination is direct or indirect is that the penalties and remedies are greater for direct discrimination.

The main purpose of the discrimination legislation is to ensure that people are not treated less favourably in their employment by virtue of belonging to one of the appropriate groups. The legislation therefore covers most aspects of the employment relationship including terms and conditions and pay. Unlike other aspects of the law that provide rights to people only during the employment contract, the legislation on discrimination extends to those seeking employment and therefore has significant relevance for recruitment and selection. The full range of legal issues is beyond the scope of this book, but selectors should ensure they are fully familiar with them. Further information can be obtained from CIPD books and conferences and from the various codes of practice.

POSITIVE ACTION AND POSITIVE DISCRIMINATION

Not all discrimination is negative. There are occasions where employers may take steps to remedy an under representation of a particular group within the workforce. Positive action occurs when an employer attempts to remove the barriers perceived by the discriminated group, for example by ensuring advertisements or notices are placed in areas where under represented groups may see them. Positive discrimination occurs where there is direct action to give more favourable treatment to the under-represented group by, for example, giving preference to Asian candidates over their white counterparts. Positive action is legally permissible whereas positive discrimination is not.

There is always a danger that equal opportunities will be seen as a 'right thing' to do, a moral obligation which needs law and activists to promote. The reality however is that the natural law of distribution dictates that there must be sufficient numbers of perfectly suitable candidates amongst different genders, races, religions, or political conviction to warrant full and proper consideration. Given that it is always difficult to find good candidates, it makes sound economic and business sense to give full and fair consideration to all candidates, or selectors will have failed to perform their role properly.

How to take steps to avoid unlawful discrimination

It can be seen that the focus of legislation against discrimination is not only on advertising and decisions on offering employment, but also 'in the arrangements that are made for the purpose of determining who shall be offered employment', which of course means the recruitment and selection practices and policies. While overt discrimination due to prejudice may be tackled through statements on equal opportunities and appropriate training, it is also true that ingrained or unthinking discrimination needs to be engineered out of the process through careful attention to recruitment practices.

- **Step 1: Set objective requirements**. The development of the person specification needs to be undertaken thoroughly. Care needs to be taken to avoid description of the previous incumbents, and the focus should be on the key requirements of the role itself. Arbitrary qualifiers such as age, qualifications, experience or physical attributes, that are not essential to the role, should be avoided as this will help create a realistic and balanced profile. A very solid platform will be provided by the use of a carefully drafted competency framework related to the key requirements of the role, identified through a proper role analysis and expressed in objective descriptions.

- **Step 2: Encourage fair and open competition**. The employment marketing strategy should ensure that any advertising or promotion is not confined to media that may be less accessible to under-represented groups. Efforts should be made to take positive action to ensure that opportunities are brought to the attention of such groups. Open recruitment practices are less likely to be discriminatory, whereas other methods have been condemned as means of perpetuating the current composition of the workforce and therefore likely to be discriminatory. These include 'word of mouth' recruitment through existing employees, restriction to internal appointment only, recruiting through families of existing employees, and through trade unions. The content of any advertising or recruitment literature needs to portray an image of a mixed workforce and should show a balance of ethnic groups, females, and various age groups. The employment marketing strategy should avoid giving the impression that higher positions are only occupied by white males, and also to avoid showing sporting or other 'physical' images which suggest that disabilities will be a bar. This is not to suggest that advertisements ought not to be imaginative or 'catchy'. There is however a tendency for imaginations to run riot, particularly in graduate recruitment where pictures of mountaineering may be intended as a metaphor for ambition, but may suggest a requirement for physical attributes and fitness wholly unrelated to the reality of the training programme. Similarly, perpetuating the milk round in certain Universities or favouring candidates from certain public schools may be seen to be practices discriminating against women or ethnic groups. Statements welcoming applicants from under-represented groups should be included in the advertisement through phrases such as 'we seek to be an equal opportunities employer and welcome applications regardless of age, gender, race or disability'.

- **Step 3: Use suitable application procedures**. The method of application should be constructed so that it is free of discrimination. A requirement for applicants to complete forms 'in your own handwriting' has the potential to be discriminatory against those whose first language is not English or against the visually impaired. Where standards of English or reading are required as essential elements of the role, then of course it is quite justifiable to incorporate such aspects, but for roles where it is not required, or where adjustments can be made for a disability, then the practice should be avoided. Similarly the content of the application form should be framed around essential elements of the role rather than 'nice to know' aspects. Asking questions about experience or 'GCSE grades' may imply an intention to discriminate, which may not actually be present. The development of biodata screening methods should ensure that the construct measures (i.e. the factors which differentiate) are not discriminatory, and that the questions are not framed in a way that assumes a 'western' education/lifestyle or predominantly male/female disposition. Telephone screening will need to take account of those with speech or hearing impairments, particularly if it is not a requirement of the role, and alternative avenues may need to be offered. The importance attached to information gathered, for making shortlisting decisions, must of course take account of alternative backgrounds and lifestyles. Paying attention, for example, to speed of promotion may discriminate against women and ethnic minorities facing greater difficulties achieving such progress due to the very effects of discrimination.

- **Step 4: Ensure any tests are proper.** The use of psychometric tests, and especially ability tests, is a particular cause for concern. It is important to ensure that the test itself is not discriminatory and, in choosing tests, employers should check carefully that the test has been tried out on samples of female, ethnic and disabled groups to ensure that it is free of bias. Particular care needs to be undertaken to ensure that the ability, which the test is measuring, is an essential prerequisite of successful performance in the role to which the person is being recruited. Many cases of unfair discrimination have been raised because of the indiscriminate use of ability tests, particularly for literacy or numeracy, where such abilities are not relevant to the position being filled. Consideration will also need to be given to helping disabled candidates to complete the test if their disability renders it difficult to do so.

- **Step 5: Use balanced and objective interviews.** Care needs to be taken in the interview with choice of questions and consistency of questions. The codes of practice, which will be taken into account in deciding claims of discrimination, advise against certain questions that might indicate an intention to discriminate. Asking female candidates about how male colleagues would respond to them, or about their plans to start a family, or about childcare arrangements may indicate the presence of discrimination. Similarly, asking ethnic minority candidates how white colleagues will react to them, or about their right to work in the UK may be seen to be discriminatory. Even 'off the cuff' conversational questions can cause concern as in the case of an Irish candidate asked questions about Guinness, which was perceived as racial stereotyping on alcoholism and detrimentally affected interview performance. Given that the Disability Discrimination Act requires employers to make provision to assist disabled persons to perform their role, it may be necessary at interview to phrase such questions carefully around the help that is needed rather than around the challenges or obstacles faced. It is highly unlikely that anyone will be more acutely aware than the disabled person of the challenges to be surmounted. It is an effective interviewing technique to maintain consistent questions and this can be particularly helpful in avoiding discrimination. A question that would be embarrassing to pose to an able-bodied white male is one that probably ought not to be asked of any candidate.

Care should also be taken with certain kinds of interviewing; it has been shown that situational interviewing – where candidates are asked to say how they would response to a future hypothetical situation – tends to be discriminatory in making it difficult for people whose first language is not English to respond effectively with the grasp of abstract language and concepts. Body language is, at the best of times, a concept of dubious authenticity; all the more so in the interview of minority candidates. For example, a well-qualified black female teacher was discriminated against as a consequence of an 'unsuccessful interview' because of failure to make good eye contact with her interviewers. However, the Employment Appeal Tribunal accepted the evidence that people of Afro-Caribbean origin often avoided eye contact with those in authority, such eye contact being regarded as impolite. In some ways the employer is between 'the devil and the deep blue sea' in that questions about the right to work in the UK would be seen to be discriminatory, but on the other hand employers would be liable for employing someone who needs, but does not have, a work certificate – regardless of whether the employer knew that they needed such certificate. Good practice may however be to incorporate this element into the status checks at the offer stage, rather than in the interview.

- **Step 6: Use only suitable exercises.** The use of exercises and work simulations needs careful consideration to ensure that the exercises themselves are not incapable of being performed by, for example, disabled people (particularly highly physical outdoor type activities) and that the purpose of the exercise is not designed to elicit information which may be discriminatory (for example looking for aggressive behaviour in team leadership exercises). Where work simulations are involved, arrangements will need to be made to adjust the workplace or equipment to accommodate disabled candidates.

- **Step 7: Make objective decisions**. The basis upon which decisions are made must also be free of discrimination. One of the more common mistakes in making decisions about candidates is stereotyping, and racial stereotyping is one such example. A carefully-drafted person specification or, better still, a clearly defined competency framework, will provide an objective benchmark against which selectors may measure candidates rather than relying on subjective criteria. Additionally, a good investment is to train interviewers and decision-makers in equal opportunities principles and ways to avoid discrimination. Providing interviewers with examples of model answers to questions in addition to examples of non-discriminatory questions can help eliminate bias, and the use of a consistent scoring mechanism, properly applied, is particularly effective in eradicating selection bias. Particular attention should be paid to avoiding over-emphasis on how the candidate will 'fit in' with the existing workforce; particularly where 'fitting in' means someone of a different gender, racial background, etc. fitting the current work group.

- **Step 8: Make consistent offers**. While legislation on discrimination forbids such discrimination in the process of recruitment and in the decisions on recruitment, it extends of course to the terms of employment offered. Care must therefore be taken to ensure that there is consistency here, because there can still be a successful claim if the terms are rejected by the applicant. Thus, for example, a female student hired for a temporary holiday job as a security guard was unfairly discriminated against by not being offered night shifts which resulted in loss of earnings (*Dunlop v Royal Scottish Academy*). Similarly, applying employment regulations in a certain way may also be discriminatory. For example, forbidding women to wear trousers has been seen to be discriminatory to Sikhs and Muslims, particularly where there is more hardship for the applicant to adhere to the rule than for the employer to change it. Conversely, while rules against the wearing of beards have discriminated against Sikh men – whose religion requires that they should wear them – it has been ruled justifiable where employers of food products insisted on the rule as part of their hygiene standards.

- **Step 9: Carry out effective induction**. Sadly, the workplace is still an environment where abuse can be manifested through sexual and racial harassment. Care needs to be taken therefore to monitor the induction period – and beyond – to ensure that such abuse does not take place and that the new employee is integrated smoothly and effectively into the workplace.

- **Step 10: Carry out on-going monitoring**. In addition to engineering-out the potential causes of discrimination, on-going vigilance will need to be maintained through the monitoring of equal opportunities. The development of an equal opportunities policy and training is a worthwhile investment. Candidates who are likely to suffer discrimination need to be identified and an equal opportunities monitoring form should be incorporated into the selection system. Such a form, seeking information on the candidate's gender, race, disabilities, religion and age should be used to gather information on the success of certain groups at each stage of the selection process. Using the information it will, for example, be possible to assess whether ethnic minority candidates have as much chance as others in proceeding to and beyond the shortlist stage, and whether the 'failure' rate at testing is disproportionate and whether interview scores are consistent with other parts of the process. Such monitoring should be established as a regular and systematic part of recruitment activity and all assignments should be accompanied by such statistical analysis. Collecting the information on the form can be a cause of concern or sensitivity and it is better collected as a separate form from the application (or a detachable portion) with an explanation to candidates of the purpose to which the information will be applied. See Figure 19.1.

*Figure 19.1 / **Example of an equal opportunities monitoring form***

We do our best to promote equality of opportunity and to ensure that people are selected for employment on the basis of their suitability and are treated fairly, regardless of race, sex, marital status, disability, age, religion or any other aspect not related to job performance. We need to be sure that we deliver on our promises, so we use this form to check on progress. The form is not used for selection purposes but to monitor the decisions made, and to ensure they are made fairly. Please help us by completing it.

Name: ....

Post applied for: ....

Location: ....

Are you: Male ☐   Female ☐

Single ☐   Married ☐   Widowed/Divorced ☐

Black-African ☐
Black-Caribbean ☐
Black other ☐
Indian ☐
Pakistani ☐
Bangladeshi ☐
Chinese ☐
White ☐
Other (specify) ....

Age   under 30 ☐   30–45 ☐   45 or over ☐

Disabled ☐
Any special facilities needed to attend interview? ....

....

Signature .... **Date** ....

20

Starting-up

INDUCTION

Selection is not a noble art pursued for its own purpose, nor is it an abstract exercise or quest for achievement in which the appointment of the most suitable candidate is the culmination of the challenge. It is in fact a work process, a production line for securing and feeding human fodder into an organisation to provide sustenance to the organisation. This may seem a bizarre caricature, but it is perhaps useful to illustrate the point that selection does not end when the candidate takes up the role. There is a cost to selection, not only in the direct cost of finding and selecting people, but also the indirect cost of disruption and learning curves. Recruitment and selection must therefore be concerned with the length of time the new person will stay in the role, how quickly they can achieve full performance, and how well performance and commitment can be sustained.

The single most important influence on labour turnover is length of service. The simple truth is, that the longer an employee has been with an organisation, the less likely they are to leave. Conversely those most at risk of leaving are new employees. The term 'induction crisis' has been coined to describe the first twelve months of an employee's service in which they will be most at risk of leaving. The first 12 weeks will be a particularly acute risk period, but normal stability does not really occur until after 12 months of service. Most organisations will find that, even if their labour turnover rates are in low single figures, labour turnover for the 12 month 'induction crisis' will be around 20 per cent. Good recruitment and selection practices must therefore be concerned with stabilising the risk and managing the integration of the new person into the role. In a recent CIPD survey over 40 per cent of respondents indicated that they were seeking to improve the induction process as a way to improve staff retention.

The first part of the induction begins long before the role is taken up. Information provided to the candidate throughout the selection process should be aimed at encouraging enthusiasm and managing expectations. In order to improve self-selection in the selection process, sufficient information should have already been given to candidates to enable them to have a very clear idea of how the role will shape up.

Once an offer has been extended and accepted, work can begin on the induction process without actually waiting for the new employee to begin work. Some organisations begin the induction process as soon as an offer is made, not waiting until the candidate accepts, so that enthusiasm and commitment can be engendered in candidates who may be wavering in their decision. There is a danger of trying to load too much information onto people before they start, because there will invariably be pressure on them in their old role to clear up and hand over. Where relocation is involved, there will also be a great deal of domestic arrangements to be handled. Nevertheless information on the organisation, its purpose, and 'culture' to supplement and expand on information already given, will help to create 'mental readiness'. There is not a great deal of point in loading organisation charts on to the new person, since these can be particularly bewildering, and only become meaningful when faces and personalities can be attached to the name, after starting. In technical or managerial positions, it is particularly useful to provide background information on current projects and initiatives and other issues as part of the mental preparation required for taking up the new challenges.

How to ensure effective induction

Once started, the new employee should follow a carefully planned induction programme which balances help and utilisation, so that plenty of assistance is provided to enable them to settle in and be able to do their work, but avoiding their attendance becoming just a 'learning' experience without getting a return on their time. The more clearly defined the role, and the greater the degree of homogeneity between organisations, then the easier it will be for the new person to adapt and become truly productive. A maintenance fitter, for example, may be able to make an immediate contribution on the first day, while a supervisor or manager will need a great degree of familiarisation with people, processes and equipment before being able to make a particularly meaningful contribution. A balance also needs to be struck between ensuring that there is sufficient information provided to speed up the induction process, while avoiding 'information overload' which will make it unnecessarily difficult for the new person to absorb all the information and is therefore counterproductive. It is useful therefore to plan the process over a few weeks rather than trying to cram everything into the first few days.

On the first day the new employee will need to be provided with 'signposts' to help them help themselves. This will include a guide to the workplace, including not only the 'physical' layout of the workplace or building/site, but also the 'virtual layout' of computer systems and other tools. Health safety and hygiene issues will need to be covered during the first day. Introduction ought to be kept to a minimum, and limited to those with whom the new hire will be in most

---

contact, but taking care not to 'snub' anyone who feels they should have been introduced. 'Introduction' is more than social introduction: it is spending time with the people to get an understanding of their role and, more pertinently, to begin building the relationship. Perhaps the most important outcome of the first day is that the new employee should go home with a good 'feel' of the organisation and its style, and the reassurance, through a warm welcome and a professional induction, that they made the right decision.

By the end of the first week, the new employee should have a clear understanding of the values and aims of the organisation, the aims and objectives of the immediate work group, a clear working knowledge of the purpose of their own role, and know their key contacts – both external and internal. The temptation to include any further 'general' induction topics during the first week should be avoided, and attention paid in the remainder of the time to the job itself. Thus, machine operators will need to be familiarised with the operation of their machine and all related aspects. Sales or marketing people will need to become familiar with products and related issues, and delivery people will need to be familiarised with routes, cycles and customers. The 'technical' aspects of the job will, in a well-run organisation, be set out in training schedules for the various positions that are likely to form the training plan for a number of weeks or months. The 'general' issues, which should be deferred beyond the first week, are the aspects related to administration or bureaucracy which, though important (particularly for large organisations), are not urgent. Aspects such as the discipline or grievance procedures, claiming expenses, the performance appraisal scheme and similar aspects need to be considered. It is also important at this stage to ensure that the new employee is provided with reference points or sources so that he or she can take responsibility for continuing their longer term induction, and is not unduly hampered in making progress on work issues by not knowing who or where to ask.

In organisations where there is a fairly regular intake of new staff (at whatever level), it is very useful to plan a regular general induction day (or half day). By setting a regular pattern, whether fortnightly, monthly or 6 weekly, it becomes easier for the organisation to slot new entrants on to the programme, whereas organising on an *ad hoc* basis is not only more work but also more uncertain in that there may not be 'enough time to get around to' organising the individual induction. It may of course seem unsuitable to have a general induction programme when the recruitment intake may be spread across a whole variety of posts and a spread of people across the 'pecking order' of the organisation. In practice, however, it works very well since people on the programme will have built up a relationship with others across the various parts of the organisation – even if the relationship is only a smiling nod in the staff restaurant – which can be important in reinforcing team culture. Status differences rarely cause problems because everyone shares a common lack of knowledge about the organisation.

Where the recruitment intake to the organisation is so low or irregular that a routine induction programme becomes unsuitable, it is useful to consider using a 'buddy' system whereby the new employee is paired up with a colleague who will help them through the induction process, arrange introductions and show them around the site. The buddy can be the prime person to be contacted for any help or any queries in the future. This is not simply a social nicety for the new employee, it is also far more efficient in eliminating the new employee wasting time in 'exploring' useless avenues of information when a quick call could put them right. The buddy system can either be a very informal arrangement or it can be formalised into the appointment of a number of very suitable people trained to deliver all the aspects of induction. The careful selection of such people will also ensure that the perception of the company is conditioned by the people the organisation values. It is sad to realise that even in today's world of work, sub-cultures of subversive and sometimes malicious groups operate; such groups rarely turn down the opportunity to 'induct' new employees into 'their' working methods and outlook.

COMPETENCY-BASED INDUCTION

Some of the difficulties faced in planning induction are often reflections of the difficulties arising from the selection process itself. Where the specification or decision, or both, are unclear it is possible that candidates are recruited because they 'seem suitable' or 'not particularly strong, but should be okay' or other vague reasons. While there may be concerns about the candidate being wholly suitable for the role, it is not easy to articulate what those concerns are and therefore not easy to plan how they should be handled when the new person starts work. Equally, even where there are no concerns, it is difficult, when appointing someone on generalisations of suitability, to be clear about individual strengths and weaknesses. The competency-based approach to selection ensures that the person specification is broken down into its constituent parts, related to performance in the role, expressed in clearly understandable terms and described in the behaviours one would expect to see in the workplace. The advantage, from an induction viewpoint, is that it is possible to be very specific about where the candidate does or does not match the specification. It then becomes easier to plan induction, development and the everyday management of that person to play on the strengths and accommodate the weaknesses. See Figure 20.1.

*Figure 20.1 / **Example from a competency-based report***

Achievement orientation

He has a much higher level of energy and drive than most people (achieving sten 9). People with his style are often perceived as very organised, disciplined and thorough. The strengths of his style are that he will readily accept responsibility and pursue his objectives energetically. He seems to have the motivation to try to make the most of what is done and get the best results (Belbin 'Shaper').

On the negative side, he may find it difficult to switch off from work. He may also find it difficult to accept people who don't have the same sense of purpose and career direction, or who have different values and standards.

Development advice

To increase his personal effectiveness, he should think about the following development points:

1. Establishing whether other people are committed to the task.
2. Considering other people's ideas and proposals and being prepared to negotiate and compromise.
3. Showing that he understands that other people may see things differently.
4. Finding ways of switching off from work.

The profile of the candidate used for making the selection decision needs to be conveyed to the person responsible for managing that individual. This is likely to have been done as part of the selection decision, since good practice will have ensured that their manager is involved in such decision, but there is a danger that once the decision is made the information may be neglected. It is important to highlight the applicability of the profile to the work situation. This will enable the manager to plan and manage the new person effectively. Thus, for example, if the profile indicates that the employee is very high on creativity and low on attention to detail, while the profile asked for above average creativity and average attention to detail, the decision may have been made that the candidate was sufficiently close to the profile to merit the selection. (The descriptions 'average' and 'below average' would not be used in practice, but are used here for illustration). While this decision may be the correct one for selection purposes, it needs to be realised that there will be implications for the way in which the role is fulfilled. It may be, for example, that the employee will be inclined to take risks, or not pay sufficient attention to implementation details of new assignments, or may be weak in project planning – other elements of the candidate profile will contribute to the picture. It may too be necessary to identify training programmes if these are appropriate (e.g. project management) or redesign the role (e.g. allocating implementation planning to another section) or paying particular attention to the potential risks in the day-to-day management and supervision of the employee.

Consideration needs however to be given to whether the competencies are innate attributes, acquired skills or adapting behaviours. Where the shortcomings are innate (i.e. underlying personality characteristics) there will be little point in arranging training programmes since they will not be effective in making a change. In such cases, attention will need to be given to the way in which the individual is managed or to redesigning or restructuring the work to build in checks and balances. Where the shortfall occurs amongst acquired competencies (i.e. knowledge, experience or qualifications) it may be appropriate to plan training and development opportunities, assuming the shortfall is not unduly difficult or expensive to make good. For shortfalls in the adapting competencies (i.e. how the individual applies natural abilities and acquired skills), particular attention will need to be paid to the early stages of an induction programme to help the employee adapt to the new role or organisation, and consideration will need to be given to providing higher concentrations of management support, particularly during periods of change.

While 'general' induction can still be delivered through general induction programmes or buddy systems, the competency approach enables the remainder of the induction to be carefully tailored to the needs of the individual and focused on the most appropriate intervention, whether training, supervision or role redesign, rather than relying on 'sheep dip' training applied indiscriminately in the hope of getting people up to speed.

PROBATIONARY PERIODS

Many organisations operate a probationary period for new staff. The principle is that a safeguard is built in to the employer's decision-making process so that if the wrong decision has been made, the employment can be brought to an end at an early stage. It may of course not necessarily be a 'wrong decision'. The new employee may have the right qualities and skills but somehow is not able to adapt successfully to this new environment, or perhaps there is a personality mismatch with the new boss or other key stakeholders. Most often, however, it was the wrong decision. Selectors know that selection is an imperfect science, that there are no 'perfect' selection techniques (as covered in the chapter on choosing techniques) and that all they can do is 'shorten the odds'. Yet, despite this knowledge, there is a great reluctance to admit when a selection decision was not right. It may thus be the case that the probationary period in many organisations is a wasted safeguard that becomes little more than a meaningless clause in the contract.

The right to claim unfair dismissal before an employment tribunal is not generally available to employees with less than one year's service. There are some significant exceptions to the rule and the opportunity to pursue claims through the civil courts for wrongful dismissal or breach of contract (see Chapter 18 on checks and offers), so it would be unwise for any employer to be cavalier about an employee's rights at any time in their employment. It is however the case that it is much easier and less costly to terminate employment correctly in the early stages of employment than at a later stage. It is important therefore to put in place a structured probationary period that includes formal assessment and confirmation of successful completion.

How to make the probation period effective

1   The first step is to include a clear clause in the offer of employment and the contract of employment to state that continued employment is dependent upon satisfactory completion of a probationary period of a specified time. The period should take account of the type of job and how long it is reasonable to expect the new employee to 'get up to speed'.

2   The second step is to provide a proper induction that ensures the employer has taken reasonable steps to help the new employee get up to speed in the job. The induction should also ensure that the rules and ways of working are clearly communicated and explained, making sure that the important rules are put in writing.

3   The third step is to clearly set out the required performance standards. This could be included in the offer stage, at induction, or in the first few days of starting. The standards may be a series of deliverables or projects or milestones, or they may be levels of output or production, or accomplishing a level of qualification or skill acquisition. Ideally these should be set out in a simple document that sets the target or standard, the timeframe, and the development plan if appropriate. The document should set down review points, preferably on a monthly basis.

4   Regular reviews, at least monthly, should be undertaken. These can be quite short but should form a discussion with the employee and state whether satisfactory progress is being made. Where progress is not satisfactory the employee should be reminded that continued employment is dependent on satisfactory completion of the probationary period. It is useful to have a 'sign off' section on the performance standards document to show the outcome of each review. For some roles, such as a production machine operative, it may be appropriate for trainers to sign off on skill acquisition with the supervisor giving an overall review.

5   The final step is to conduct an assessment at the end of the probationary period to confirm that the standards have been achieved. The performance standards document should be signed off where everything is satisfactory. In the event that the performance, behaviour or attendance is not satisfactory, a decision will need to be taken on whether to extend the probationary period

---

or terminate the employment. This is often a difficult decision, but in the absence of extenuating circumstances it is highly likely that someone failing to fulfil the probationary demands will become a long-term problem if they are retained. In the event that employment is terminated the disciplinary procedure should be followed. It is preferable to incorporate specifically the probationary procedure in the disciplinary procedure. A case conference should be held with the line manager and recruiter to review the recruitment process and identify whether it is appropriate to adjust the person specification, the recruitment techniques, advert or induction in the light of the employee's failure. Care should however be taken to avoid assumptions that anything was wrong in the process, as recruitment is not a perfect science. In the event that the probationary period is satisfactorily completed, a formal letter – preferably from the most senior person in the organisation – should be promptly sent to the employee to congratulate them on satisfactorily completing the probation and confirming their continued employment. This is a simple but very important detail.

USING INFORMATION

All organisations need good information in order to operate effectively. Invariably, decisions on marketing strategy will be informed by research on customers and markets, decisions on investment will be informed by financial predictions and the utilisation forecasts. The decisions on the organisation's human resource strategies will be no different in requiring information for their formulation. The difficulty however is that many organisations do not use the information which is available to them. A great deal of information is collected during the selection process and subsequently abandoned when the assignment has been completed. Organisations need to capture by-product information and key data during the selection process and make it available to appropriate people afterwards.

The by-product information is all the intelligence on markets, competitors and developments, which is 'down loaded' from candidates during the selection process. This is not to say that sensitive information disclosed in confidence, perhaps during the interview, should be abused, but that the vast range of other information freely given may be very useful to the organisation in seeing trends and developments and thereby keeping abreast of current business affairs. Similarly, information on types of people available or the kind of work being sought or not sought (including variations on working themes) is important to shape future decisions. There may be, for example, the opportunity to put on an extra part-time night shift, or a need to reconsider expansion plans if there are early signals of problems in the labour market. Similarly, early news of the likely closure of the factory down the road may have an adverse effect on services or products supplied to them or have the effect of releasing extra cash into the local economy to increase demand for products or service. By-product information is not essential, it is simply additional knowledge which may from time to time prove useful.

There is furthermore some key data which is often ignored beyond the selection process. In planning future work, organisation structure or resource requirements it is important to have the information on issues such as skill levels, working time, flexibility and availability. The assessment of future training needs and current training effectiveness requires information on the abilities and potential of employees. Decisions on pay structures need to take account of the motives, values, and expectations of employees if they are to be effective. Organisation development and culture change require an understanding of the psychology of the workforce. The work, and expense of gathering such information when the various initiatives are proposed may be so daunting, expensive or contentious that it is simply not gathered. It seems strange that often in these cases the raw data is sitting in employee files or selection assignment folders, and was not funnelled into an aggregated information database. This type of database could prove an invaluable guide to the development of human resource policies and practices. Although computerised human resources information systems are in place in many organisations – and frequently the systems provide a bridge from 'candidate' to 'employee' and integrate selection with other HR details – the information seems to be used for administrative purposes rather than research intelligence. However simple the selection process in an organisation, it is likely to be the most in-depth look that the organisation will take into an employee's work record, domestic circumstances, aptitude and personality at any stage in their employment. It seems a great pity that such a potentially useful insight does not continue to play a meaningful role in planning the individual and collective management of that person.

21

Measurement and evaluation

STATISTICS

It is important to measure the success of the selection activity. At the simplest level this means following through to see that the new employee is able to fulfil the requirements of the role. It is not unthinkable that the selection decision could have been wrong and that the individual is not suited to the role. This is the importance of probationary periods and proper induction that are covered in the previous chapter on 'Starting up'. It is also necessary to evaluate the success of the selection function itself. This means looking at the fairness and effectiveness of selection activity. Examining fairness involves the following activities:

- to ensure that the process does not discriminate against protected groups

- to monitor how such groups survive each stage or technique in the selection process

- to ensure that such groups are properly represented as a proportion of the workforce.

Assessing the effectiveness of the selection function, although important, is not a common practice and there is also a great deal of disagreement between researchers on appropriate measures of effectiveness. The basic premise is that the natural laws of distribution will apply to employees and candidates as much as they apply to anything else. Thus, taking a group of people and measuring them against some criterion such as height, weight or age, there will be a distribution pattern that equates to a bell-shaped curve. The proportions either side of the mid point will be equal at half each and most people will be nearer to, but either side of, the mid point. In statistical terms the bell-shaped curve is known as the 'normal distribution curve', and the difference between the smallest and greatest measure is the range, which is divided into sections known as 'standard deviations' so that 68 per cent of people will be within one standard deviation either side of the mid point, 95 per cent of people will be within two standard deviations either side, and 99 per cent will be within three standard deviations either side.

Put simplistically, if the adult male population of a city were to be weighed, and the average weight was 11 stone with a range from 8 to 14 stone, we should expect to see 34 per cent of the people between 10 and 11 stone, and 34 per cent between 11 and 12 stone (i.e. 34 per cent will be one standard deviation above or below the mean). Similarly we can expect that 95 per cent of the population will be within two standard deviations from the mean, so we can say that 85 per cent of the population will not weigh more than 12 stone. Such statistical analysis is an important element of occupational psychology. If a set of weighing scales were to be regarded as an ability test and we subsequently weighed newcomers to the city to see whether they would be lighter or heavier than the present population, we could say that any male greater than 12 stone was at the 85th percentile. That is to say: he would weigh as much, or more than 85 per cent of the general adult male population of the city, and therefore provide some meaningful comparison or benchmark for his weight. Using these principles, in trying to select people, we are attempting to see how they would compare to the rest of the 'population'. See Figure 21.1.

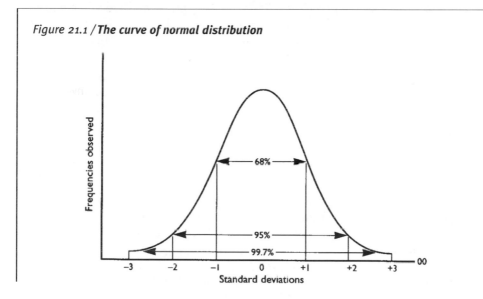

*Figure 21.1 / **The curve of normal distribution***

UTILITY ANALYSIS

One of the main arguments, in proposing that the effectiveness of selection techniques should be evaluated, is to say that by improving the techniques, selectors should be able to select those who are at the higher levels of performance, i.e. those at the higher range of the bell-shaped curve. Thus selectors ought to be looking to recruit those from the top 15 per cent of performance or, to put it simply, trying to attract the best. Two problems emerge: what is the 'population' and how can all employers recruit 'the best'?

In looking at the population, should we be looking at a wide group of people or only those suitable to undertake the role? Using these principles two researchers, Brogden and Hunter, developed a statistical method, called utility analysis, to assess the cost benefit of improved selection procedures. The utility analysis is expressed as the following equation:

$$(V \times Sr \times SDy \times l \times n) - (c \times n) = £benefit$$

where:

- **V** stands for the predictive validity of the particular technique or techniques used. This will range from 0 for no better than chance selection, to 1 for perfect selection. For more information on validity see the chapter on using the right tools and techniques in Chapter 7

- **Sr** stands for the selection ratio which, broadly speaking, is the proportion of people who would be suitable to fill the role. This is a tricky point since it does not relate to the whole population. Thus, for example, if we were looking to recruit brain surgeons we may say that the proportion of the population able to fill the role would be very small, but that the selection ratio would be taken not from the population as a whole, but those suitable to be considered, i.e. suitably qualified surgeons. The selection ratio would be those suitable to fill the role. This is a strange concept given that all of them should be capable of doing the role: the ratio should be derived by looking at how many were appointed from the candidate pool. Thus if 20 people applied and four were selected as suitable, then the selection ratio would be 0.20 (one in five). One of the difficulties with this concept is that it assumes that those not selected are not suitable, but it may be the case that the number of suitable candidates outstripped the availability of positions. Although the figure of 0.20 was used to illustrate this example, it is not quite so simple to derive a selection ratio, and in the 1930s Taylor and Russell developed a set of statistical tables that have been universally applied.

- **SDy** relates to the financial value of differences in performance. Thus taking the normal distribution curve, what is the greater or lesser financial worth for a standard deviation above or below the mean? Put simply, how much better are the better performers than the performers in financial terms to the organisation? In looking at a sales force, for example, it is possible to derive the normal distribution curve of performance by looking at sales generated (allowing for extraneous factors) and it is then possible to see how much more income is derived from the better performers. For service organisations and knowledge roles, this may not be so straightforward. Some researchers, in trying to quantify this, have tested managers and supervisors on the value of better performance and concluded, as a generalisation, that one standard deviation is equivalent to around 40 per cent of salary. This is partly attributable to research in the 1930s by Clark Hull which showed that, in skilled and semi-skilled jobs, the best performers achieved better productivity than the worst performers in a scale of ratios from 1.5: 1 to: 2: l.

- **l** equals the length of service of the appointed people.

- **n** is the number of positions being filled.

- **c** is the cost of the particular technique.

Thus, using a worked example for financial planning consultants, selling life insurance and related policies, it was decided to upgrade the selection system that consisted of an application form and interview, and change to a system that involved the application form, a structured interview, an ability test and a personality test. This would provide an improved predictive validity of 0.2. The selection ratio was 0.33, average length of service was around three years and 60 consultants were to be employed. The differences in income generated from various level of performers in the current population was analysed and determined to be £36,000. The additional cost of the improved selection was £35 per person. The equation worked out at:

$(0.2 \times 0.33 \times £36k \times 3 \times 60) - (£35 \times 60) = £426k$

Researchers are particularly keen to improve techniques of utility and analysis as a way of persuading practitioners to accept improved techniques for selection, and the associated additional cost. It is interesting to note therefore that it is not a widely used method for evaluating the effectiveness of the selection function. Recent research has shown that many line managers are not interested in the concept of the financial value of different performance levels. This may, at first, seem a strange finding and not wholly rational. It is worthwhile considering, nevertheless, the selection criteria for purchasing a car where prospective purchasers have the following characteristics:

- They rate safety highly when they regard the probability of an accident involving them as remote.

- They pay attention to the 0 – 60 acceleration and top speed when the law will not let them take advantage of it.

- They are very unlikely to take a test drive.

- They pay little regard to depreciation, running costs, and related aspects.

It is unlikely that decisions on selection techniques are any more rational than decisions on buying a car.

One of the interesting aspects of utility analysis is that it demonstrates that there is little point in investing in greatly improved selection techniques where the proportion of candidates eligible to succeed is fairly high, since their cost benefit will be marginal.

Interesting though utility analysis may be, it is of limited use as a sales technique for persuading others to adopt improved practices, and it does not provide a refined basis for on-going evaluation of the effectiveness of the selection procedure used. It is however useful as a general guide in making decisions about the techniques to be used.

How to measure the effectiveness of selection

Given the difficulties of obtaining 'off the shelf' methods to assess the usefulness of techniques and the potential payback, it is important to develop measures internally which can be used as the quality control, and pinpoint problems and opportunities. Measures should be looked at from the perspectives of individual performance and organisation performance.

The measures of **individual performance** may include the following aspects:

- productivity (whether measured in output or sales or some similar measure)

- performance against quality criteria such as error rates, level of competency, length of service in the organisation, speed of promotion, levels of absence, etc.

By gathering individual data on such measures, and comparing and contrasting with similar data for other employees, it is possible to see whether the people recruited were a good choice, and therefore reflect on quality of the selection process and decisions.

Organisation-wide measures can also be a useful indicator, particularly where there is a large proportion of recruitment intake which can influence the organisation on a dynamic basis. Such measures include:

- productivity

- quality measures, e.g. error rates or downtime, absence rates, labour turnover, and measures of motivation and morale.

The argument may be raised that these issues are too remote from decisions on selection to be a reflection on the quality of the selection process. The reality, however, is that they are all indicators of a potential mismatch between the people and the organisation, whether it be a mismatch with the role requirements or the organisation's aims. The purpose of selection is to ensure that there is a good match, which comes back to the comments on the normal distribution curve.

Some organisations take a holistic view of their human resources strategies and seek to identify how effective HR policies can translate into business success. This is often called 'Human Capital Measurement' and is beyond the scope of this book. It is however an aspect that should be considered in measuring selection effectiveness.

The question has been posed: 'What happens if all employers try to improve their selection practices and aim to recruit the top 15 per cent?' The answer is of course that 'the top 15 per cent' is a myth; there are no 'best' people, simply the most suitable people. It is the reason that selection cannot be looked at as a competition between candidates, or a competition with other employers to grab 'the best'. The primary role of recruitment and selection is to define the requirements which the organisation has for a certain kind of person, to go out and look for that kind of person, make them want to join the organisation, check that there is a match, bring that person into the organisation, and bring them up to speed at the earliest opportunity. Therefore, measures of selection effectiveness cannot be external. They cannot be the product of academic research or other third-party views and must be internal measures based on the organisation's aims and purpose.

Bibliography

ARGYRIS, C. (1962) Interpersonal Competence and Organisational Effectiveness. London: Tavistock Publishing.

ARGYRIS, C. (1971) *Management and Organisational development: The Path from XA to YB.* Maidenhead: McGraw-Hill.

BARRICK, M. and MOUNT, M. (1991) The Big Five Personality Dimensions and Job Performance; Meta-Analysis. *Personnel Psychology.* Vol. 44, 1-26.

BARRICK, M. and ZIMMERMAN, R. (2005) Reducing voluntary and avoidable turnover through selection. *Journal of Applied Psychology.* Vol 90, 159-166.

BARTRAM, D. (1997) Distance Assessment; Psychological Assessment Through the Internet. *Selection & Development Review.* Vol 13, No.2, 10-14.

BARTRAM, D., LINDLEY, P., MARSHALL, L. and FOSTER, J. (1995) Recruitment and Selection of Young People by Small Businesses. *Journal of Occupational and Organisational Psychology.* Vol 68, 339-358.

BELBIN, R. (1984) *Management Teams: why they succeed or fail.* London, Heinemann.

BOAM, R. and SPARROW, P. (1993) *Designing and Achieving Competency.* Maidenhead: McGraw-Hill.

BOYATZIS, R. (1982) *The Competent Manager.* New York: John Wiley & Sons.

CAMPION, M., PURSELL, E. and BROWN, B. (1988) Structured Interviewing; Raising the Psychometric Properties of the Employment Interview. *Personnel Psychology.* Vol. 41, 25-42.

CASCIO, W. and RAMOS, A. (1986) Development and Application of a New Method for Assessing Job Performance in Behavioural Economic Terms. *Journal of Applied Psychology.* Vol. 71, 20-28.

COLLINSON, D. (1987) Who Controls Selection? *Personnel Management.*

COOK, M. (1991) *Personnel Selection and Productivity.* London: John Wiley & Sons.

COOPER, C. (1981) *Psychology and Management; a Text for Managers and Trade Unionists.* London: British Psychological Society.

DALESSIO, A. and SILVERHART, T. (1994) Combining Biodata Test and Interview Information; Predicting Decisions and Performance Criteria. *Personnel Psychology.* Vol. 47, 303-315.

EYSENCK, H.T. (1947) *Dimensions of Personality.* London: Routledge.

FORSYTH, P. (1993) *Marketing for Non-Marketing Managers.* London: Institute of Management.

FOX, S., BIZMAN, A., HOFFMAN, N. et al. (1995) The Impact of Variability in Candidate Profiles on Rater Confidence and Judgement Regarding Stability and Job Situation. *Journal of Occupational and Organisational Psychology.* Vol. 68, 13-23.

FURNHAM, A. and GUNTER, B. (1994) *Business Watching; Understanding Business Life.* London: ABRA Press.

FURNHAM, A., STEELE, H. and PENDLETON, D. (1993) A psychometric assessment of the Belbin team role self-perception inventory. *Journal of Occupational Psychology.*

GALBREITH, D. and WILSON, W. (1964) Reliability of the Grapho-Analytical Approach to Handwriting Analysis. *Perceptual and Motor Skills.* Vol. 19, 615-618.

GRAVES, L. and POWELL, G. (1995) Effects of Sex Similarity on Recruiters Evaluations of Applicants. *Personnel Psychology.* Vol. 48, 85-98.

GUNTER, B. and FURNHAM, A. (1993) *Consumer Profiles; an Introduction to Psychographics.* London: Routledge.

GUNTER, B., FURNHAM, A. and DRAKELEY, R. (1993) *Biodata; Biographical Indicators of Business Performance.* London: Routledge.

HERRIOT, P. and WINGROVE, J. (1984) Decision processes in graduate pre-selection. *Journal of Occupational Psychology* 57, 269-275.

HIGGINS, C. and JUDGE, T. (2004) The effect of applicant influencing tactics on recruiter perceptions of fit and hiring recommendations: a field study. *Journal of Applied Psychology.* Vol. 89, 553-561.

HONEYBALL, S. and BOWERS, J. (2002) *Textbook on Labour Law.* Oxford University Press.

HULL, C.L. (1920) Qualitative aspects of the evolution of concepts *Psychological Monographs* 123.

HULL, C.L. *Principles of Behaviour.* New York: Appleton Century.

KEINAN, G., BARAK, A. and RAMATI, I. (1984) Reliability and Validity of Graphological Assessment in the Selection Process of Military Officers. *Perceptual and Motor Skills.* Vol. 58, 881-821.

KING, S. (1995) Graphology: Writing on the Wall. *Management Development Review*. Vol. 7, No. 5, 26-28.

KLINE, P. (1995) Models and Personality Traits in Occupational Psychological Testing. *International Journal of Selection & Assessment*. Vol. 3, No.3, 186-190.

LATHAM, G. and WHYTE, G. (1994) The Futility of Utility Analysis. *Personnel Psychology*. Vol. 47, 31-46.

LAWLER, E. *(1981) Pay and Organisation Development.* Reading, Mass: Addison Wesley.

LYNCH, B. and WILSON, R. (1985) Graphology: Towards a Handpicked Workforce. *Personnel Management.*

MAEL, F., CONNERLEY, M. and MORATH, R. (1996) None of Your Business; Parameters of Biodata Invasiveness. *Personnel Psychology*. Vol. 49, 3, 613-650.

McCLELLAND, D. (1961) *The Achieving Society*. Princeton NJ: Van Nostrand.

McCLELLAND, D. and BOYATZIS, R. (1982) Leadership motive pattern and long term success in management. *Journal of Applied Psychology*. Vol. 67, 737-743.

McCRAE, R. and COSTA, P. (1989) More reasons to adopt the five-factor model. *American Psychologist*. Vol. 44, 451-452.

McDOUGALL, W. (1932) *The Energies of Man*. London: Methuen.

McHENRY, R. (1997) Finding the Norm for Psychometric Tests. *People Management*. January.

MINTZBERG, H. (1994) *The Rise and Fall of Strategic Planning*. Hemel Hempstead: Prentice Hall.

OOSTHUIZEN, S. (1990) Graphology as Predictor of Academic Achievement. *Perceptual and Motor Skills*. Vol. 71, 715-721.

PEARN, M. and KANDOLA, R. (1988) *Job Analysis*. London: Institute of Personnel Management.

PITT, G. (1995) *Employment Law,* 2nd edn. London: Sweet & Maxwell.

PLUMBLEY, P. (1974) *Recruitment & Selection,* 2nd edn. London: Institute of Personnel Management.

PULAKOS, E. and SCHMITT, N. (1995) Experience Based and Situational Interview Questions: Studies of Validity. *Personnel Psychology*. Vol. 48, 289-308.

RANKIN, N. (ed). (1997) The State of Selection: Developments in Basic Methods. *Employee Development Bulletin*. Vol. 89, May.

RANKIN, N. (ed). (2004) Survey of Selection. *IRS Employment Review*. Vol. 796, March.

SACKETT, T. and ROTH, L. (1996) Multi-Stage Selection Strategies. *Personnel Psychology.* Vol. 49, 3, 549-572.

SATOW, R. and RECTOR, J. (1995) Using Gestalt Graphology to Identify Entrepreneurial Leadership. *Perceptual and Motor Skill.* Vol. 81, 263-270.

SCHMIDT, F. and HUNTER, J. (1998) Validity and utility of selection methods in personnel psychology: practical and theoretical implications of 85 years of research findings. *Psychological Bulletin.* Vol. 124, 262-274.

SCHMIDT, F. and ZIMMERMAN, R. (2004) A counterintuitive hypothesis about employment interview validity and some supporting evidence. *Journal of Applied Psychology.* Vol. 89, 553-561.

SMITH, M. and ROBERTSON, I. (1991) *Advances in Selection and Assessment.* Manchester: John Wiley & Sons.

TAYLOR, H.C. and RUSSELL, J.T. (1939) The Relationship of Validity Co-efficience to the Practical Effectiveness of Tests in Selection: Discussion and Tables. *Journal of Applied Psychology.* Vol. 23, 565-578.

TERPESTRA, D. (1996) Recruitment and Selection: the Search for Effective Methods. *HR Focus* 16-17, May.

TETT, R., JACKSON, D. and ROTHSTEIN, M. (1991) Personality Measures as Predictors of Job Performance; a Meta-Analytic Review. *Personnel Psychology.* Vol. 44, 703-742.

THERESON, C., BLIESE, P., BRADLEY, J. and THERESEN, J. (2004) The Big Five Personality Traits – individual job performance growth trajectories in maintenance and traditional job stages. *Journal of Applied Psychology.* Vol. 89, 835-853.

TOPLIS, T., DULEWICZ, V. and FLETCHER, C. (1991) *Psychological Testing; A Manager's Guide,* 2nd edn. London: Institute of Personnel Management.

WALSH, J. (1996) Multinational Management Strategy and HR Decision Making in the Single European Market. *Journal of Management Studies.* Vol. 33, 663-648.

WARNER, L. (1991) Apply in Writing: the Case for Graphology. *Human Resources.* 153-155, Autumn.

WHINCUP, M. (1995) *Modern Employment Law: A Guide to Job Security and Safety.* Oxford: Butterworth Heinemann.

WOOD, R. (1997) The Interview: Just When You Thought It Was Safe ... *Selection & Development Review.* Vol. 13, No. 2, 15-17.

WOODRUFFE, C. (1990) *Assessment Centres.* London: Institute of Personnel Management.

Index

Also from CIPD Publishing . . .

Becoming an Employer of Choice

Judith Leary-Joyce

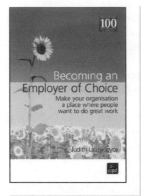

Being an 'employer of choice' can make a huge difference to your organisation's performance. If you create a great working environment, not only do great people want to work for you but everyone will strive to deliver their very best.

But how do you become an employer of choice? The companies that the Sunday Times has listed as the 'best places to work' can tell you. From ASDA and Microsoft to Timpson and Bromford Housing Association, all these organisations have one thing in common. They have created an environment in which employees feel valued and respected; in which they feel so connected to the company that they willingly give the effort required to deliver great results.

Judith Leary-Joyce has spoken to leaders, managers and employees within those companies and others to discover the secrets that have made them fantastic places to work. Her book will help you assess your organisation's current claim to greatness and make the business case for creating the sort of truly great company atmosphere that will attract great people who will deliver great results. It will help your organisation become an employer of choice.

Order your copy now online at www.cipd.co.uk/bookstore or call us on 0870 800 3366

Judith Leary-Joyce is an expert in leadership and management. She is CEO of Great Companies Consulting, which she established in 2002 after spending the previous year working on the Sunday Times' '100 Best Companies to Work For' list. She is a board member of the Servent Leadership Centre and, from 1979–1990, was MD of the Gestalt Centre, a psychotherapy training insititute.

| Published 2004 | 1 84398 057 6 | Paperback | 224 pages |

The Chartered Institute of Personnel and Development is the leading publisher of books and reports for personnel and training professionals, students and all those concerned with the effective management and development of people at work.

Membership has its rewards

Join us online today as an Affiliate member and get immediate access to our member services. As a member you'll also be entitled to special discounts on our range of courses, conferences, books and training resources.

To find out more, visit www.cipd.co.uk/affiliate or call us on 020 8612 6208.